D1554631

Some Quaint, Old-fashioned Advice

For all the
talented, hard-working,
extraordinary students
entering college and university
in the twenty-first century

Titles in this series

Some Quaint, Old-fashioned Advice

For all the
talented, hard-working,
extraordinary students
entering college and university
in the twenty-first century

A. Troglodyte, O.F.

COLLEGE PUBLICATIONS
LONDON

© 2022
All rights reserved
Revised June 2022

ISBN 978-1-84890-396-8

Published by College Publications
http://www.collegepublications.co.uk

All rights reserved. No part of this publication may be
reproduced, stored in a retrieval system or transmitted in any
form, or by any means, electronic, mechanical, photocopying,
recording or otherwise without prior permission, in writing,
from the publisher.

Cover image: Charles Darwin

Nullius in verba[†]

Contents

Preface[1]

This book has been written to help students get the most from their time at university. It has also been written to give potential students a glimpse into college and university life – its rewards, its challenges, its character.

The first year of undergraduate study can be intimidating. Being away from home for the first time can sometimes be lonely. To do well, it helps to get advice from someone who has been around colleges and universities for a while, first as a student, then later as a professor.

Numerous student survival guides populate the shelves of university bookstores. Even so, few discuss what is most distinctive about university life. Some discuss how to prepare for admissions exams. Others focus on how to make (and stick to!) a budget, how to cook one's own meals, or how to find the best deals on everything from student accommodations to smart phones. These are all valuable skills, but they do little to help students understand what's special about universities and why a university education can be valuable.

This book is different. Rather than giving suggestions about how best to navigate one's newfound *social* independence, this book is designed to help students (both young and old) take advantage of their newfound *intellectual* independence. It says something about the opportunities a university offers and about the difference between studying at university and studying in high school. It also includes some concrete suggestions about how to write essays and study for exams. As one colleague tells her students, "To do well at university you need to know more than where to put your bicycle. You need to know where to put your head."

In the pages that follow, it is assumed that anyone who has decided to devote four or more years and untold dollars (or pounds or euros) to obtaining a degree is right to think there is something special about a university education. It is also assumed that anyone enrolling at university will have the capacity – and the desire – to make the most of the opportunity, and that having some basic knowledge of what universities do and how they function will make it easier to take advantage of the many benefits universities offer. Finally, it is assumed that, given their busy schedules, students should not have to find the time to read this book cover to cover in a single sitting. Instead, they should be able to dip into different chapters here and there, depending on their interests and time commitments.

It should also be noted that the book is unusual since it has been written by a troglodyte, by someone whose views may initially seem a little quaint – perhaps even old fashioned – especially when compared to those of other, more progressive colleagues. As much as it pains me to admit it, I confess that my own time as an undergraduate was long ago, when reading was done primarily with scrolls, books and newspapers, rather than with the kinds of modern, hand-held communication devices that now allow users to have at their fingertips more computing power than the entire mission-control room that launched the Apollo astronauts to the moon.

Perhaps it is because of such changes that some think today's universities should become places of training rather than education, or of activism rather than reflection. As others are quick to suggest, perhaps universities should give up being centres of elite learning. These are all thoughtful suggestions, to be sure. But wrong.

Today's high-school and university students are part of an exceptional generation. Intelligent, hard-working and highly motivated, they are hungry for new challenges and eager to learn as much as they can about the world they are about to inherit, regardless of their background. They also have enough common sense to know that learning from someone who already knows how to navigate the institution they are about to enter will help them find their own way. My hope is that this book will also inspire them to follow their dreams wherever they might lead, and to remind them that a good education will help them succeed in whatever path they choose to take, just as it has done for generations past.

Today's university is rightly a time-honoured institution. Originally composed of independent colleges, universities today come in all shapes and sizes. As society has evolved, so too has the university. In some contexts, it is still helpful to distinguish between colleges and universities, but in others the terms "college" and "university" have come to be largely synonymous.

Regardless of such changes in lexicon, at its core today's university remains much as it was hundreds of years ago. Central to the mandate of all universities is the simple idea that *knowledge matters*. As the economist John Maynard Keynes reminds us, the ideas people have, both when they are right and when they are wrong,

> are more powerful than is commonly understood. Indeed, the world is ruled by little else. Practical men, who believe themselves to be quite exempt from any intellectual influences, are usually the slaves of some defunct economist. Madmen in authority, who hear voices in the air, are distilling their frenzy from some academic scribbler of a few years back. I am sure that the power of vested interests is vastly exaggerated compared with the gradual encroachment of ideas.[2]

It is this basic insight – that knowledge and ideas matter – that motivates people who work and study in universities today, just as it motivated the founders of the first medieval universities some eight or nine hundred years ago. More than anything else, it is awareness of this insight that transforms the lives of university students.

Admittedly, since its most recent expansions in the 1960s and 2000s, the university has become a more complex institution than it once was. Traditional arts and science faculties vie with professional programs for student enroll-ments. Educators vie with researchers for scarce space and resources. Worries about grade inflation, declining educational standards, political bias in the classroom and budget shortfalls abound.

Despite all this, the essence of university life has remained largely unchanged. New literature, new music, new scientific advances and new medical technologies appear side by side in the classroom – and on library shelves and in files on your smart phone – with the greatest thinkers and greatest books of the past. The result is an institution that not only meets the changing needs of each new generation of students, but each generation's many unchanging needs as well.

Chief among the latter is the need to be introduced to a world of ideas beyond that of our own limited experience. It is for this reason that university students are given access to many of the world's best libraries, lecture halls, museums, performing arts centres, hospitals and research laboratories. It is also for this reason that they are given access to many of the world's most talented writers, researchers and lecturers, and are given the opportunity to participate in student and alumni organizations that connect them to people and institutions around the world.

Despite these many involvements, today's university also remains what it always has been – a place set apart from society, a place where young people and others are given an opportunity to think about who they are, where they have come from and what's important to them before taking their place in the outside world. Universities remain, as they always have been, places in which students are able to experience the *intellectual enjoyment* that comes with encountering new ideas and learning about the amazing world in which we find ourselves.

To anyone who recently has been accepted into college or university, congratulations!

Your adventure is about to begin.

Some Quaint, Old-fashioned Advice

Chapter 1

Be Curious

"In spite of all that can be said against our age, what a
moment it is to be alive in!"[1]

These are the words of the Australian writer James McAuley.
They are as true today as they were when McAuley first wrote
them over half a century ago. In McAuley's day, the Cold War
was in its ascendency, modernism in the arts had come close to
exhausting itself, science was beginning to unpack the secrets
of the universe, religion was in decline and social change was
everywhere.

Today, many things are different, but many things remain
the same. The Cold War is over, only to be replaced by new
forms of international tension. In the arts, modernism has been
replaced by post-modernism, only to be replaced by something
that again looks surprisingly like modernism. Populations have
swollen, not only in countries such as China and India, but
around the world. For better or worse, religion has re-emerged
as a significant social force that needs to be studied to be
understood. The civil rights movement has led to greater social
inclusivity, not only in the United States but in Canada, South
Africa, Australia, Europe, and most of the Western world, and
cancel culture has emerged as both an impediment to free
speech and an incentive for people inside and outside the

university to re-evaluate some of their most fundamental assumptions.[2]

Since McAuley's day, science has continued to transform the world in which we live. Watson and Crick's double-helix model of DNA and the massively ambitious Human Genome Project have given us a much fuller understanding of who we are. Computers have evolved from enormous machines that once filled large, air-conditioned rooms to small, portable devices now used as fashion accessories. The information and communications revolution has made it harder for military dictatorships, theocracies and other forms of state-imposed thuggery to control the spread of information within unwilling populations. The world's first generation of space telescopes – the European Hipparcos telescope, the American Hubble telescope, and the Canadian MOST telescope[3] – has given us more insight into the history and nature of the universe than generations of astronomers ever dreamed possible. And at the centre of all these remarkable changes are those amazing engines of discovery, our universities.[4]

In spite of all that can be said against our age, what a moment it is to be at university!

Part centre of knowledge, part custodian of culture, part conduit of social change, the university remains, as it has been for centuries, one of the world's most vibrant institutions, animated by ideas and brimming with opportunity.

Jobs, jobs, jobs. What draws most people to university? Here's what one author tells us:

> Why do people go to college? In an idealistic world, they might go to develop a capacity for critical thinking, enhance an already grounded knowledge of the sciences and world culture, learn further how to deal with other people's diversity of opinion and background, and in general become better citizens. They might go for fun, for friendship, for a network of contacts. They might go for spiritual enrichment or for pragmatic honing of skills.

4

In the real world, though, mostly they go to college to make money.[5]

Perhaps this is true; and, if so, there's nothing wrong with it. Doing well in life, earning enough to support one's family and perhaps do a little more are respectable goals.

It is also true that a university education isn't for everyone. Many excellent careers do not need a university degree. Many good jobs provide on-the-job training. Studying at university places genuine demands on people. Being a student requires not just a significant commitment of time but a fair amount of intellectual focus and hard work. It can also be costly.[6] People who register for classes simply in the hope that doing so will help them get better jobs are often disappointed. For those who don't enjoy independent work, spending time in a college or university library can be a purgatorial prospect. For those who need to borrow unreasonably large amounts of money to cover their expenses, more education isn't always a sound financial investment.[7] If you'd prefer to jump straight into the job market, there is nothing wrong with doing so. If you'd rather take an online course that gives you immediate job-related skills, this can be an ideal career path. And if you change your mind a year or a decade later, your local university will still be waiting for you.

But for students who genuinely want to learn, there is no better place to expand their horizons. For people who enjoy the thrill of discovery, few institutions give greater opportunity. Even if you are sure you want to be an engineer, it never hurts (and often helps!) to learn some history or a second language. Even if you are sure you want to major in the humanities, learning some mathematics or some computer science or some law will help you become a better journalist or novelist or history teacher.

The school of hard knocks. One thing that distinguishes formal education from life without school is the opportunity to learn from other people's mistakes. The fact that architects and engineers can build buildings and bridges that support the enormous weights they do comes as much from past trial and error as from *a priori* theorizing. The same is true in other areas as well. In his 1925 essay *What I Believe*, the Nobel laureate Bertrand Russell reminds his readers that in the Middle Ages, "when pestilence appeared in the country, holy men advised the population to assemble in churches and pray for deliverance; the result was that the infection spread with extraordinary rapidity among the crowded masses of supplicants."[8] The result was death on a massive scale, something that can be avoided in an age of new pandemics, provided we have the common memory of such historical events to pass on to future generations. No wonder that life without education used to be called 'the school of hard knocks.'

Something else worth emphasizing is the intellectual freedom universities give their students. University students are free to think about *anything* – about the changing world around them, about where they have come from and where they are going, about what they believe and about what the future might bring.

Just as importantly, universities also give students access to unimaginable resources: to almost everything important that has ever been written, to experts in almost every field who are willing to answer students' questions, to equipment and research environments that allow them to investigate almost any question imaginable. Without such resources, each of us constantly would be having to reinvent the wheel. With them, as Isaac Newton said, we are able to stand "on the shoulders of giants" – although scholars still argue over whether the sometimes-vindictive Newton intended this comment as a compliment when he wrote it in a letter to his long-time rival, Robert Hooke, or, given Hooke's diminutive stature and poor posture, as an insult.[9]

There is also the passing of exams and the awarding of degrees. Exams give students objective feedback about how much they've learned and about what they've been able to accomplish. Grades are also helpful indicators when it comes time to obtain professional certification, whether as a teacher or a toxicologist, a pharmacist or a philosopher. Even so, as significant as these things are, there is an important sense in which they are also merely the incidental features of a good university education. The famous Greek philosopher Socrates wasn't talking about the pleasures associated with passing a first-year calculus exam when he told his friends that "the unexamined life is not worth living."[10] Instead, Socrates believed that education involves acquiring an appetite for excellence, or what the ancient Greeks called *virtue*, and allowing this appetite to guide you throughout your life.

Naturally, some people see university primarily as a stepping-stone to a future career. This is fine, but doing so with any seriousness will very soon draw you into the world of ideas. Perhaps you've enrolled in an MBA program and you want to learn how to grow a small Mom-and-Pop business into a national chain. Some people succeed when they try to do this. Many more fail. What distinguishes successful attempts from unsuccessful ones? Is it just luck? Or are there some underlying principles that are useful to learn? Perhaps you've enrolled in an engineering program and you want to build a better human-computer interface. What is the computing culture going to look like a year from now? Or ten years from now? Will quantum computing be a reality by then? What can we learn from condensed matter physics or other materials sciences about how to construct such devices? Perhaps you want to go to law school. Why are there different standards of proof in civil and criminal trials? Should property rights include the right to patent newly discovered forms of life? What is a right, anyway?

These questions remind us that sharp boundaries rarely exist between the practical and the theoretical, that a good education helps us excel in even the most practical of fields. Recognizing this, universities unashamedly promote the view that there are advantages to being introduced to what the Victorian poet Matthew Arnold famously called "the best that has been thought and said,"[11] that there is something valuable for everyone about the life of the mind.

Here is how the late University of Chicago professor Allan Bloom puts it:

> What does a first-rank college or university present today to a teen-ager leaving home for the first time, off to the adventure of a liberal education? He has four years of freedom to discover himself … In this short time he must learn that there is a great world beyond the little one he knows, experience the exhilaration of it and digest enough of it to sustain himself in the intellectual deserts he is destined to traverse. He must do this, that is, if he is to have any hope of a higher life. These are the charmed years when he can, if he so chooses, become anything he wishes and when he has the opportunity to survey his alternatives, not merely those current in his time or provided by careers, but those available to him as a human being. The importance of these years … cannot be overestimated. They are civilization's only chance to get to him.[12]

At their best, universities not only give students an opportunity to discover who they are but who they want to be.

The production, promotion, preservation and application of knowledge. Universities shouldn't be idealized. They have all the normal failings and shortcomings of any human institution. They also struggle with numerous real-world challenges – increasing enrollments, unpredictable budget shortfalls, changing social expectations and evolving educational standards. Despite this, universities have at their core the simple observation that *knowledge matters*, that knowledge is one of the things that help us live better, safer, happier lives.

Practically speaking, this means that universities play a role in the production, promotion, preservation and application of knowledge. They do so by being involved in *research, teaching* and *archiving*. As the Canadian philosopher Mark Mercer explains, research has at its centre three types of activity: *inquiry, interpretation* and *appreciation*.[13] *Inquiry* is the activity of trying to discover the ways of the world. It is the effort we put into trying to figure out how things in fact are. *Interpretation* is the activity of trying to appraise and criticize cultural artefacts and expressions. It is the effort we put into trying to read and imagine literary and artistic work. Sometimes we do this by thinking about what people believe and value; sometimes we do so by creating new stories, new music and new works of art in response to what we have read or seen or heard. *Appreciation* is a type of emotional and intellectual response to the world that we have come to understand through inquiry and interpretation. Teaching and archiving, in turn, help pass on the results of this research to those who follow us.

Other institutions are often involved in these kinds of activities too. Many private companies fund research laboratories. Schools and academies of various sorts teach students about any number of subjects. Numerous libraries, museums, galleries and archives have been created to preserve important collections of various kinds.

Two things separate universities from these other institutions. The first is that most people working in universities believe that these tasks are all intimately connected. They believe that each is done better when done together: Research – the discovery of new knowledge and the creation of new culture – is improved when students are present to ask questions. Libraries, museums and archives gather more valuable collections when they are informed by the best available research. Learning is more exciting when students are taught by people who are actively involved in advancing scholarship in their chosen fields.

Today, students shouldn't be surprised if their computer science professor helped develop some of the software they find on their computers, or if their chemistry professor contributed to some of the discoveries they learn about in their lectures. They shouldn't be surprised if, in addition to being a university instructor, their music professor is a noted composer

WHAT IS A UNIVERSITY?

Universities produce, promote, preserve and apply knowledge. At their best, they not only give people an opportunity to explore the world of ideas and the resources to follow their curiosity wherever it may lead, they also serve as creators and custodians of the world's culture, of "the best that has been thought and said."

Most contemporary universities are divided into faculties: arts and humanities faculties (with departments such as history, philosophy, English, French, music and drama); formal science faculties (with departments such as mathematics and computer science); natural science faculties (with departments such as physics, chemistry and biology); social science faculties (with departments such as economics, political science and psychology); and professional faculties (such as law, medicine, library science, engineering, architecture, journalism and business).

Following a period of residency, and upon sufficient achievement, students are admitted to life-long membership in their universities through the awarding of degrees.

or their drama teacher is a well-known playwright, or if their law professor or economics professor was present at the cabinet table, serving as an advisor, when an important government decision was being made. Of course, it is a stretch to think your archeology professor was actually present during the Archaic Period some twenty-five hundred years ago, but he or she may have been part of a dig that uncovered some of the artifacts that taught us how people lived when the famous Greek democrat Pericles was a boy.

The second thing that separates universities from other institutions is the freedom they give students and professors alike. While at university, people are free to follow their curiosity wherever it may lead. Unlike the commercial researcher who has been hired to work on a specific project, university professors are free to pursue purely curiosity-driven research. This same privilege applies to students. Not only are students free to choose their programs of study, almost all degree programs include large numbers of course electives that allow students to explore a wide variety of ideas and disciplines. This is not done by accident. The ancient custom of apprenticeship is still one of the best ways of imparting certain types of knowledge. Sometimes apprenticeships even form part of modern degree programs. Even so, apprenticeships alone can never fully replace a university education. The reason is simple: freedom of inquiry over a wide range of areas is a core part of any modern university education and it is this freedom of inquiry that helps distinguish a good college or university education from other types of learning.

Curiosity-driven research. One mistake people sometimes make is thinking that research occurs only in the sciences. But this would be like thinking that people can be curious only about things in the natural world and never about literature or music or law. Recognizing this, universities encourage students to ask questions, not only about the basic building blocks of nature but about *anything.* Why are we moved by some works of literature and not others? Why do some social movements grow while others collapse? Why are some proposed criminal laws met with wide-scale acceptance, while others result in violent protest?

Equally important is the role universities play as active custodians of what has already been discovered and created. Once discovered, scientific knowledge needs to be preserved, both in the library and in the classroom. Once created, works of art, literature and music not only need to be archived, they need to be experienced anew by each generation. If we never discovered a single new thing about Milton or Shakespeare or Mozart or Gershwin or Galileo, this might be disappointing, but it wouldn't detract one bit from the benefits each generation gets from re-discovering their accomplishments. To some extent, this marks an important distinction between the two main types of work done at any university. Some work is intended to *discover the new.* Other work is intended to *re-discover the old.* Neither is less or more important than the other. Mastering either requires curiosity and skill on the part of students and professors alike.

This distinction between discovering the new and re-discovering the old is something to remember when it comes time to choose your electives. Some courses are designed to encourage creativity. Some are intended to teach research skills and to introduce us to the latest scientific discoveries. But many are simply designed to introduce us to ideas and concepts already known to be important. This intellectual heritage, passed on by previous generations, shouldn't be undervalued. For all its strengths and shortcomings, it tells us not only what has been of value in the past; it prepares us, as much as anything can, for an unpredictable future.

Pure versus applied research. Another distinction to keep in mind is the distinction between *pure* and *applied* research. Some research leads very quickly to practical applications. Other research serves more theoretical purposes. For the practically minded, it is sometimes unclear why universities value both equally.

Applied research has clear and immediate benefits. During the Second World War, the United States, the United Kingdom and Canada coordinated their efforts to develop a new form of weaponry using fissionable materials.[14] Code-named the Manhattan Project, researchers worked day and night under the direction of University of California Berkeley professor Robert Oppenheimer. Within three years they had succeeded in producing the first atomic bomb.

In May of 1961, U.S. President John F. Kennedy announced to a joint session of Congress that he was committed "to achieving the goal, before this decade is out, of landing a man on the Moon and returning him safely to the Earth."[15] By July 20, 1969, both Neil Armstrong and Buzz Aldrin had reached the surface of the Moon. Four days later they returned to Earth with a successful splashdown in the Pacific Ocean.

Innumerable commercial groups have also done important applied research. Commercial R & D (Research and Development) labs focus their energy on everything from new pharmaceutical products and new communications equipment to new navigation aids for vehicles on both the surface of the Earth and the surface of Mars. The results of this work often transform how we live. Beginning with the idea of a trackball invented by the Royal Canadian Navy in the 1950s and an early primitive prototype developed by Doug Engelbart at the Stanford Research Institute in the 1960s, Bill English came up with the idea of the first ball-driven computer mouse while working at Xerox PARC in the 1970s.[16] The result led to the invention of track pads and touch screens and revolutionized the personal computer industry.

In Scotland, Touch Bionics released the i-Limb, the first commercially available hand prosthesis with five individually powered fingers. Work towards a more ambitious version of a similar prosthesis is being done by DARPA – the U.S. Defense Advanced Research Projects Agency – the same agency that developed stealth technology and the original global positioning system (or GPS). DARPA's goal is to develop a completely thought-controlled arm-and-hand prosthesis that will perform, look and feel like a natural limb, something now close to being a reality.[17]

In contrast to such projects, the goals of purely theoretical research are often much less predictable. Even so, for many people, satisfying their curiosity is an important end in itself.[18] The desire to learn something new or re-discover something old is part of what makes us human.

It is also important to remember that even the most applied work can't flourish without a solid theoretical foundation. As the social psychologist Kurt Lewin writes, "There is nothing so practical as a good theory."[19] Or as Leonardo da Vinci reportedly told his students, "He who loves practice without theory is like the sailor who boards ship without a rudder and compass and never knows where he may be cast."[20] In short, just as the purest research has intimate connections with how we live and how the world works, even the most practical of projects requires a foundation of pure research. It turns out that good academic work requires an awareness of both.

PURE VERSUS APPLIED RESEARCH

"We must not forget that when radium was discovered no one knew that it would prove useful in hospitals. The work was one of pure science. And this is a proof that scientific work must not be considered from the point of view of the direct usefulness of it. It must be done for itself, for the beauty of science, and then there is always the chance that a scientific discovery may become like the radium a benefit for humanity."

Marie Curie (1867-1934)
Winner of the 1903 Nobel Prize in Physics
Winner of the 1911 Nobel Prize in Chemistry

Without Niels Bohr's early shell model of the atom (in which electrons travel in discrete orbits around an atom's nucleus, and in which chemical properties are determined by the electrons in the outermost orbit), it is unlikely advances could have been made in any number of areas, from the invention of plastic pipes and microwave ovens, to atomic clocks and medical scanning technologies. Without the writings of historians such as Thucydides and of political theorists such as John Locke, it is unlikely modern democracies would have flourished as they have. In all intellectual work, theory is the lifeblood of application, just as application is the litmus test of theory. Neither pure nor applied research can long exist in isolation from the other.

Although most people remember Isaac Newton for his work on a unified theory of gravitation, it was his much more practical work on tides that originally made him famous.[21] During the age of exploration, Britain sought to develop the first detailed understanding of the physical properties of tides. Being able to predict the rise and fall of the Earth's oceans was an advantage every sea-faring nation wanted but few had the ability to achieve. Developing the correct, underlying theory required not just close collaboration between sailors, harbor-masters and the British Admiralty, it also required a detailed understanding of how the moon affected the rise and fall of the

Earth's largest bodies of water. This in turn required the development of a unified theory of gravitation and it was this theoretical work of Newton's that turned out to have such long-lasting importance.

This same interaction between theory and practice characterizes the work Bertrand Russell and Alfred North Whitehead did in formal logic during the first part of the 20th century, work that helped initiate the modern computer revolution. It is also found in Alexander Fleming's work on bacteriology, work that led to his accidental discovery of penicillin, and in Marie Curie's theoretical work on radium. Curie, who along with American Maria Goeppert Mayer and Canadian Donna Strickland, is one of only three women ever to have won the Nobel Prize for Physics, famously makes the point as follows:

> We must not forget that when radium was discovered no one knew that it would prove useful in hospitals. The work was one of pure science. And this is a proof that scientific work must not be considered from the point of view of the direct usefulness of it. It must be done for itself, for the beauty of science, and then there is always the chance that a scientific discovery may become like the radium a benefit for humanity.[22]

This is true whether the work in question is being done in the natural sciences, the social sciences, the arts or the humanities.

Huxley's game of life. Being a university student means having genuine intellectual independence. It means having, not just the social freedom of an adult but the intellectual freedom as well. It means being able to think for yourself about any number of issues. Being a university student thus means having quite different opportunities than in high school. It also means that it is important to be able to reason critically – to be able to give sound reasons for what you believe – and to be able to recognize when others have done the same. This is not a trivial skill. It is for this reason that Harold Macmillan, prime minister of Britain from 1957 to 1963, used to quote his classics tutor at Oxford:

> Nothing you will learn in the course of your studies will be of the slightest possible use to you in the afterlife [in life after you leave university], save only this: That if you work hard and diligently you should be able to detect when a man is talking rot. And that, in my view, is the main, if not the sole purpose of education.[23]

Completing a university degree means having the opportunity to discover important connections between the world of ideas and the world in which we live. Whether it is learning about the difference between a real science like astronomy and a non-science like astrology, or about the difference between democratic governments bound by the rule of law and authoritarian governments that are not, a university education helps us understand things that otherwise might seem mysterious.

Students who come to university with a curious attitude and who are eager to explore the world around them will gain an intellectual maturity that will serve them well throughout their lives. For most of us, overcoming intellectual challenges teaches us how to approach new problems critically. Taking courses in a variety of areas helps us discover connections among diverse phenomena. A good university education helps us discover why events unfold as they do and what needs to be done to bring about effective change.

This point was made over a hundred years ago by the famous British naturalist, Thomas Huxley:

> Suppose it were perfectly certain that the life and fortune of every one of us would, one day or other, depend upon his winning or losing a game of chess. Don't you think that we should all consider it to be a primary duty to learn at least the names and the moves of the pieces; to have a notion of a gambit, and a keen eye for all the means of giving and getting out of check? Do you not think that we should look with a disapprobation amounting to scorn, upon the father who

allowed his son, or the state which allowed its members, to grow up without knowing a pawn from a knight?

Yet it is a very plain and elementary truth, that the life, the fortune, and the happiness of every one of us, and, more or less, of those who are connected with us, do depend upon our knowing something of the rules of a game infinitely more difficult and complicated than chess. It is a game which has been played for untold ages, every man and woman of us being one of the two players in a game of his or her own. The chess-board is the world, the pieces are the phenomena of the universe, the rules of the game are what we call the laws of Nature.[24]

As Huxley suggests, education is what gives us the chance of winning at the game of life. Education, says Huxley, is what lets us master the rules of this "mighty game":

In other words, education is the instruction of the intellect in the laws of Nature, under which name I include not merely things and their forces, but men and their ways; and the fashioning of the affections and of the will into an earnest and loving desire to move in harmony with those laws. For me, education means neither more nor less than this. Anything which professes to call itself education must be tried by this standard, and if it fails to stand the test, I will not call it education, whatever may be the force of authority, or of numbers, upon the other side.[25]

Put in other words, the freedom we have at university gives us an amazing opportunity. With this freedom comes the opportunity to learn about "things and their forces" and "men and their ways." This in turn helps us understand, not only the great world around us but also events in our own quiet lives. With this understanding we are able to discover, not just where we have come from, but how to succeed at what we want to do and who we want to be.

Further reading

Anders, George, *You Can Do Anything: The Surprising Power of a "Useless" Liberal Arts Education*, New York: Little Brown and Company, 2017

Andrew, Caroline and Steen B. Esbensen, *Who's Afraid of Liberal Education? / Qui a Peur Del 'Education Generale?* Ottawa: University of Ottawa Press, 1989

Bird, Caroline, *The Case against College*, New York: D. McKay Co., 1975

Bok, Derek, *Beyond the Ivory Tower: Social Responsibilities of the Modern University*, Cambridge: Harvard University Press, 1982

Huxley, T.H., *Science and Culture and Other Essays*, New York: D. Appleton and Company, 1882

Huxley, T.H., *Science and Education* (Collected Essays, vol. 3), London: Macmillan and Co., 1893

Klassen, Thomas R. and John A. Dwyer, *How to Succeed at University (and Get a Great Job!)*, Vancouver: UBC Press, 2015

Kimball, Roger, *Tenured Radicals: How Politics has Corrupted Our Higher Education*, New York: Harper Collins Publishers, 1990

Neilson, William, and Chad Gaffield, *Universities in Crisis: A Mediaeval Institution in the Twenty-First Century*, Montreal: Institute for Research on Public Policy, 1986

Russell, Conrad, *Academic Freedom*, London, New York: Routledge, 1993

Rybak, Jeff, *What's Wrong with University – and How to Make It Work for You Anyway*, Toronto: ECW Press, 2007

Sowell, Thomas, *Intellectuals and Society*, New York: Basic Books, 2009

Stross, Randall, *A Practical Education: Why Liberal Arts Majors Make Great Employees,* Stanford: Redwood Press, 2017

Traub, James, *City on a Hill: Testing the American Dream at City College*, New York: Addison Wesley, 1994

Chapter 2

Be Brave

ى‌ه ه‌ى

Bertrand Russell was perhaps the most influential English-speaking philosopher of the 20th century. He was the grandson of a respected British Prime Minister and in 1931, upon the death of his older brother, he became the third Earl Russell. In 1908 he was elected to the Royal Society for his work in mathematical logic and in 1950 he received the Nobel Prize for Literature. Even so, as a young man he was notoriously shy. In his *Autobiography* he tells the story of his first trip to Cambridge:

> My father had been at Cambridge, but my brother was at Oxford. I went to Cambridge because of my interest in mathematics. My first experience of the place was in December 1889 when I was examined for entrance scholarships. I stayed in rooms in the New Court, and I was too shy to enquire the way to the lavatory, so that I walked every morning to the [train] station before the examination began.[1]

While writing his examinations, Russell was invited to dine at High Table with the College Master, something that can't have been easy for either the younger or the older man:

> I was alarmed by so formidable a social occasion, but less alarmed than I had been a few months earlier when I was left

tête-à-tête with Mr. Gladstone [the four-time British Prime Minister]. He came to stay at Pembroke Lodge [Russell's boyhood home], and nobody was asked to meet him. As I was the only male in the household, he and I were left alone together at the dinner table after the ladies retired. He made only one remark: "This is very good port they have given me, but why have they given it me in a claret glass?" I did not know the answer, and wished the earth would swallow me up. Since then I have never again felt the full agony of terror.[2]

Somehow, everyone muddled through.

The courage to ask questions. Despite the bravery it takes to raise one's voice, one can't help but think that Russell's time at Cambridge might have been just a little easier had he been able to summon the courage to ask someone the location of the nearest toilet. This is a lesson for us all: Asking questions is often the most efficient route to obtaining new knowledge.

Like everyone else, academics have their full measure of faults and shortcomings. Some are not known for their social graces. Some seem to have their heads in the clouds (to use a metaphor introduced by the ancient Greek dramatist Aristophanes 2,400 years ago). Some take time to become good teachers. If Russell the student found it took courage to ask questions, it is quite possible that Russell the young lecturer found it took just as much courage to stand in front of a group of undergraduates and give a lecture. Depending on the people involved, not every question-and-answer session is guaranteed to be successful.

There is also room for misunderstanding. During the 1960s and 1970s when the Apollo moon program was underway, the twenty-four astronauts who travelled to the moon brought back some of the most remarkable photographs ever taken. Many of the most striking images came from the cameras of the twelve men who walked on the surface of the moon. Some were hauntingly beautiful. Others showed the courage it took to survive in that desolate place. Yet others gave the Earth-bound observer some small insight into the technological achievements that had to be made for such fragile creatures to live and work in such a hostile environment. But if you look carefully and notice the sharp contrast in these pictures between the white surface of the moon and the dark, black sky, you'll see not a single star. Why are there no stars?

Normally there are two reasons we're unable to see something: either the object is too far away or something is blocking our view. We know that stars aren't too far away to be seen. And since there's no atmosphere on the surface of the moon it is hard to imagine exactly what could be blocking our view. It is a puzzle.

Unfortunately, if you ask a working astrophysicist why there are no stars in the Apollo moon photos, it is quite possible your question may spark a misunderstanding. The reason is simple: for some reason, people who challenge scientists on this point often turn out to be conspiracy theorists, people with a hidden agenda who want to prove the moon landings were a hoax. To them, the missing stars somehow prove their point. Having been down this road once too often, your friendly, neighborhood astrophysicist may become uncharacteristically condescending and perhaps even a little rude, telling you that there are just not enough hours in the day to spend time debating with conspiracy theorists about whether there really was a moon landing just 66 years after the invention of the airplane.

Of course, there is nothing special about astrophysicists. (Well, at least not in this respect.) Members of every teaching discipline, from political science to social work, from medicine to music, have to deal with their fair share of eccentrics. Even the best lecturer will sometimes misunderstand the purpose of a question. But if you have an honest question, it pays to be persistent. If you don't receive a satisfactory answer, don't give up. Try again, either with the same person or with someone else. If there's no atmosphere on the surface of the moon, why are there are no stars in the photographs taken during the Apollo missions?

HOW TO IMPRESS YOUR FRIENDS

Ask a question in class – everyone else will be glad you did!

The answer turns out to be that the stars are too faint to be seen. Put another way, the sky is dark in the Apollo photos because it is underexposed. When the aperture and f-stop on a camera are set to expose the moon's bright surface correctly, the shutter is not open long enough for starlight to register. This makes sense once we realize that even though the sky is black, the photographs were all taken during daytime! We can't see stars from the bright side of the moon for the same reason we can't see them from the bright side (the daytime side) of the Earth: there's just too much sunlight. (In contrast, it turns out there are plenty of stars visible in photos taken from the dark side of the moon.)

But this leads us to at least one more interesting question, and this question shows why it is good to be persistent. It shows why, if you have a question that's puzzling you, you shouldn't give up trying to find the answer.

Why is the sky dark at night? Why, we might ask, is the sky dark at night? Since there are so many trillions of stars, why don't they illuminate the night sky more brightly? Why doesn't their combined light completely fill the night sky? If the only thing blocking our view of a distant star is another, closer star, shouldn't the night sky, whether on the moon or on the Earth, be just as bright as during the day?

Whatever the correct answer, this is an interesting question. It is also an important one, and one that numerous astronomers have puzzled over.[3] If the light emitted from a common candle is defined as one candela (or 1 cd) of light, then the average starry-night luminance is about 0.00006 cd/m^2. In contrast, the average daytime luminance given directly from the sun is about 1,600,000,000 cd/m^2. The ratio between the two is about 1 to 26 trillion.[4] In other words, if all we saw in the sky were one giant sun, the sky's brightness would exceed ordinary sunlight by such a huge margin that we would all be vaporized in seconds. So this is a *big* discrepancy! Why does it arise?

To answer this puzzle, let's start with some assumptions. For simplicity, let's assume that the universe is infinite in size, or at least that it is very large. Next, let's assume that all light-emitting objects (stars, galaxies, etc.) are distributed more-or-less uniformly throughout space, in other words that the universe is roughly homogeneous. Third, let's assume that light has the same intensity regardless of its direction of measurement, in other words that radiation is roughly isotropic. Fourth, let's assume that the interstellar absorption of light is so small it can be ignored. In other words, let's assume that radiation sent from distant galaxies doesn't 'disappear' on its way to the Earth, either because the only material blocking it will be other, equally bright galaxies, or because any other material absorbing such radiation would eventually get hot and glow just like a star. At least initially, all of these assumptions seem plausible. Our question can now be thought of as follows:[5]

We know that background radiation becomes fainter at greater distances. In fact, it has been shown to decrease at a predictable rate. We also know that the greater the number of galaxies, the greater the intensity of radiation, and that this radiation increases at a rate that is also capable of being calculated. In other words, even though radiation is fainter from greater distances, provided the universe is homogeneous and the interstellar absorption of light can be ignored, this faintness will be offset by the much greater number of galaxies found at these distances. (For example, if you think of a section of space as viewed from the surface of the Earth as being pie-shaped, the further away from the Earth you go, the larger the outer edge – the piecrust – becomes. Or if you prefer to think in three dimensions, think of an ice-cream cone. If you double the height of the cone, you'll more than double the amount of ice cream it holds.) Looking at these two factors together, it seems that the greater the distance, the greater the amount of radiation we should be observing. Since we are assuming that the universe is infinite – or at least very large – it follows that the amount of observable radiation should increase proportionately until the whole sky appears as if covered by one giant sun! So why isn't this the case?

What the experts say. For the sky to be dark at night, at least one of our four assumptions (infinity, homogeneity, isotropy and absorption neutrality) must be incorrect. Apparently, the universe is not infinite, or not homogeneous, or radiation is not isotropic, or radiation somehow disappears on its way to the Earth. During the 19th century, the most widely accepted solution was to deny homogeneity, to assume that galaxies must be clustered in a relatively small number of spots throughout the universe. Initially this may have seemed plausible, but 20th-century observations made out to distances of thousands of mega-parsecs give no indication of this kind of localization. (A parsec is a unit of distance used in astronomy: one parsec, or the 'parallax of one arcsecond,' equals approximately 31 trillion kilometers. This is the same as about 19 trillion miles, or approximately 3.262 light-years. A mega-parsec is a million parsecs.) As a result, astronomers have concluded that we are likely to be mistaken about one or more of our other three assumptions. For example, it now seems possible that we live in a universe that is finite in age or, at least, that light has existed for only a finite amount of time. If so, then the volume of space that we are able to observe will be finite as well. In addition, it also seems likely that the systematic motion of galaxies may affect the intensity of the radiation we observe.

Today, there is broad agreement among scientists that that universe (or at least, the universe in its present form, since it is this point that our mathematical models cease to be useful) is a little less than 14 billion years old. Initially, we might think that this means that the light from any galaxies that might be further than 14 billion light years away won't have had time to reach us. However, as cosmologists Charles Lineweaver and Tamara Davis point out, "because the universe is expanding, the space traversed by a photon expands behind it during the voyage. Consequently, the current distance to the most distant object we can see is about three times farther, or 46 billion light-years."[6] Things are also complicated by the fact that the rate of expansion of the universe seems to be accelerating. Even so, since the time for radiation to reach the Earth from very distant galaxies would have to be greater than the age of the universe itself, it follows that the volume of space we are capable of observing must be finite. (As an aside, this explains how astronomers are able to learn so much about the very early history of the universe. Light from distant galaxies that takes billions of years to reach us tells us, not how those galaxies might look today, but how they looked billions of years ago, near the time of their formation.)

Today there is also broad agreement that the systematic motion of galaxies affects the intensity of the radiation we observe. Because of the big bang, the universe turns out to be expanding. As a result, galaxies end up moving away from one another with speeds roughly proportional to their distance apart. On average, the further a galaxy is from the Earth, the faster it will be moving relative to the Earth and the greater will be the weakening of the radiation we observe from it.

Confirmation of a finite, expanding universe comes from several independent sources. Here is how one contemporary astronomer, Paul Wesson, summarizes our current state of knowledge:

> The age of a given galaxy can be determined by dating its oldest stars. This can be done by comparing the abundances of the elements in the stars with the theory of how simple elements are converted to more complex ones by thermonuclear reactions. Remarkably, the ages of different galaxies turn out to be approximately the same ... This by itself is enough to suggest that the galaxies were formed in some ancient cosmic cataclysm, and more evidence exists in

favour of this idea. For example, there is a field of long-wave-length radiation filling space that appears to be the cooled-down aftermath of some primeval fireball. Also, the abundances of a few special elements in the universe cannot be explained solely in terms of nuclear cooking inside normal stars, but instead require the existence in the past of some even hotter environment.[7]

Putting these pieces of evidence together, most astronomers think that some form of gigantic explosion must have occurred a little less than fourteen billion years ago. However, as Wesson also tells us, "this explosion was of a rather peculiar type, that happened everywhere at the same time,"[8] and it was following this 'big bang' that the material scattered throughout the universe is thought to have begun to cool and condense into galaxies.

The expansion of the universe and the finite age of galaxies thus explain a great deal of what working astronomers and astrophysicists observe. But of these two factors, is one more important than the other for answering our question about the night sky? Is one more important than the other for explaining why the sky is dark at night? It turns out the answer is yes. As Wesson has discovered, the main reason the sky is dark at night is that galaxies have finite age. Both factors reduce the brightness of space, but the finite age of galaxies does so to a much greater degree. It does so in two ways.

First, the amount of light that stars have been pumping into empty space turns out to be finite since it is restricted by the age of each star. Second, since it takes time for light from distant galaxies to reach the Earth, at any time only a fraction of the light produced by a distant galaxy will have had a chance to reach us. In other words, even if the universe turns out to be significantly larger than what we can observe, we still will be able to see only sources of radiation from within a limited volume of space.

The constant receding of galaxies also means that the intensity of observable radiation is more limited than it would be in a static universe. Two reasons again account for this limitation. As Wesson tells us, this happens

> partly because the volume of intergalactic space increases, so the number density of photons decreases, and partly because the energy of the photons emitted by receding galaxies decreases in accordance with the redshift or Doppler effect. To understand the latter better, it is helpful to recall how the motion of the source affects emitted waves in acoustics and optics. The sound waves from a train whistle decrease in pitch or frequency as the train recedes. (The redshift mechanism in the big-bang theory is really more subtle than this, and involves expansion as distinct from velocity, but the two words are commonly taken to imply each other and this is done here also.) By Planck's law, the redder light is the less energetic it is. So, the recession of the galaxies, besides diluting the light by increasing the volume of space, also lowers its intrinsic energy.[9]

In other words, taking into account the expansion of the universe means that there will again be a corresponding reduction in observable radiation.

Of these two factors – the expansion of the universe and the finite age of galaxies – the expansion of the universe turns out to have comparatively little effect on what we observe. Computer models developed by Wesson and others reveal almost the same levels of radiation regardless of whether the universe is expanding or not. In other words, although the expansion of the universe results in some reduction of radiation, it is the finite age of galaxies that is the real reason the sky is dark at night.

A moral. What is the moral of all this? It is that, if asked sincerely, almost any question – even the most obvious, such as 'Why is the sky dark at night?' – can turn out to be important.

Even the most elementary questions play a role in the development of new theories: Why do we dream? Why should we be moral? How do governments gain legitimacy? Why do

A FEW FAMOUS QUESTIONS

Homer	Why must we fight?
Plato	Why be moral?
Aristotle	What constitutes proof?
Leonardo da Vinci	Why is the sky blue?
Niccolò Machiavelli	Is it better to be loved or feared?
William Shakespeare	To be or not to be? That is the question.
Galileo Galilei	Does the Earth move?
Thomas Hobbes	Why do we leave the state of nature?
John Locke	How do governments gain legitimacy?
Isaac Newton	Why does an apple fall?
Gottfried Leibniz	Why is there something rather than nothing?
Jean-Jacques Rousseau	Why is there inequality?
Adam Smith	Why does cooperation occur without coercion?
Heinrich Olbers	Why is the sky dark at night?
Thomas Malthus	Must population growth always exceed food supply?
Charles Darwin	How do new species arise?
Frederick Douglass	Why am I a slave?
Susan B. Anthony	Are women persons?
Gregor Mendel	Why are some traits dominant and some recessive?

some species adapt and survive, and others not? Does adolescence always have to be an unhappy time? Asking such elementary questions may seem initially like a waste of time, but over the centuries it is questions like these that have motivated many of the world's greatest discoveries.

It is also important to remember that not every question leads directly to new knowledge. Some questions simply don't have answers – not because we haven't yet discovered how to answer them but because they are ill formed. If someone asks you the diameter of the largest crater on the surface of

A Few Famous Questions

Francis Guthrie	Can any map be coloured using just four colours?
Friedrich Nietzsche	Is God dead?
Georg Cantor	Is there just one size of infinity?
Sigmund Freud	Why do we dream?
Marie Curie	What causes radioactivity?
John Raskob	How high can we build?
Albert Einstein	What would it be like to travel at the speed of light?
Lester Pearson	How can there be peace?
Friedrich Hayek	Who plans best?
Margaret Mead	Is adolescence always going to be an unhappy time?
Isaiah Berlin	Is it better to be free from or free to?
Alan Turing	Can machines think?
Arthur C. Clarke	Are we alone?
Nelson Mandela	Are human beings inherently evil?
Isaac Asimov	How can robots be made safe?
Martin Luther King, Jr	Where do we go from here?
Alice Munro	Who do you think you are?
Bob Dylan	What else can you do for anyone but inspire them?

Jupiter's largest moon, you might not know the answer, but given enough time and a large enough research budget, this is something you or someone else should be able to discover. In contrast, if someone asks you the diameter of justice, or the colour of a cosine, or the mass of the note middle C, most of us will recognize right away that, unless we are speaking metaphorically, a mistake has been made.

Distinguishing well-formed from ill-formed questions is not always easy. Some questions appear to be well formed even though they contain the kinds of mistaken assumptions that make them nonsensical and that prohibit fruitful investigation. For many years the question, "How do we cure cancer?" hampered cancer research. Built into the question was the mistaken assumption that cancer is a single disease admitting of a single cure. Only once it was realized that different types of cancer require different types of treatment, and that there is not one cure for cancer but many, did cancer research become as successful as it is today. Here, as in so many other cases, just getting the question right turned out to be a major accomplishment.

Finally, it is worth remembering that if you have a question that is difficult to answer, it is important not to give up. If you can't find a satisfactory answer, share your question with your friends, your teaching assistants and your professors. As the Nobel-prize-winning physicist, Isidor Rabi, tells us, it is often the ability to ask good questions that leads to academic success:

> My mother made me a scientist without ever intending it. Every other Jewish mother in Brooklyn would ask her child after school: "So? Did you learn anything today?" But not my mother. She always asked me a different question. "Izzy," she would say, "did you ask a good question today?" That difference – asking good questions – made me become a scientist![10]

Further reading

Brooks, Michael, *13 Things that don't Make Sense: The Most Baffling Scientific Mysteries of Our Time*, Toronto: Anchor Canada, 2009

Chaikin, Andrew, *A Man on the Moon: The Voyages of the Apollo Astronauts*, New York: Viking Penguin, 1994

Chaikin, Andrew, *Voices from the Moon: Apollo Astronauts Describe Their Lunar Experiences*, New York: Viking Studio, 2009

Clark, Ronald William, *The Life of Bertrand Russell*, London: J. Cape, 1975

Epstein, Richard, L., *The Pocket Guide to Critical Thinking*, 4th edn, Socorro, NM: Advanced Reasoning Forum, 2011

Harrison, Edward Robert, *Darkness at Night: A Riddle of the Universe*, Cambridge (MA): Harvard University Press, 1987

Lovell, James, and Jeffrey Kluger, *Lost Moon: The Perilous Voyage of Apollo 13*, New York: Houghton Mifflin, 1994

Mermin, N. David, *Boojums All the Way Through: Communicating Science in a Prosaic Age*, Cambridge (UK), New York (USA): Cambridge University Press, 1990

Peacock, John, *Cosmological Physics*, Cambridge: Cambridge University Press, 1999

Pickover, Clifford A., *Archimedes to Hawking: Laws of Science and the Great Minds Behind Them*, New York: Oxford University Press, 2008

Russell, Bertrand, *My Philosophical Development*, London: George Allen and Unwin, 1959

Singh, Simon, *Big Bang: The Most Important Scientific Discovery of All Time and Why You Need to Know about It*, London: Fourth Estate, 2004

Zakaria, Fareed, *In Defense of a Liberal Education*, New York: W.W. Norton & Company, 2015

Chapter 3

Get Involved

ఞ ఞ

Today's universities have their roots in medieval Europe. It is from the medievals that we've inherited the idea of "privileged corporate associations of masters and students with their statutes, seals and administrative machinery, their fixed curricula and degree procedures."[1] This is true, but there is something else common to all university students from the Middle Ages to the present: the need for money.

Here is how one medieval father sums things up: "A student's first song is a demand for money and there will never be a letter which does not ask for cash."[2] There is even evidence that medieval universities taught students how to write home to ask for funds. One much-copied exercise lists twenty-two different ways to approach authority figures (ranging from parents to your local bishop) on this delicate subject. Here is one such letter that, the translator tells us, was written originally in "uncommonly bad Latin":

> B. to his venerable master A., greeting. This is to inform you that I am studying at Oxford with the greatest diligence, but the matter of money stands greatly in the way of my promotion, as it is now two months since I spent the last of what you sent me. The city is expensive and makes many demands; I have to rent lodgings, buy necessaries, and provide for many other things which I cannot now specify. Wherefore I respectfully beg your paternity that by the

promptings of divine pity you may assist me, so that I may be able to complete what I have well begun.[3]

Of course, not all recipients of these letters were immediately swayed by such appeals. Here is a reply to a similar letter written on the other side of the English Channel, no doubt dictated and delivered with all possible affection:

> To his son G. residing at Orleans, P. of Besançon sends greetings with paternal zeal. It is written, "he also that is slothful in his work is brother to him that is a great waster." I have recently discovered that you live dissolutely and slothfully, preferring license to restraint and play to work and strumming a guitar while the others are at their studies, whence it happens that you have read but one volume of law while your more industrious companions have read several. Wherefore I have decided to exhort you herewith to repent utterly of your dissolute and careless ways, that you may no longer be called a waster and your shame may be turned to good repute.[4]

What is the poor student to do? How is the ordinary student to survive? The short answer, of course, is to get a job. But where? And how? It is at this point that the modern university places students at a tremendous advantage. Almost every modern university has numerous interesting part-time jobs for which students can apply.

Getting a job on campus not only means more money, it also means discovering more about university life. Students may not realize it, but working in the university bookstore, or at the athletics centre, or in a university theatre connects them to their university in important and lasting ways. If possible, it is also a good idea to spend some time living on campus, at least initially. Living and working on campus make it easier to participate in a variety of university activities. This makes it easier to meet people and make connections.

Meeting new people, whether in class, at work or over a meal, not only makes it easier to discover what universities do

HOW TO GET INVOLVED

- Live on campus!
- Work on campus!
- Attend a concert!
- Go to a game!
- Join a club!
- Join a choir!
- Join a team!
- Learn to dance!
- Learn an instrument!
- Learn a new language!
- Learn to swim!
- Start a book swap!
- Form a study group!
- Become an actor!
- Get elected!
- Write for a campus newspaper!

and how they function. It also helps students develop many of the skills that will serve them well later in life. Regardless of your future profession, spending time with other people will be a large part of your job description. This is something often overlooked. Whether you want to work as an accountant, a journalist, an artist, an engineer, a lawyer or a librarian, a great deal of your time will be spent working with others, often as a part of a team. Almost every career requires, not only that you master the technical skills associated with a particular field, but that you also learn to work with others. Communication skills, listening skills, the ability to discover other people's goals, talents and ambitions – all are essential.

For most of us, these skills are not something we learn while attending lectures. Instead, they come from spending time and interacting with others. So, whether you play a sport, join the debate club or audition for a role in a play, it is important to get out from behind your computer screen and spend time with people. Often the best advice for students new to a university is simply to *get involved.*

Working on campus. Too much outside employment can distract students from their education. Having to devote time to both study and work can also place unnecessary stress on students. For students who are able to earn enough money during their summer vacation to last the year, it is helpful to be able to focus on their lectures and readings without having to hold down one or more part-time jobs. But for students who need the money, working in a lab, a library or a university museum can help them succeed academically. Working in a college or university residence is a good way to make new friends.

Working as a research assistant is a good way to learn more about your discipline. Working on campus in any capacity lets you meet people who have the potential to be valuable sources of advice. Many universities have co-op programs designed to integrate academic study with work experience done outside the university. These programs allow students to get paid while gaining real-life work experience in areas relevant to their programs of study.

For those who choose not to work during term, being without large amounts of money is not the end of the world. As the famous New Zealand physicist Ernest Rutherford said during the Great Depression of the 1930s, "We have less money, we must think harder."[5]

Borrowing an exciting new book from the library is often of more long-term benefit than buying the latest electronic gizmo. Going for a regular run is just as good for your health as buying an expensive gym membership. The challenge for many students is simply to find the right balance. Not enough paid employment makes it hard to pay one's bills. Too much outside work makes it hard to find the time to read, study and explore new ideas.

Living on campus. Living on campus has its own set of re-wards. Students who live in residence have immediate access to libraries, laboratories and professors. They also save large amounts of time otherwise spent commuting, something especially important at the end of term when exams are approaching and every hour counts.

In addition to student residences, some universities have systems of federated colleges – autonomous institutions within the university that provide accommodation to students and faculty alike. Different colleges often have different specializations. Some emphasize connections with the natural sciences or liberal arts. Others have connections to pro-fessional schools or accept only graduate students. Being a member of a college often makes it easier to meet and socialize with students and professors from disciplines other than your own. At many universities, colleges also provide some of the best sporting opportunities and some of the best food services available on campus.

On many North American campuses fraternities and sororities also maintain university chapter houses. Easily recognizable because of their Greek names – the names of most fraternities and sororities consist of two or three Greek letters that abbreviate their mottos – many fraternities and sororities emphasize a particular form of community service, social function or professional affiliation. Others emphasize academic achievement. Yet others have a particular ethnic or religious emphasis, although debate still takes place on many university campuses about how best to balance the competing social goods of maintaining communities supportive of particular ethnic and religious groups on the one hand and of creating open, non-discriminatory entrance requirements on other. Greek Rush Week is a time when fraternities and sororities open their doors to the public and invite potential members to tour their facilities.

For students who sometimes struggle with academic work (and even those who don't), living on campus makes it easier to find peer tutors – older students who've already figured out

PART-TIME JOBS ON CAMPUS

Alumni assistant	Marker
Athletics assistant	Martial arts instructor
Bartender	Museum docent
Bookstore worker	Music instructor
Cafeteria worker	Office worker
Cashier	Research assistant
Childcare worker	Residence advisor
Clerical worker	Retail worker
Computer advisor	Security guard
Dance instructor	Software tester
Dorm monitor	Sports writer
Editorial assistant	Student councillor
Equipment manager	Student note-taker
Fitness instructor	Survey administrator
Graduate instructor	Swimming instructor
Grounds keeper	Teaching assistant
Hospital intern	Theatre usher
Kitchen worker	Tour guide
Lab assistant	Tutor
Library assistant	Waiter
Lifeguard	Webmaster

what is important in a subject and what is not. It also makes it easier to join a study group and easier to socialize. In short, living on campus helps students pick up information about their university easily and quickly, information that might otherwise be difficult to obtain.

Even in an age of Zoom meetings and international teleconferencing, learning how to shake hands and meet new people will also always have its benefits. Sharing meals and going to social events together is a great way to learn about people other than yourself. It is part of the glue that holds societies together.

Of course, despite its benefits, community living needn't be forever. After living on campus for one or two years, many students prefer to move off campus. Even so, spending at least some time living in a college or university residence is often a highlight of many people's time at university.

Socializing on campus. Another benefit of attending university is the opportunity to make new friends. For students living away from home for the first time, universities sometimes can be lonely places. Saying goodbye to family can be difficult. Not having a network of friends to talk to and share experiences with can be painful. Even if you haven't moved away from home, at some point it may seem that everyone has a boyfriend or girlfriend except you. As counterintuitive as it may seem in such circumstances, it is important to realize that you are not alone. At one time or another, everyone has such feelings. So, if you find yourself feeling lonely, try to make an effort to go out and meet new people.

Universities attract interesting people from all around the world. Whether on a bus or in a cafeteria, the person sitting next to you will often have an interesting story to tell. At the start of each new course, take a moment to introduce yourself to the people sitting next to you. Being new to the course is something you will have in common. Try not to be shy. If someone asks you to join a team, a club or a study group, or to write something for the local campus newspaper, your first instinct should be to say yes.

Many universities and colleges have strong sporting traditions. Others emphasize different forms of competition or social activity. Many have student organizations devoted to public service as well as to having fun. At the beginning of each academic year, most universities have a Club Day, a time when clubs and other organizations have an opportunity to introduce themselves to new students. As interesting as they are, don't make the mistake of thinking the only clubs on campus will be the Debate Club and the Math Club (as enjoyable as these two clubs are).

At the University of Florida there is a Rock-Paper-Scissors Club. Carleton College in Northfield, Minnesota, is famous for its Mustache Club. The Expedition Club at Waseda University in Japan likes to go monster hunting in Papua New Guinea. Princeton has a Mime Company. Harvard has a Tiddlywinks Society. (Its motto is *In Levitate Veritas.*) Several universities have clubs intended to educate chemistry and engineering students about the proper use of explosives. The University of London Society of Change Ringers promotes the art and science of church-bell ringing. The Cambridge University Combined Boat Clubs encourages all students at Cambridge to row.

Several universities have chapters of Students for an Orwellian Society. In Toronto, students are welcome to join the Trinity College James Bond Society. (Black tie is required for voting.) At the University of Saskatchewan there is a Stockman's and Rodeo Club. The Russellian Society at Sydney University meets every week in the local pub. The same is true for the Queen's Players at Queen's University in Kingston. Perhaps surprisingly, the Campus Anarchist Network is well enough organized to have multiple chapters and a nicely organized website. Yale University's Political Union is home to the oldest student debating society in America.

Two clubs that I've never encountered but that would be worth starting would be a Banned Books Club and a New Ideas Club. Each term a Banned Books Club could read and discuss a different book that was once banned. A New Ideas Club could require each member to present a new idea for discussion once each term. I've been waiting a long time to be able to buy golf balls with GPS chips inside them. Instead of spending hours in the rough searching for my ball, I could just turn on my smart phone and a compass would point me to the ball. Whenever I'm stuck in traffic, I also think it might be a good idea for someone to pass a bylaw requiring all road repairs to be done at night. And I bet we could almost eliminate traffic accidents if drivers were required to tie babies to their bumpers, although I suppose some overly sensitive parents might object. Still, it would be helpful to hear if anyone has any better ideas for finding golf balls, reducing commuting time and eliminating traffic accidents.

Regardless of which clubs you join, one of the best features of membership is the life-long friendships you are likely to form. Whether you become president of the local ski club or you are just an occasional visitor to your local chapter of Doctors without Borders or Engineers without Borders, you are likely to meet at least a few people you will have as friends for the rest of your life. The fact that some clubs are so welcoming to guests also explains why they are successful when other clubs last only a year or two before they disappear.

Some clubs are created to help advance social or political causes. The Heretics Club, founded in 1909 by C.K. Ogden, worked with people like J.B.S. Haldane, Jane Harrison and Ludwig Wittgenstein to help promote rationalist thought at Cambridge a century ago. More recently, many LGBTQ+ (Lesbian, Gay, Bisexual, Transgendered, Queer and Other) clubs have helped countless young people find friends at a time when being gay was often believed to be, not just a sin but also a mental illness and a crime. Regardless of a club's mandate, it is helpful to remember that the best clubs are always welcoming to guests and new members. Clubs that see the world differently achieve very little by tearing down each other's posters. Instead, if your club and another see the world differently, even dramatically differently, find an opportunity to host a joint social event together. Learning to disagree without being disagreeable is one of the great opportunities we all have while at university.

Sports and athletics. Some of us have the potential to become elite athletes. Others don't. Some of us hear the call for the youth of the world to unite every four years at the next Olympic or Paralympic Games. Others may simply want to keep active and lose a few pounds. Regardless of our circumstances, the benefits of sport are many. Greater strength, speed, skill, stamina and suppleness – the five main

SOME FAMOUS (AND NOT-SO-FAMOUS) STUDENT CLUBS

Amnesty International
amnesty.org

Australian National University ANU for Bees
anusa.com.au/life/club/7586/

Cambridge University Footlights Club
cambridgefootlights.org

Canadian University Field Lacrosse Association
cufla.ca

Cornell University Curling Club
cornell.campusgroups.com/ccc

Doctors without Borders
doctorswithoutborders.org

Engineers without Borders
www.ewb.ca/en, www.ewb-uk.org, www.ewb-usa.org

Harvard University Hasty Pudding Theatricals
hastypudding.org

London School of Economics Debating Society
lsedebating.blogspot.com/p/welcome.html

Michigan State Fencing Club
michiganstatefencing.com/

Oxford Union
oxford-union.org

Purdue University Hurling Club
purduehurling.club

Queen's Debating Union
queensdebatingunion.org

Simon Fraser University Pipe Band
sfupipeband.com

Stanford University Federalist Society
law.stanford.edu/federalist-society

Students for an Orwellian Society
studentsfororwell.org

SOME FAMOUS (AND NOT-SO-FAMOUS) STUDENT CLUBS

University of Aberdeen Lairig Club
www.ausa.org.uk/sports/club/lairig/

University of British Columbia Concrete Toboggan Team
www.ubctbog.com

University of Edinburgh Shinty Club
shinty.eusu.ed.ac.uk

University of London Society of Change Ringers
ulscr.org.uk

University of Manitoba Debating Union
www.facebook.com/uofmdebate

University of Michigan Fencing Club
websites.umich.edu/~fencing

University of Pennsylvania Philomathean Society
philomathean.org

University of Queensland Underwater Club
unidive.org

University of Saskatchewan Men's Hockey
huskies.usask.ca/sports/mens-ice-hockey

University of St Andrews Riding Club
www.facebook.com/UStARiding

University of Sydney Piano Society
www.usydpianosoc.org/

University of Toronto Toastmasters
uofttoastmasters.com

University of Victoria Juggling Club
web.uvic.ca/~juggling

University of Warwick Riding Club
www.warwicksu.com/societies-sports/sports-clubs/riding

University of York Bellringing Society
yusu.org/activities/view/bellringing

Yale Whiffenpoofs
whiffenpoofs.com

components of fitness – lead to improved health, increased energy, greater mental acuity and clearer complexions.

There are few places better than universities to learn about and participate in organized physical activities. Not only do many universities have excellent playing fields, gymnasiums and other athletic facilities, they also have experts able to answer almost any question you might have about the sporting world, from the best way to improve your jump shot to how to make a career out of an activity you love. Human kinetics departments not only specialize in physical education training, they have experts in everything from sports medicine to the sociology of sport. Importantly, too, universities have experts who look critically at the culture of sport, studying not just the benefits but also the shortcomings of the amateur and professional sporting worlds.[6] One shortcoming is drug use.

Occasionally the suggestion is made that little harm would result from dropping restrictions on steroid use and allowing professional athletes to use whatever drugs they wanted. This is a mistake. It overlooks the fact that the health risks associated with unrestricted drug use at the top of the sporting pyramid would very soon trickle down to college and high-school locker rooms even more than they have today. Such a change wouldn't affect the health of just a few well-paid, professional, adult athletes. It would harm the health of generations of young women and men hoping to reach higher levels in baseball, football, hockey, track and field, basketball and every other sport.

One of Greece's great gifts to the world has been the Olympic Games. Initiated some 2,800 years ago along with the Pythian Games, the Nemean Games and the Isthmian Games, the ancient Olympic Games had many of the same short-comings modern sporting competitions have today.[7] Some athletes were famous for trying to win at any cost. Sometimes pickpockets succeeded in ruining the day of more than a few spectators. Far from stopping war, the famous Olympic truce did little more than allow athletes safe passage so they could compete against one another without the threat of imprisonment or execution. Even so, the Games continued to inspire athletes for over a thousand years. It wasn't until the year 393 that the Roman Emperor Theodosius I finally disbanded them.

Today, the opportunity to gather together to meet at the modern Olympics continues to motivate not just athletes but also coaches, trainers, fundraisers and spectators. The fact that Olympic athletes also publicly promise to compete drug free, and that many of the world's best chemists work to ensure that this happens, serves as an important reminder to both young people and their parents that cheating is incompatible with success at all levels of organized sport.

It also has long been recognized that, despite its short-comings, sport builds character. The ability to accept a loss and try harder the next time is a skill more people wish they had. The ability to shake hands with your opponent after a hard-fought match and wish him or her well is something that will serve you well in life regardless of your future career. So whether you only play the occasional pickup game, or whether you make sport a daily part of your routine, remember that exercise is an important part of any healthy life. While at university, find a sport you enjoy and become active.

The Arts. Do you have a story to tell? A song to share? A film that demands an audience? Do you enjoy listening to music on your iPhone, watching the occasional movie with a friend, or visiting a museum? For all of us, universities are some of the best places to become involved in the arts. Almost all universities have their own movie theatres. Many have world-class museums and concert halls. And almost every degree requires students to take at least a few required or elective courses in music, art or language. This is not something done by accident. As the scientist Charles Darwin tells us in his autobiography, "If I had my life to live over again, I would have made a rule to read some poetry and listen to some music at least once every week."[8]

Music especially seems to bring out the best in people, both as performers and as audience members. Even the characters in J.K. Rowling's *Harry Potter* give music its due: "Ah, music," Dumbledore said, wiping his eyes. "A magic beyond all we do here!"[9] Perhaps this is because music somehow prompts emotion in a way that is sometimes less common with mere words. As Beethoven reminds us, "To play a wrong note is insignificant. To play without passion is inexcusable!"[10] Somehow, something of this passion rubs off on even the most casual of listeners.

Historically, the arts have been divided into four main groupings: the fine arts, the decorative arts, the performing arts and the language arts. The *fine arts* (including painting, sculpture, architecture, music and poetry) have sometimes been characterized as focussing exclusively on beauty. They also have been said to be unencumbered by practical considerations (such as function), although as long ago as Plato and Aristotle, such descriptions were controversial. The *decorative arts* focus on work that is both beautiful *and* functional. They include creative activity in ceramics, metalwork, jewellery design and furniture design, as well as in fashion and textiles. The *performing arts* focus primarily on theatre and dance, and the *language arts* on listening, speaking, reading and writing. Today, these divisions remain helpful, even though many recent forms of artistic expression (photography, videography, ice dancing, automobile design, computer graphics) can sometimes blur the boundaries between them.

The language arts sometimes fail to get their fair share of recognition in today's often prosaic world. Even so, the ability to express oneself clearly without ambiguity or exaggeration is a skill to be valued in even the most workaday of contexts. Perhaps more exciting are the advantages that come with learning a new language. The International Organization for Standardization (ISO) lists over 7,800 known natural and artificial languages arranged under 58 "macro-languages," so if you want to study language, even choosing where to start might seem daunting. Even so, learning just a hundred words in another language will help you order a taxi, pay a bill, find a washroom and say thank you to your host when visiting another country, or even another region in your own country. Learning a language in greater depth will introduce you, not just to words, but to the culture and emotion of a people who might otherwise be quite distant from you. As an old Arab Proverb reminds us, "Learn a language and you'll avoid a war."

Creativity Squared. As in so many areas, something that distinguishes contemporary activity in the arts from that of previous generations is the availability of computers. For the consumer, the online world gives us access to a seemingly unlimited amount of music, literature, imagery and performance. To see an original Rembrandt, you may still have to visit the Rijksmuseum in Amsterdam, but online images are now so authentic and precise, travelling the world virtually without the bother of going through airport security is a privilege unparalleled in human history. The information revolution has had its downsides, but the enormous democratizing of information is one of the great benefits of living in today's connected world.

For the creator – the artist, the author, the designer, the composer – computer technology can be of equal benefit. Not only does it allow for the wide, public distribution of newly created artwork, it opens the door to completely new forms of innovation and creativity. Not only can older works now be digitally re-mastered, previously unimaginable sounds and sights can be created. Computer-generated imagery (CGI) is not found just in movies.

Perhaps it goes without saying that not all of us have the creative impulse of a musician or an artist. And not all of us have the computer skills we need to take advantage of new, cutting-edge technologies. It is here that universities can be of special help. Universities are some of the few places where students in the technological sciences and students in the creative arts can interact and work together. One option is to register for a course; but a second is simply to join a study group, a performance group or a computer club.

Admittedly, it can take courage to ask for help in an area where you might have little or no experience. It can take courage to attend a club meeting if you are the only one there from another discipline or another faculty. But if so, ask a friend to join you; and once there, ask people what courses they are taking and whether they have chosen a major. Eventually you will find something in common to talk about.

Something that may come as a surprise is that not all technically talented people have the best social skills. (Whether they could become more socially adept if they wanted to put some effort into it is another matter.) It may sound harsh, but just as some people would rather spend time with their nose in a book, others would rather spend time online. But are they generous with their time when they are asked for help? Absolutely. If you attend a computer club and if you have a question about technology, you may not be greeted with a smile or a warm handshake. But if you ask for help, you won't go away disappointed.

Student politics. There are two main schools of thought about student politics. The first is the admittedly somewhat extreme view that student politics – along with college or university politics more generally – are positively harmful to all concerned. This view is summed up in the old adage, "Don't vote, it only encourages them."

Contrary to this view is the more moderate position that student politicians, like all politicians, have the potential to do some genuine good for the people who elect them. Since politics also has the potential to be tremendously good fun, many people give in to the temptation and seek election. Even so, according to the classics scholar F.M. Cornford, the supposed benefits of a political life are often illusory. Despite the fact that Cornford taught at the University of Cambridge over a century ago, his tongue-in-cheek analysis of academic politics still has about it an air of familiarity. As he tells us, many aspects of political life can be singularly unrewarding:

> My heart is full of pity for you, O young academic politician. If you will be a politician you have a painful path to follow, even though it be a short one, before you nestle down into a modest incompetence.[11]

The reason for this frustration, says Cornford, is that rather than being a noble calling of the intellect, politics is really a disagreeable endeavor in which self-interest and corruption rule:

> I take it that you are in the first flush of ambition, and just beginning to make yourself disagreeable. You think (do you not?) that you have only to state a reasonable case, and people must listen to reason and act upon it at once. It is just this conviction that makes you so unpleasant. There is little hope of dissuading you; but has it occurred to you that nothing is ever done until everyone is convinced that it ought to be done, and has been convinced for so long that it is now time to do something else? And are you not aware that conviction has never yet been produced by an appeal to reason, which only makes people uncomfortable? If you want to move them, you must address your arguments to prejudice and the political motive.[12]

Cornford was clearly not without a sense of humor. He is, after all, the man who defined *propaganda* as "that branch of the art of lying which consists in very nearly deceiving your friends without quite deceiving your enemies."[13] Some of his advice also found its way into the famous BBC TV comedy series *Yes Minister*.

Cornford also points out that the very most an academic politician should hope to achieve is the absence of harm. Here are the arguments that he suggests all politicians need to master if they are going to be able to achieve this rather modest end:

NATIONAL MUSEUMS

Australia – National Museum of Australia
www.nma.gov.au

Canada – National Gallery of Canada
gallery.ca

China – National Museum of China
en.chnmuseum.cn

Egypt – National Museum of Egyptian Civilization
nmec.gov.eg

France – Louvre Museum
louvre.fr

Germany – Germanisches National Museum
www.gnm.de

Greece – National Archaeological Museum of Athens
www.namuseum.gr

India – National Museum New Delhi
www.nationalmuseumindia.gov.in/en

Israel – Israel Museum
www.imj.org.il/en

Italy – National Roman Museum
museonazionaleromano.beniculturali.it

Japan – Tokyo National Museum
www.tnm.jp

Korea – National Museum of Korea
www.museum.go.kr

Netherlands – Rijksmuseum
www.rijksmuseum.nl/en

Russia – Hermitage Museum
www.hermitagemuseum.org

United Kingdom – British Museum
britishmuseum.org

United States – Smithsonian Museum
si.edu

Vatican City – Vatican Museums
www.museivaticani.va

First, there is the *Complexity Argument*. This is an argument that the world is so complex that we are never able to foresee the consequences of our actions: "It follows at once that the only justifiable attitude of mind is suspense of judgment; and this attitude, besides being peculiarly congenial to the academic temperament, has the advantage of being comparatively easy to attain."[14]

Second, there is the *Wedge Argument*. This is the argument that, even if you think you know which action is right, acting would cruelly raise people's expectations that you might act on their behalf again in the future, something unrealistic in the extreme.

Third, there is the *Dangerous Precedent Argument*. This is the argument that, should you be certain which action is right, and should you actually have the courage to do it, doing the right thing even once would set a dangerous precedent about other, quite dissimilar actions. As a result, "Every public action which is not customary, either is wrong, or, if it is right, is a dangerous precedent. It follows that nothing should ever be done for the first time."[15]

Next is the *Fair Trial Argument*, which advances the view that it is essential that the current system be given a fair trial before being changed, even though it is never explained "why a Fair Trial ought only to be given to systems which already exist, not to proposed alternatives."[16]

Finally, there is the *Time is not Ripe Argument*, a general-purpose argument that can always be invoked even though, as Cornford reminds us, time unfortunately "has a trick of going rotten before it is ripe."[17]

Underlying Cornford's humorous remarks is a general skepticism about politics that not everyone accepts. For many, French President Charles de Gaulle got it right when he said, "I have come to the conclusion that politics are too serious a matter to be left to the politicians";[18] or as Aristotle put it over two thousand years earlier, "if liberty and equality, as are thought by some, are chiefly to be found in democracy, they will be best attained when all persons alike share in the government to the utmost."[19]

In other words, if democracy is to flourish, there will always be a need for talented young men and women to have the courage to let their names stand for public office. Such people are often able to achieve great goods, but as with any other activity, preparation and training are essential to success. Just as no one should expect to succeed at a sport without an appropriate amount of coaching and practice, trial and error, the same is true in politics. Like so many other activities, running for political office is something that, for many of us, is first tried most profitably while at university.

Further reading

Berry, Mary Frances, *Ripples of Hope: Great American Civil Rights Speeches*, New York: Basic Civitas Books, 2003

Bowen, William, and Sarah A. Levin, *Reclaiming The Game: College Sports and Educational Values*, Princeton: Princeton University Press, 2003

Cornford, F.M., *Microcosmographia Academica: Being a Guide for the Young Academic Politician*, Cambridge: Bowes & Bowes Publishers Ltd, 1908

Deacon, Richard, *The Cambridge Apostles: A History of Cambridge University's Elite Intellectual Secret Society*, New York: Farrar Straus & Giroux, 1986

Gruending, Dennis, *Great Canadian Speeches*, Markham (ON): Fitzhenry & Whiteside Ltd., 2004

Haskins, Charles Homer, *The Rise of Universities*, Ithaca: Great Seal Books / Cornell University Press, 1957

Heffer, Simon, *Great British Speeches*, London: Quercus Books, 2007

Kagan, Donald, *Pericles of Athens and the Birth of Democracy*, New York: The Free Press, 1991

Pound, Dick, *Inside the Olympics: A Behind-the-scenes Look at the Politics, the Scandals and the Glory of the Games*, New York: John Wiley and Sons, 2004

Robson, Pamela, *Great Australian Speeches*, Sydney: Pier 9, 2009

Safire, William, *Lend Me Your Ears: Great Speeches in History*, Scranton, Pennsylvania: W.W. Norton & Co Inc, 1992

Spivey, Nigel, *The Ancient Olympics: A History*, New York: Oxford University Press, 2004

Swaddling, Judith, *The Ancient Olympic Games*, 2nd edn, Austin: University of Texas Press, 1999

Chapter 4

Be an Active Reader

When Amazon released its first Kindle in 2007, many people said reading was about to change forever. Were they right?

Probably not. Kindles, iPads, smart phones and other electronic book-readers haven't put an end to traditional books, at least not yet. Even though they let readers carry in their pockets entire libraries of books and other digital media, many people still prefer reading the printed page rather than an electronic screen. (Others do just fine without the feel of paper in their hands, thank you very much.) Of course, there are advantages to being able to retrieve countless volumes of electronic information, but it is important not to confuse retrieving information with reading. Many sources of information are not intended to be read. They're meant to be checked, or scanned, browsed or inspected. They've been created to consult, to leaf through, to glance at, to skim. No one *reads* a business directory or a birth registry.

Reading involves more than just checking a source or looking up a fact. It means following a train of thought. It means understanding an author's goals and intentions. It means evaluating an argument. Reading is a skill that develops in parallel to learning. It shouldn't be rushed and can't be cursory. It requires attention and focus in a way that surfing the web does not. As Booker Prize chair and English professor John Sutherland puts it, reading is not a spectator sport but a participatory activity. Done well, a good reading is as creditable as a 10-scoring high dive. It is, I would maintain, almost as difficult to read a novel well as to write one well. Which is greater, Henry James the critic or Henry James the novelist?[1]

Learning to read well involves more than just discovering the meanings of words. It means discovering connections between ideas and evaluating an author's thoughts. It means learning to retrieve meanings that time and distance may have made obscure. It means climbing inside someone else's head.

Where to read. The Australian philosopher David Stove lists three things necessary for learning: leisure, quiet and access to the learning of others.[2] By leisure he means time free from pressing pursuits such as the search for food and shelter. After all, it is from the Greek word for leisure, *schole*, that we derive the English words 'school' and 'scholar.' It is in this context that Stove quotes Charles Darwin's *The Descent of Man*:

> The presence of a body of well-instructed men, who have not to labour for their daily bread, is important to a degree which cannot be overestimated, as all high intellectual work is carried on by them, and on such work, material progress of all kinds depends, not to mention other and higher advantages.[3]

Finding a good place to read, a place to exercise your leisure, a place where you will not have to labour for your daily bread or be distracted by other, more pressing matters is therefore crucial. The same is true of Stove's other two points: the need for quiet and for access to the learning of others. By access to the learning of others Stove means, at a minimum, access to libraries, but in many cases this access can also come, at least initially, through good teachers and trusted friends. Even so, for most of us, this is probably why attending university involves spending at least some time each day in the quiet of the library.

Of course, some people prefer reading in a cafeteria. Others find it just as easy to read on a bus. While at home, some enjoy having music play in the background. These places can all be conducive to reading of a certain sort, especially if the music is not too loud and there is someone on the bus to remind you when you've reached your stop. But even so, reading with full understanding requires a lack of distraction. This is true whether you are reading a chemical formula or a Victorian novel. When it comes time to do your most important reading, make sure you are in a quiet place with nothing and no one to disturb you.

When to read. Some reading is best done early in the morning so you have the rest of the day to think about it. Other reading can be done almost anytime, provided you have the time and ability to focus. Textbooks and other course materials should be read at least twice: once before the relevant lecture and then again afterward. Reading before a lecture helps you prepare for the lecture. It gives you an opportunity to make a list of the topics you don't understand so you can ask questions in class. It also means you will be familiar with the lecture's main themes. As a result, you won't be tempted to try to take notes about things you already know. Instead, you'll be able to relax and focus on new or more challenging material, something that makes note taking much easier. Re-reading your course materials again after the lecture gives you an opportunity to focus on key issues with greater understanding. It also means being able to compare what is written in your textbook with what was said during the lecture.

Regardless of the particular times you choose to do your reading, reading regularly for comparatively short periods of time is always more effective than trying to cram all your reading into one long session late in the term. Regular reading over many years will also give you insights and abilities that will serve you long after you leave college. As the 18th-century English reformer and pamphleteer, William Cobbett, commented during his first trip to the New World in the 1790s, reading does more than just inform, it helps the reader develop character:

> There are very few really ignorant men in America of native growth. Every farmer is more or less of a reader. ... They are all well-informed; modest without shyness; always free to communicate what they know, and never ashamed to acknowledge that they have yet to learn. You never hear them *boast* of their possessions, and you never hear them *complaining* of their wants. They have all been readers from their youth up; and there are few subjects upon which they cannot converse with you, whether of a political or scientific nature.[4]

Reading introduces us to the many parts of the world we haven't experienced first-hand. It gives us insight and a maturity that otherwise would be hard to acquire.

How to read. Different materials need to be read differently. Some materials can be read relatively quickly. Others need to be read slowly and more carefully. A mistake undergraduates often make is thinking technical material can be read just as quickly as ordinary writing. This is not so. Some scientific and mathematical formulas *should* take hours to read and understand. Regardless of what you are reading, reading should never be a race. It is better to read and understand five pages than to skim and misunderstand fifty.

New terminology and new symbols can be challenging to read, but they are really no different from words in English or any other natural language. The only real difference is efficiency. Technical symbols allow writers to pack larger amounts of information into a small space. In chemistry, for example, different symbols are used to represent different chemicals. Success in reading a chemical formula therefore depends on knowing the meaning of each of these basic symbols. The symbol 'C' represents an atom of carbon, 'H' represents an atom of hydrogen, and 'O' represents an atom of oxygen. A molecule of table salt, or sodium chloride, is represented by 'NaCl,' since 'Na' represents sodium and 'Cl' represents chlorine. The chemical chlorine is referred to as 'chloride' in this case because of its connection to sodium.

A chemical equation can then be understood as describing a chemical process. For example, the equation

$$AgNO_3(aq) + NaCl(aq) \rightarrow AgCl(s) + NaNO_3(aq)$$

tells us what happens when two chemicals, $AgNO_3$ (silver nitrate) and NaCl (sodium chloride), are mixed together under normal conditions. The substances mixed together are called the *reactants*. The substances resulting from the reaction are called the *products* of the reaction. The arrow, $\rightarrow$, separating reactants and products is read as *yields*. If a triangle appears above the arrow, this means that energy needs to be added to begin the reaction. Often this information is given in more detail by replacing the triangle with a specific temperature (say 500° C), pressure (say, 100 atm), or amount of energy (say, 1,000 cal).

Chemical equations also often indicate the state of each chemical substance. For example, '(s)' means the substance is a solid, '(l)' means the substance is a liquid, and '(g)' means the substance is a gas. The abbreviation '(aq)' for aqueous means that the substance is dissolved in water. Subscripts (or coefficients) indicate the relative amounts of each substance, expressed either in molecules or moles. When no subscript is shown, a 1 is assumed.

The equation for photosynthesis – the converting of light energy into chemical energy stored in sugar, together with oxygen – is perhaps the most important chemical equation for life as we know it:

$$\overset{674 \text{ cal}}{6\ CO_2 + 6\ H_2O \rightarrow C_6H_{12}O_6 + 6\ O_2.}$$

In other words, mixing carbon dioxide together with water, along with light from the sun, yields glucose (a type of sugar), together with oxygen.

Understanding a chemical formula in this way shows us that it is not surprising that it takes more time to read some types of writing than others, or that the key to understanding technical writing comes with understanding the alphabet, vocabulary and grammar of each new expression. It is also important to notice that nothing in the above example pertains solely to the natural sciences. An exactly parallel example could have been given from mathematics or computer science or music. Just imagine trying to read a piece of music if all the instructions were printed entirely in English, without the use of staffs, clefs, notes, rests, accidentals, key signatures and all the rest. A single line of music might easily fill an entire page of ordinary English text and, even if completely accurate, it would still be of no practical use to a performer. Understanding any technical expression – whether in science, music or accounting – requires that we take the time to read it carefully and that we have the patience to learn what each different symbol and combination of symbols means.

These examples also point to another important difference between technical and non-technical writing. Technical writing strives to include all relevant information in one place. After first carefully defining one's terms, the author hopes to give an exact, unambiguous, complete account of whatever needs to be said. This has many virtues, but it also shows why technical writing can sometimes appear dense, and why it requires detailed training to understand. Non-technical writing, in contrast, is often meant to be more evocative than complete. As the Canadian literary theorist Northrop Frye reminds us,

> The connections of literature are with the imagination, not with the reason, hence the ideal in literature is one of intensity and power rather than of precision or accuracy, as in science. There can be no intensity without precision, but to aim directly at precision is trying to seize the shadow.[5]

Shakespeare's famous couplet from *Romeo and Juliet* provides a helpful example:

What's in a name? that which we call a rose
By any other name would smell as sweet.[6]

These famous words may evoke strong feelings and memories. They may draw to mind the names of people closest to you, or a spring day when you once walked through a rose garden with someone you loved. What this couplet doesn't try to do is give a complete account of some object, event or encounter. Similarly, with Shakespeare's lines,

What a piece of work is a man!
How noble in reason!
How infinite in faculties!
In form and moving how express and admirable!
In action how like an angel!
In apprehension how like a god!
The beauty of the world!
The paragon of animals!
And yet, to me, what is this quintessence of dust?
Man delights not me: no, nor woman neither,
though by your smiling you seem to say so.[7]

The reference to man noble in reason might remind you of a favourite relative or teacher. The reference to an angel might remind you of a famous piece of art. The reference to dust is intended to remind you of the passage "earth to earth, ashes to ashes, dust to dust" from *Genesis*.[8] The success of these lines comes not from giving a complete account of some phenomena, and not just from Shakespeare's joke at the end, but from Shakespeare's ability to prompt numerous previously unconnected ideas and feelings to come together in the mind of the reader.

This is also why machine translation from one language into another has proved to be such a challenge. Evocative language intentionally lacks the precision necessary for unambiguous translation. One probably apocryphal example is that when the phrase "The spirit is willing but the flesh is weak"[9] was given to an early computer program designed to translate between Russian and English, the result was the less-than-accurate translation, "The vodka is good but the meat is rotten."

READING WITH COMPREHENSION

Different languages have been developed in different contexts for different purposes. Reading requires an understanding of a language's alphabet, vocabulary and grammar. Because reading involves following an author's train of thought, reading with comprehension can't be rushed.

Braille	⠐⠁⠇⠇ ⠓⠥⠍⠁⠝ ⠃⠑⠊⠝⠛⠎ ⠁⠗⠑ ⠃⠕⠗⠝ ⠋⠗⠑⠑ ⠁⠝⠙ ⠑⠟⠥⠁⠇ ⠊⠝ ⠙⠊⠛⠝⠊⠞⠽ ⠁⠝⠙ ⠗⠊⠛⠓⠞⠎⠲
C	`printf("hello, world\n");`
Chess	1 e4 e5, 2 Qh5 Nc6, 3 Bc4 d6, 4 Q×f7 mate
Chinese	千里之行始于一步
Chemistry	$6 CO_2 + 6 H_2O \rightarrow C_6H_{12}O_6 + 6 O_2$
English	It was the best of times, it was the worst of times.
French	Je pense, donc je suis.
German	Verweile doch, du bist so schön.

Whether in the humanities or the sciences, it is worth noting that much of the best writing can be read over and over, each time with new insight and greater understanding. Partly this is because good writing is a pleasure to read, but partly it is because good writing is packed with meaning. As the American poet Ezra Pound tells us, "It is as important for the purpose of thought to keep language efficient as it is in surgery to keep tetanus bacilli out of one's bandages. ... Great literature is simply language charged with meaning to the utmost possible degree."[10]

Regardless of what you are reading, don't confuse high-lighting with note taking. Some people like to highlight passages in their textbooks or on their computer screens. This can be useful but it is not the same as note taking.

READING WITH COMPREHENSION

Greek	ὁ δὲ ἀνεξέταστος βίος οὐ βιωτὸς ἀνθρώπῳ.
Japanese	国境の長いトンネルを抜けると雪国であっ
Latin	Scientia et potentia humana in idem coincident.
Mathematics	$e^{\pi} + 1 = 0$
Morse Code	● ● ● — — — ● ● ●
Music	(musical notation)
Physics	$E = mc^2$
Russian	Но линия, разделяющая добро и зло, пересекает сердце каждого человека
Spanish	El arte es una mentira que nos hace comprender la verdad.

Most of us read, not only to understand and learn, but also to remember. Only by *writing down in your own words* the important ideas of a book or article will you fully master and remember its content.[11]

What to read. There are two schools of thought about what to read. Both seem plausible. The first is that it is good to read everything, to read wherever your curiosity might take you. The second is that it is better to focus your reading more narrowly, to read only what's important.

Reading widely introduces readers to the richness of the world and to the wide scope of human thought. It helps build connections in the mind, making it easier to retain information. Like a muscle, the brain is strengthened by exercise. Reading in only one area is like exercising only one part of the body. A strong, healthy mind requires exposure to a wide variety of ideas.

Reading widely also helps fuel the imagination. Of course, imagination alone is never enough to advance knowledge. As the 20th-century mathematician Alfred North Whitehead tells us,

> Youth is imaginative, and if the imagination can be strengthened by discipline this energy of imagination can in great measure be preserved through life. The tragedy of the world is that those who are imaginative have but slight experience, and those who are experienced have feeble imagination. Fools act on imagination without knowledge, pedants act on knowledge without imagination. The task of a university is to weld together imagination and experience.[12]

Reading widely prompts our imagination. It exposes us to new ideas and previously un-thought possibilities. Even so, it is only when imagination is informed by knowledge that it is able to generate ideas of practical value.

It is at this point that our second school of thought becomes relevant. Unless we want to spend our lives re-inventing the wheel, it is often better to focus large amounts of our reading on what's important. Rather than reading every crackpot idea ever advanced, it is often more efficient to read comparatively narrowly, to learn which sources of information are most reliable and to concentrate our reading there. This is especially true in the age of the internet, when reliable and unreliable information can be posted side-by-side on a web page and it is sometimes hard to distinguish between the two.

This brings us to the role of teachers. As Whitehead also reminds us,

The universities are schools of education, and schools of research. But the primary reason for their existence is not to be found either in the mere knowledge conveyed to the students or in the mere opportunities for research afforded to the members of the faculty.

Both these functions could be performed at a cheaper rate, apart from these very expensive institutions. Books are cheap, and the system of apprenticeship is well understood. So far as the mere imparting of information is concerned, no university has had any justification for existence since the popularization of printing in the fifteenth century. Yet the chief impetus to the foundation of universities came after that date, and in more recent times has even increased.

The justification for a university is that it preserves the connection between knowledge and the zest of life, by uniting the young and the old in the imaginative consideration of learning. The university imparts information, but it imparts it imaginatively. At least this is the function which it should perform for society. A university which fails in this respect has no reason for existence.[13]

There is much that is true in this quotation. For most people, the "zest for life" that accompanies learning is real and long lasting. As Whitehead goes on to say, a good teacher is able to transform bare words on a page into something vibrant and alive: "A fact is no longer a bare fact: it is invested with all its possibilities. It is no longer a burden on the memory: it is energizing as the poet of our dreams, and as the architect of our purposes."[14] This bears repeating. Think of those facts and ideas that have been a burden to learn. Then compare them to those facts and ideas that you've been able to remember effortlessly. The difference is simple. Some ideas are easy to remember because they energize and excite us. They stick in our mind because, as Whitehead says, they become "the architect of our purposes." Knowing this can help you remember even the dullest of facts.

Even so, universities and professors also have another, more prosaic purpose. This is to help make learning *efficient*. It is part of the teacher's job to guide the student towards paths most likely to be successful, to act as a filter, explaining why some readings are more likely to be profitable than others. At a time when almost *everything* is available online, this role becomes even more central and important.

Centuries ago, when we didn't live in the midst of an information hurricane and when much less information was available to the average person, the stories, histories, plays and songs that people had access to were central to their lives in a way that today is difficult to understand. They were told and retold around campfires, in outdoor theatres and in town squares until they became a defining part of one's culture. Today there is an irony in that, as information has become more easily accessible, our most important stories have come to have less cultural significance. Many of our greatest books sit side-by-side on the shelf or in our computers or on our smart phones, indistinguishable from the latest passing fads. Perhaps things have always been this way. Even so, it is helpful to remember that not all ideas are equally important and not all reading will be equally profitable. Unless we get good advice about where to begin, it is easy to spend a lifetime running down blind alleys, taking years to discover what many people have already long known.

Further reading

Bald, Margaret, *Banned Books: Literature Suppressed on Religious Grounds*, New York: Facts on File, 1998

Bryson, Bill, *Shakespeare: The World as Stage,* New York: Harper Collins, 2007

de Botton, Alain, *How Proust can Change Your Life*, New York: Vintage, 1998

Downs, Robert B., *Books that Changed the World*, New York: New American Library, 1983

Frye, Northrop, *Anatomy of Criticism: Four Essays,* Princeton: Princeton University Press, 1957

Frye, Northrop, *The Educated Imagination*, Bloomington: Indiana University Press, 1964

Giltrow, Janet, *Academic Reading: Reading and Writing in the Disciplines*, 2nd edn, Peterborough (ON): Broadview Press, 2002

Karolides, Nicholas J., *Banned Books: Literature Suppressed on Political Grounds*, New York: Facts on File, 1998

Pound, Ezra, *How to Read*, London: Desmond Harmsworth, 1931

Quiller-Couch, Arthur, *On the Art of Reading*, Cambridge: Cambridge University Press, 1920

Sova, Dawn B., *Banned Books: Literature Suppressed on Sexual Grounds*, New York: Facts on File, 1998

Sova, Dawn B., *Banned Books: Literature Suppressed on Social Grounds*, New York: Facts on File, 1998

Sova, Dawn B., *Banned Plays: Censorship Histories of 125 Stage Dramas*, New York: Facts on File, 2004

Sutherland, John, *How to Read a Novel*, New York: St Martin's Press, 2006

Whitehead, Alfred North, *The Aims of Education and Other Essays*, New York: The Macmillan Company, 1929

Wiker, Benjamin, *10 Books that Screwed Up the World, and 5 Others that didn't Help*, Washington (DC): Regnery Publishing, 2008

Chapter 5

Be a Demanding Writer

ৼ ঌ

During his lifetime, David Hume was most famous as a historian. His six-volume *History of England* (1754-1762) was a bestseller, earning him not only a large public following but also enormous sums of money. Originally entitled *The History of Great Britain*, the work has appeared in over a hundred editions. A leading figure of the Scottish Enlightenment, Hume also played a fundamental role ushering in the modern age of reason. Together with other famous Scots such as Francis Hutcheson, Adam Smith, Thomas Reid and John Playfair, Hume made popular the idea that it is reason and observation – rather than other forms of authority – that hold the key to progress in fields as diverse as history, philosophy, engineering, the natural sciences, medicine, law, architecture, agriculture and economics. In fact, Hume's conviction that people could improve their circumstances through reason and observation soon came to characterize, not just his century, but an entire age. Despite this, Hume was unable to get a job teaching at a Scottish university. The problem was his atheism.

During the 18th century, critics of Christianity still needed to express themselves carefully. As late as 1697, men were still being hanged in Britain for blasphemy and other crimes of the mind.[1] As a result, Hume published several of his most influential works anonymously,[2] and neither his *Dialogues concerning Natural Religion* (1779) nor his *Essays on Suicide and the Immortality of the Soul* (1783) appeared in print until after his death and, even then, devoid of a publisher's imprint. Despite the risk, Hume remained forthright in his public condemnation of religion throughout his life. As he writes in his 1748 *Enquiry concerning Human Understanding,*

> we may conclude, that the Christian religion not only was at first attended with miracles, but even at this day cannot be believed by any reasonable person without one. Mere reason is insufficient to convince us of its veracity: And whoever is moved by *Faith* to assent to it, is conscious of a continued miracle in his own person, which subverts all the principles of his understanding, and gives him a determination to believe what is most contrary to custom and experience.[3]

Eventually he was charged with heresy. Perhaps surprisingly, he was acquitted on the ground that, although technically still a Christian, his atheism showed that he effectively had resigned from the Church. This meant that he fell outside the purview of the Church's power, an unusually enlightened judgment for its day.[4] Despite this legal success, because of petitions from influential members of the clergy, Hume failed to obtain teaching posts at both the University of Edinburgh and the University of Glasgow. If he couldn't get something as basic as belief in God right, one can hear his critics saying, then what reason is there to think he might be trusted on other, more controversial matters?

Hume's three rules. Where even Hume's most fervent critics agree is that Hume is a master stylist. It is no accident that his *History* was so well received or that so many of his other writings continue to be read to the present day. They remain not just full of insight but a pleasure to read. Many quotations might be cited giving advice to writers, but three are especially worth repeating.

First, when considering one's *writing style*, it is fun to note Hume's observation that

> Amidst all this bustle 'tis not reason, which carries the prize, but eloquence ... The victory is not gained by the men at arms, who manage the pike and the sword; but by the trumpeters, drummers, and musicians of the army.[5]

Perhaps this metaphor overstates things slightly. It is unlikely that in Hume's day musicians alone, without the aid of cavalrymen, infantrymen or the pike, won many battles. But Hume's underlying point, stripped of hyperbole, remains true: for successful writing, style is just as important as content. Unless people *want* to read what you've written, it is unlikely they will take the time and effort to do so. Unless what you write is clear and interesting, readers are unlikely to make the effort to understand what you have to say. When writing, we ignore issues of presentation at our peril.

Second, Hume reminds us of the importance of being able to articulate a *core argument*. We know from experience how unsatisfactory discussions can be when people speak at cross-purposes. Often what motivates people to hold a particular point of view is completely ignored by their critics. As a result, no matter how articulate a critic might be, no progress is made since the main point at issue is never engaged. To help us realize this, Hume introduces a second military metaphor:

> Here then is the only expedient, from which we can hope for success in our philosophical researches, to leave the tedious lingering method, which we have hitherto followed, and instead of taking now and then a castle or village on the frontier, to march up directly to the capital or centre ... .[6]

In other words, Hume is reminding us that intellectual battles, like military ones, are won at the centre. Unless we focus on the core point of dispute, until we convince our opponents that their most important assumptions, arguments or conclusions are incorrect, we will never change anyone's mind. Progress at the fringes may be tactically helpful at times, but it can never replace a strong, core argument.

HUME'S THREE RULES FOR SUCCESSFUL WRITING

Hume's 1st Rule   Pay attention to style.
Hume's 2nd Rule   Go quickly to the heart of the issue.
Hume's 3rd Rule   Don't' overstate or understate your conclusion.

Finally, when considering the construction and evaluation of one's central ideas, Hume reminds us that

A wise man, therefore, proportions his belief to the evidence.[7]

In other words, when crafting an argument, it is important not to overstate or understate your conclusion. It is important to find the conclusion that is best supported by the evidence you are able to marshal, not vice-versa. Thinking we know what is true in advance of investigation and then attempting to find arguments in support of our pre-conceived notion of what is right is always a dangerous way to proceed.

Together, we might summarize Hume's three observations as follows: First, pay attention to style. Second, go quickly to the heart of the issue. Third, don't overstate or understate your conclusion.

Some helpful guidelines. Hume's three rules take us some distance towards understanding the nature and importance of good writing, but a few more concrete guidelines are also helpful. Here are several rules of thumb that students often find worth remembering:

Identify your main goal. Why are you writing? What do you want to achieve? Sometimes we write to explain. Other times we write to entertain. Sometimes we write just to keep a record of something that has happened. But often we write to defend a specific claim or point of view. Regardless of your particular goal, identify your main goal and go quickly to the heart of the

---

STYLE GUIDES 1

General

Aaron, Jane E. and Elaine Bander, *The Little, Brown Essential Handbook for Writers*, Don Mills, ON: Addison Wesley Longman, 1999

Fowler, H.W., *A Dictionary of Modern English Usage*, 2nd edn, Oxford: Oxford University Press, 1968

Garner, Bryan A., *A Dictionary of Modern American Usage*, New York: Oxford University Press, 1998

Gibaldi, Joseph, *The MLA Style Manual and Guide to Scholarly Publishing*, 2nd edn, New York: Modern Language Association of America, 1998

Judd, Karen, *Copy Editing: A Practical Guide*, Los Altos, CA: Crisp Publications, Inc., 1990

Strunk, William, and E.B. White, *The Elements of Style*, 4th edn, New York: Pearson Longman, 1999

University of Chicago, *The Chicago Manual of Style*, 15th edn, Chicago: University of Chicago Press, 2003

Virag, Karen, *Editing Canadian English: A Guide for Editors, Writers and Everyone Who Works with Words*, 3rd edn, Toronto: Editors' Association of Canada, 2017

Student Writing

Davis, Roger, Laura K. Davis, Kay L. Stewart and Chris J. Bullock, *Essay Writing for Canadian Students with Readings*, 7th edn, Toronto: Pearson, 2013

Gibaldi, Joseph, *MLA Handbook for Writers of Research Papers*, 7th edn, New York: Modern Language Association of America, 2009

Turabian, Kate L., *A Manual for Writers of Term Papers, Theses, and Dissertations*, 7th edn, Chicago: University of Chicago Press, 2007

Turabian, Kate L., et al., *Student's Guide to Writing College Papers*, 4th edn, Chicago: University of Chicago Press, 2010

---

matter. Your readers need to understand exactly what it is you want to achieve and why it is important. The sooner you are able to convey this information to them, the better.

Identify your main audience. For whom are you writing? What background knowledge should you assume? What unfamiliar terms need to be defined? When writing, it is important to meet your reader half way. Take the time to explain what your reader needs to know in addition to taking the time to report what it is you want to say. Craft your argument to meet your audience's needs. As Aristotle put it over twenty-three hundred years ago, it is "equally foolish to accept probable reasoning from a mathematician and to demand from a rhetorician scientific proofs."[8]

Write clearly. Writing style is important. Not only is it important to write clearly, it is also important to make sure you chose a style that is appropriate to your goal and audience. Take the time to polish your work. Do your best to eliminate typographical errors. Try not to hand in work containing spelling or grammatical errors. Even though Mark Twain tells us "It is a weak mind that can think of only one way to spell a word,"[9] readers tend to mistrust authors who make careless mistakes. Try to avoid complex sentences. Spelling mistakes and difficult sentence constructions distract the reader from the message the writer is wanting to convey. Define any technical terms you may be using. Never use a big word when a small one will do.

Work in stages. Work first on the heart of your paper. Then, after you have developed your central claim, begin work on the structure of your paper. What structure will make it easier for readers to understand what you have to say? What structure will make readers *want* to read what you have to say? Then polish, polish, polish.

Write multiple drafts. Many authors find it helpful to remember that good writing needs to go through numerous drafts. Six, seven, eight or more drafts are not uncommon. Remembering this reminds us not to be too critical of our first efforts and helps us to avoid writer's block. One of the most liberating things about writing – unlike, say, brain surgery – is that writers don't have to get things right the first time! Your first, second and third drafts *should* contain errors.

STYLE GUIDES 2

The Arts & Humanities

History – Storey, William Kelleher, *Writing History: A Guide for Students*, 3rd edn, New York, Oxford: Oxford University Press, 2009

Philosophy – Vaughn, Lewis, and Jillian Scott McIntosh, *Writing Philosophy*, Don Mills (ON): Oxford University Press, 2009

The Natural Sciences

Biology – Council of Science Editors, *Scientific Style and Format: The CSE Manual for Authors, Editors, and Publishers*, 7th edn, Reston (VA): Council of Science Editors (in cooperation with Rockefeller University Press), 2006

Chemistry – American Chemical Society, *The ACS Style Guide: Effective Communication of Scientific Information,* 3rd edn, Washington (DC): American Chemical Society, and New York: Oxford University ty Press, 2006

Physics – American Institute of Physics, *AIP Style Manual*, 4th edn, New York: American Institute of Physics, 1990

The Social Sciences

Psychology – American Psychological Association, *Publication Manual of the American Psychological Association*, 5th edn, Washington (DC): American Psychological Association, 2001

Sociology – American Sociological Association, *American Sociological Association Style Guide*, 3rd edn, Washington (DC): American Sociological Association, 2007

Don't get sidetracked. What is your job today? Researching? Writing? Editing? Proofreading? Don't get sidetracked fact checking if today's main job is writing. If you find yourself easily diverted when working in the evening, try doing your most important writing in the morning. It is often best to leave the writing of your introduction and conclusion until after all the other sections of your paper are complete.

Learn from criticism. Feedback from friends, teaching assistants and others is important, especially with regard to writing. If someone tells you that something you've written is unclear or unconvincing, don't be dismissive. Even if you're sure that a reader has misunderstood your point, take a moment to figure out why the misunderstanding occurred. Ensuring clarity is the job of the writer, not the reader.

A final check. After you've finished your penultimate draft, read what you've written *out loud* to yourself from start to finish. (If you don't want anyone to see your lips moving, lock yourself in your bedroom before you begin.) Why did you pause? Was something unclear? Why did you stumble? Do revisions need to be made? Why did you want to take a break? Was the section you were reading a little repetitive? A little boring? It never hurts to remember that polishing and proofreading often take longer than planned, so try to complete your penultimate draft early.

What practical value do these guidelines have? In essence, they tell us that it is important to know what goal we want to achieve. (What is your main purpose in writing what you do? Who is your main audience?) They also remind us that it is important to keep in mind a few concrete suggestions about how to go about achieving our goal. (Write clearly. Write in stages. Write multiple drafts. Don't get sidetracked. Learn from criticism. Check your work.) Finally, it is important to notice what these guidelines *don't* say. They don't say that there is any single, mechanical way to write. In fact, just the opposite is true.

When thinking about how to improve your writing, it also sometimes helps to compare your writing to that of someone else. For example, consider the opening sentence from Charles Dickens' *A Tale of Two Cities*:

> It was the best of times, it was the worst of times, it was the age of wisdom, it was the age of foolishness, it was the epoch of belief, it was the epoch of incredulity, it was the season of Light, it was the season of Darkness, it was the spring of hope, it was the winter of despair.[10]

STYLE GUIDES 3

The Professions

Journalism & Communication – Associated Press, *Associated Press Stylebook and Briefing on Media Law*, 43rd edn, New York: Basic Books, 2009

Law (Australia) – Kirwan, Lucy, and Jeremy Masters, *Australian Guide to Legal Citation*, 2nd edn, Melbourne: Melbourne University Law Review Association Inc., 2002

Law (Canada) – McGill Law Journal, *Canadian Guide to Uniform Legal Citation*, 6th edn, Toronto: Carswell, 2006

Law (UK) – French, Derek, *How to Cite Legal Authorities*, London: Blackstone Press, 2003

Law (USA) – Harvard Law Review Association, *The Bluebook: A Uniform System of Citation*, 18th edn, Cambridge (MA): Harvard Law Review Association, 2005

Medicine, Dentistry & Health Sciences – American Medical Association, *AMA Manual of Style: A Guide for Authors and Editors*, 10th edn, New York: Oxford University Press, 2007

In contrast, here is a quite different opening sentence. This one comes from J.D. Salinger's *The Catcher in the Rye*:

> If you really want to hear about it, the first thing you'll probably want to know is where I was born, and what my lousy childhood was like, and how my parents were occupied and all before they had me, and all that David Copperfield

kind of crap, but I don't feel like going into it, if you want to know the truth.[11]

Here are two more. The first is from Gabrielle Roy's novel, *The Tin Flute*:

Where was the young man who had given her so many admiring glances yesterday?[12]

This one comes from George Orwell's *Nineteen Eighty-Four*:

It was a bright cold day in April, and the clocks were striking thirteen.[13]

There is not a lot in common between these four famous sentences. Two are by British authors, one is by an American and one by a Canadian. Two are short. Two are long. Two seem to begin at the beginning. Two don't. The content in all four is different, as is the language. The earliest was written in 1859, the latest in 1951. Three were written by men, one by a woman. What they share – perhaps the only thing they share – is that they all make their readers *want to read more*. More than anything else, this probably tells us all we need to know about the essence of good writing.

One other point to note about good writing is the power it gives the author. As Northrop Frye tells us, "a literate person is first and foremost an articulate person, one who has the power to say what he means, which sounds simple but is immensely difficult."[14] In other words, it is a common but fundamental mistake to believe "that you can have ideas without being able to put them into words."[15] It isn't until you are successful at putting your ideas into words that you can be confident in what you believe. Perhaps more than anything else, being able to express your ideas in clear, understandable language will give you a tremendous advantage as you go through life.

Academic writing. Academic writing poses its own set of challenges. Partly this is because different disciplines have their own technical vocabularies. Partly it is because some academic writing requires the reporting of detailed data and calculations. Partly it is because different disciplines have different conventions concerning style and citations. Historians, for example, prefer to write in the past tense:

> As Aristophanes *wrote*, 'Under every rock lurks a politician'.

Philosophers prefer to write in the present tense:

> As Aristophanes *writes*, 'Under every rock lurks a politician'.

Philosophers like to pretend they can still have back-and-forth conversations with authors who are long dead. Historians know better than to pretend about such things. Despite such differences, good academic writing always has at least two things in common: the clear use of language and the careful defence of a thesis or evaluation of a hypothesis.

The clear use of language requires that we be aware of ambiguities and equivocations, of small errors and infelicities that might otherwise go unnoticed. One amusing example comes from Frye:

> I remember a *New Yorker* cartoon of a milkman who found the notice "no milk" on a doorstep, and woke up the household at four in the morning to enquire whether he meant that he had no milk or that he wanted no milk. I suspect that the milkman was a retired teacher of English: certainly he reflects the disadvantages of being sensitive to the nuances of expression.[16]

Being sensitive to the nuances of expression while you read will not only help you understand other writers. It will also help you become clearer in your own writing.

The requirement to defend a thesis or evaluate a hypothesis makes it relatively easy to establish an essay's overall structure. Each thesis or hypothesis needs to be stated clearly. Technical terms need to be carefully defined. Evidence in favour of or against the thesis or hypothesis needs to be marshaled and a conclusion needs to be drawn.

In this context, it is important to avoid a few common but elementary mistakes:

- Don't confuse *considering* a view with *advocating* that view. Many authors ask their readers to consider a variety of views. Being able to consider an idea without necessarily accepting it gives us the opportunity to evaluate a wide range of options that otherwise might go unnoticed.

- Don't confuse *advocating* a view with *defending* that view. Merely describing an idea or a point of view and saying that you accept it is not the same as defending it. Merely claiming that a proposition is true is not the same as giving good reasons for its adoption. Most academic writing requires you to explain, not just *what* you think is true, but *why* you think it is true.

- Don't confuse *good rhetoric* with *good logic*. Rhetoric is the science of successful persuasion. Logic is the science of sound reasoning. Don't confuse the two. We all want to persuade our readers that our thesis or hypothesis is correct but, when doing so, be sure to give your reader good reasons for accepting your position. Just because an argument happens to have a true conclusion doesn't mean it's a good argument.

Here are a few more guidelines specifically designed to help you write in an academic context:

Be careful to answer the question(s) asked of you. Academic assignments are often quite specific. When they are, be sure to answer exactly the question(s) you've been asked. If you've been asked to write an essay on, say, just-war theory, it is unlikely you will have been asked simply to write down everything you can discover about the idea of a just war. Much more likely is that you'll be asked to focus on a specific aspect of this general topic.

Let's assume, for example, that you've been taught that the traditional definition of a just war requires any morally defensible war to satisfy six criteria. Specifically, the war must be

- Initiated by a legitimate authority
- Initiated for an important purpose
- Initiated for a morally defensible purpose
- Initiated as a last resort
- Initiated with a reasonable chance of success, and
- Likely to have significantly greater benefits than harms.

Different instructors might now ask you quite different questions. In a history course, you might be asked to write about the history of this definition. For example, who introduced it and when? How has the idea changed over the centuries? In a political science course, you might be asked to explain how the definition has worked in practice. When nations have gone to war, have they been influenced by this definition of a just war? Or has it been largely irrelevant? In a law course, you might be asked to compare this definition to modern legal practice. Is it reflected in contemporary Supreme Court decisions? In international treaty obligations? In a philosophy course, you might be asked to evaluate the definition. Are the above six criteria accurate? Are they sufficient? Are the criteria listed above true of defensive, as well as offensive, wars? Is there even such a thing as a just war?

State your thesis clearly. Every academic paper needs to have a thesis or hypothesis. Explaining the purpose of your paper not only involves identifying your main thesis or hypothesis, it also means explaining why it is interesting or significant.

Sometimes it helps to state your main goal right at the beginning. Sometimes it helps to create a name for the position you're defending. In any case, make sure you are able to state your thesis clearly and concisely.

Develop your argument. What evidence can you give in support of your thesis or hypothesis? Not only should you marshal evidence and build an argument in favour of your conclusion, if the argument is long and complex you may need to help your readers navigate their way through your writing by including some "sign-posting." Comments that summarize your argument's various components, or that say things like "I'll return to this objection later ....," help readers keep track of connections that otherwise might be lost. Do whatever is necessary to help your reader understand both the content and structure of your writing.

Evaluate your argument critically. Evaluating your argument involves raising plausible objections to your main thesis or hypothesis, and then explaining why these objections fail. In doing so, you will need to exercise good judgment. Try to ask yourself what objections a typical reader might raise against your thesis or hypothesis and then respond to each of them. Not every objection may be worth pursuing but many will be.

Use reliable sources. Don't use general search engines such as Bing, Google or Yahoo in place of academic searches. Wikipedia can often be a good place to find a first, rough overview, but it can't replace carefully written, peer-reviewed academic work. Ask your librarian which databases are most relevant to your work. Good academic sources (whether found online or on a library shelf) will be peer-reviewed. This means that prior to publication they will have been checked and corrected by experts in the field. In contrast, some online information sources (including Wikipedia) may allow anyone – even those with a vested interest or ideological bias[17] – to post or edit material. Especially when dealing with controversial material, it is always a good idea to try to confirm information you want to use by looking for it in a variety of independent sources.

Fully reference all quotations and citations. Give complete references for all quotations. Add a footnote or endnote every time you rely on another person's words or ideas.

Never cut and paste from the internet. Remember to mark omissions from within a quotation using an ellipsis ("..."). Mark additions to quotations using square brackets ("[...]"). Since different disciplines use different referencing methods, ask your librarian or teaching assistant which style guide is most appropriate for your discipline.

Summarize your conclusions. Once you've finished writing the main body of your essay, be careful to summarize your conclusions accurately. Be clear about what you've accomplished. Don't overstate or understate what you've been able to achieve.

When writing, it also helps to know the meaning of several elementary editing marks. This makes it easier to revise and proofread your own work. It also makes it easier to read the corrections put on your paper by your graders. Whether you are writing an essay for a course, contributing a column to a student newspaper, writing a business plan as part of an application for a bank loan, or writing a press release for a political event, knowing how to edit your work will be a great advantage. *Copy editor's marks* are generally used to suggest minor changes, for example changes in spelling or punctuation or typeface. *Style editor's marks* are generally used to indicate more substantial changes, for example the insertion or removal of larger amounts of text. They are also used to give suggestions about word choice, sentence structure, argument structure and grammar.

COPY EDITOR'S MARKS

Task	Symbol	Mark in Text
Delete a character	✓ or ⁊	delete a character
Return to original	stet	return to ~~original~~
Add a space	⧢	add aspace
Close a space	◡	close a s pace
Space evenly throughout	eq #	space evenly throughout
Set in *italics*	ital	set in italics
Set in **boldface**	bf	set in boldface
Return to roman	rom	return to *roman*
Set in SMALL CAPS	sm cap	set in small caps
Set in CAPS	cap	set in caps
Return to lower case	lc	return to LOWER CASE
Return to upper case	cap	return to upper case
Set in subscript: H_2O	∧	set in subscript: $H2O$
Set in superscript: πr^2	∨	set in superscript: $\pi r2$
Add hyphen-here	(−) or |H|	add hyphen/here
Add en-dash–here	⅟N or |N|	add en-dash/here
Add em-dash—here	⅟M or |M|	add em-dash/here
Add (parentheses)	(/)	add/parentheses
Add [brackets]	[/]	add/brackets
Add period.	⊙	add period⊙
Add colon:	⊙	add colon⊙
Add semi-colon;	⊙	add semi-colon⊙
Add comma,	⋏	add comma⋏
Add apostrophe'	∨	add apostrophe∨
Add 'single quotes'	⸌/⸍	add single quotes
Add "double quotes"	⸌⸌/⸍⸍	add double quotes
Change to "smart quotes"	smart	change to smart quotes
Return to "straight quotes"	straight	return to straight quotes
Fix spelling	sp	fix speling
Fix wrong font	wf	change font
Fix wrong word	wrong	less than ten articles

STYLE EDITOR'S MARKS

Task	Symbol	Mark in Text
Delete a word or phrase	⌫ or ⊢	delete a ~~word~~ word or ~~phrase~~
Insert some text	∧ or ⋏	insert text _(some)_
Transpose	∿	transpose (words)(these)
Start new line	⌐	the end. The beginning
Start new paragraph	¶	the end. The beginning
Run in with previous line	⟋	the end. The beginning
Insert indent	⌐	Insert indent
Remove indent	⊏	Remove indent
Abbreviate	(abbr)	six (volumes)
Expand abbreviation	(exp) or (sp)	six (vols)
Change to active voice	(active)	(is preferred by readers)
Change to passive voice	(passive)	(readers prefer)
Fix awkward wording	(awk)	awkward (wording here)
Fix dangling participle	(dp)	(While walking home, the bank alarm went off.)
Fix grammar	(gram)	(the readers and her)
Fix *non sequitur*	(non seq)	He dances well, (so he must be good at math.)
Fix pagination	(pg #)	page (14)
Fix run-on sentence	(r-o)	and on (and on and on)
Fix sentence fragment	(frag)	(And afterward.)
Remove colloquialism	(coll)	it was (a quick-and-dirty) fix
Remove irrelevant text	(irr)	He arrived Tuesday (the 14th.)
Remove repetitive text	(rep)	He came (and arrived.)
Add missing citation	(cit)	He arrived in June 1914.
Check fact	(check) or (ok?)	He taught (after the war.)
Check (or provide) translation	(trans)	(Je pense, donc je suis.)
Needs clarification	(?)	(He was unclear.)

The virtue of memorable prose. Finally, it is worth remember-ing that even the best writers need to polish their work and then polish it again. It is one thing to be able to articulate a general idea. It is another to find the words that make the idea memorable. Here is a famous example:

> We hold these truths to be self-evident, that all men are created equal, that they are endowed by their Creator with certain unalienable Rights, that among these are Life, Liberty and the pursuit of Happiness. That to secure these rights, Governments are instituted among Men, deriving their just powers from the consent of the governed ...[18]

The quotation comes from the preamble to the American *Declaration of Independence*, written in 1776 by Thomas Jefferson when he was thirty-three years old. (Jefferson later went on to become the third President of the United States.) Here is his original 'first draft':

> We hold these truths to be sacred & undeniable; that all men are created equal & independent, that from that equal creation they derive rights inherent & inalienable, among which are the preservation of life, & liberty, and the pursuit of happiness; that to secure these ends, governments are instituted among men, deriving their just powers from the consent of the governed ...[19]

Of these two versions, which is better? Why? Is it that sometimes three words ("sacred & undeniable") have been replaced by one ("self-evident")? Is it that sometimes the impersonal ("that from that equal creation they derive rights inherent & inalienable") has been replaced by the personal ("that they are endowed by their Creator with certain unalienable Rights")? Is it that sometimes an awkward phrase ("the preservation of life, & liberty, and the pursuit of happiness") has been replaced by a more memorable one ("Life, Liberty and the pursuit of Happiness")?

It is by considering possible changes like these in our own writing on a daily basis – whether in an academic essay, a lab assignment or an email letter home to family – that our own writing improves. And with improvement comes not just memorability but influence.

Further reading

Bryson, Bill, *The Penguin Dictionary of Troublesome Words*, New York: Penguin Books, 1984

Day, Robert A., and Barbara Gastel, *How to Write and Publish a Scientific Paper*, 6th edn, Cambridge: Cambridge University Press, 2006

Fish, Stanley, *How to Write a Sentence: And How to Read One,* New York: Harper Collins, 2011

Germano, William P., *Getting It Published: A Guide for Scholars and Anyone Else Serious about Serious Books*, 2nd edn, Chicago: University of Chicago Press, 2008

Giltrow, Janet, *Academic Writing: How to Read and Write Scholarly Prose*, 3rd edn, Peterborough (ON): Broadview Press, 2002

Goldstein, Tom, and Jethro K. Lieberman, *The Lawyer's Guide to Writing Well*, 2nd edn, Berkeley, Los Angeles: University of California Press, 2002

Harvey, Gordon, *Writing with Sources*, 2nd edn, Indianapolis, IN: Hackett Publishing Company, 2008

Harvey, Michael, *The Nuts and Bolts of College Writing*, Indianapolis, IN: Hackett Publishing Company, 2003

Kennedy, X.J., Dana Gioia and Mark Bauerlein, *Handbook of Literary Terms*, 2nd edn, New York: Pearson Longman, 2009

Matthews, Janice R., and Robert W. Matthews, *Successful Scientific Writing: A Step-by-Step Guide for the Biological and Medical Sciences*, 3rd edn, Cambridge: Cambridge University Press, 2007

Quiller-Couch, Arthur, *On the Art of Writing*, Cambridge: Cambridge University Press, 1916

Rountree, Cathleen, *The Writer's Mentor: A Guide to Putting Passion on Paper*, San Francisco: Conari Press, 2002

Weston, Anthony, *A Rulebook for Arguments*, 4th edn, Indianapolis: Hackett Publishing Co., 2009

Williams, Joseph M., and Ira B. Nadel, *Style: Ten Lessons in Clarity and Grace,* Toronto: Pearson Education Canada, 2005

Chapter 6

Calculate Mechanically, Think Creatively

What would life be like without music? Whether you prefer Diana Krall or Randy Bachman, Ben Heppner or Jon Vickers, Mozart's *The Marriage of Figaro* or Shania Twain's *Man! I Feel like a Woman*, music is an essential part of any good life. Whether you would rather listen to Aaron Copeland's *Fanfare for the Common Man* or Oscar Peterson's *Hymn to Freedom* or Vince Guaraldi's *Linus and Lucy*, taking a course about the history of music will be inspiring.

Learning something about the fine arts also helps us clarify the difference between creativity and discovery and, with it, the difference between the arts and the sciences. A story about the famous scientist Werner Heisenberg is helpful for understanding the distinction. Heisenberg is the physicist whose uncertainty principle (also called the principle of determinacy) shows that, in quantum mechanics, there is a limit to the accuracy with which the values of certain pairs of physical quantities (such as the position and momentum of an electron) can be calculated. Even if all the relevant initial conditions have been specified, both values can't be calculated together with certainty.

As the historian John Nef tells it, when visiting Cambridge Heisenberg was asked to play something on the piano:

He sat down at the piano and played from beginning to end Opus 111, the last sonata of Beethoven, which is an absolutely unique work. All the dons were more and more overwhelmed by this music, and there wasn't a sound when he finished.

Heisenberg is reported in this connection to have discussed the difference between science and art. "If I had never lived, someone else would probably have formulated the principle of determinacy. If Beethoven had never lived, no one would have written Opus 111."[1]

The suggestion Heisenberg is making is that scientific discovery is in some sense objective and perhaps even deterministic. The world is out there, just waiting to be discovered. With enough work and a bit of luck, objective features of the world can always be discovered and described. In contrast, artistic creation – story-telling, music and other creative arts – owes as much to its creators as to the world itself.

True as this might be, inquiry into even the most objective subjects is helped by having a creative mind. Even in mathematics, perhaps the most objective of all disciplines, discovery is something more than mere rule following. Even in the most mathematical of the sciences, we calculate mechanically, but we discover creatively.

One of the most often-told stories of mathematical genius is about a young German prodigy named Carl Gauss. The story concerns Gauss's discovery of how to sum a series of numbers. As an adult, Gauss made fundamental contributions to almost every field of mathematics, including number theory, analysis, differential geometry and statistics, but even as a child his talents were apparent:

Shortly after his seventh birthday Gauss entered his first school, a squalid relic of the Middle Ages run by a virile brute, one Büttner, whose idea of teaching the hundred or so boys in his charge was to thrash them into such a state of terrified stupidity that they forgot their own names. More of the good old days for which sentimental reactionaries long. It was in this hell-hole that Gauss found his fortune.[2]

During his first few years in the school, Gauss kept his head down. But when he was nine, he began his first class in arithmetic.

> As it was the beginning class none of the boys had ever heard of an arithmetic progression. It was easy then for the heroic Büttner to give out a long problem in addition whose answer he could find by a formula in a few seconds. The problem was of the following sort, $81297 + 81495 + 81693 + ... + 100899$, where the step from one number to the next is the same all along (here 198), and a given number of terms (here 100) are to be added.
>
> It was the custom of the school for the boy who first got the answer to lay his slate on the table; the next laid his slate on top of the first, and so on. Büttner had barely finished stating the problem when Gauss flung his slate on the table: "There it lies," he said – "*Ligget se*" in his peasant dialect. Then, for the ensuing hour, while the other boys toiled, he sat with his hands folded, favored now and then by a sarcastic glance from Büttner, who imagined the youngest pupil in the class was just another blockhead. At the end of the period Büttner looked over the slates. On Gauss' slate there appeared but a single number. To the end of his days Gauss loved to tell how the one number he had written down was the correct answer and how all the others were wrong. Gauss had not been shown the trick for doing such problems rapidly. It is very ordinary once it is known, but for a boy of ten to find it instantaneously by himself is not so ordinary.
>
> This opened the door through which Gauss passed on to immortality. Büttner was so astonished at what the boy of ten had done without instruction that he promptly redeemed himself and to at least one of his pupils became a humane teacher. Out of his own pocket he paid for the best textbook on arithmetic obtainable and presented it to Gauss. The boy flashed through the book. "He is beyond me," Büttner said; "I can teach him nothing more."[3]

How had Gauss solved the problem? Presumably he had noticed that the pair-wise addition of terms from opposite ends of the list yields identical sums. For example, say we want to sum all the numbers from 1 to 100. If we list all the numbers in ascending order and then, underneath them, we list the same numbers in descending order, each pair will sum to 101:

1	2	3	4	5	...	98	99	100
100	99	98	97	96	...	3	2	1
101	101	101	101	101	...	101	101	101

Since there are a hundred such pairs, the total of the two series together will be 100×101, or 10,100, and the sum of the first series alone will be half this number, or 5,050. In other words, the total will be the pair-wise sum (101) multiplied by half the length of the series (50).

Applying this same insight to Gauss's original problem, we get

81,297	81,495	81,693	81,891	....	100,899
100,899	100,701	100,503	100,305	....	81,297
182,196	182,196	182,196	182,196	....	182,196

Once again, since there are 100 pairs, the total of the two series together will be $100 \times 182{,}196$, or 18,219,600, and the sum of the first series alone will be half this number, or 9,109,800. In other words, the total once again will be the pair-wise sum (182,196) multiplied by half the length of the series (50).

Generalizing from these two cases, and letting r be the initial number in the series, s the final number in the series, and n the total number of terms in the series, we get the formula

$$n/2 \times (r + s).$$

Gauss's calculation and this formula tell us much about mathematics. For example, they show us both the simplicity and the complexity of mathematical calculations. They also help us understand the difference between rule following and proof, and introduce us to questions about large numbers and perhaps even infinity. All of these ideas are important.

Of course, one doesn't have to be a mathematical genius to enjoy mathematics, just as we don't need to be gifted performers or composers to enjoy music. But such enjoyment is always helped by knowing a little music. Or a little mathematics.

Algorithms. An algorithm is a rule (or sequence of instructions) that, if followed, will generate an answer to a problem. Most calculations, whether in mathematics, computer science or the natural sciences, rely on algorithms. For example, to solve Gauss's problem, we decided to let r be the first number in the series, s the final number in the series, and n the total number of terms in the series. We then simply added r to s and multiplied this sum by half of n.

To work, an algorithm needs to satisfy three conditions: First, it needs to be *finite*. Second, it needs to be *mechanical*. Third, it needs to be *effective*. Being *finite* not only means that the rule can be stated using a finite number of words. It also means that when the rule is followed, the calculation will be completed in a finite period of time using a finite number of steps. Being *mechanical* means that following the rule won't require imagination (or even understanding) of any kind. Being *effective* means that following the rule correctly will always result in the correct answer. Flipping a coin to decide which stocks will maximize your investment return is both finite and mechanical but isn't going to be effective.

Understanding how algorithms work shows us why *calculating* is such a small part of mathematics. Recalling Gauss's example above, we see immediately that once we knew the algorithm, doing the calculation was easy. Much harder was *discovering* the algorithm in the first place. *Discovering* an algorithm – as Gauss did – often requires imagination and persistence. Rarely is it mechanical.

ALGORITHMS

For a procedure or rule to be an algorithm, it must be

    (i)   Finite
    (ii)   Mechanical
    (iii)   Effective.

Gauss's example also leads us to another distinction. This is the distinction between *discovering* an algorithm and *proving* that the algorithm is effective. In the above example, although most of us will likely agree that the formula $n/2 \times (r + s)$ seems to provide an effective way of calculating our desired result, it is important to note that this is something we haven't yet proved. We've seen the formula work in two cases. But we have not yet shown it to be effective more generally. Two types of proof often used in mathematics are proof by *reductio ad absurdum* and proof by *mathematical induction*.

In the case of the formula $n/2 \times (r + s)$, a proof will require looking, not just at one or two cases (as we did above) but at all possible cases. This requires the use of proof by mathematical induction.

Proof by mathematical induction. Let's ask ourselves why we think the formula

$$n/2 \times (r + s)$$

works. In the above example we saw that it worked in the case where $r = 1$, $s = 100$, and $n = 100$. We also saw that it worked when $r = 81,297$, $s = 100,899$, and $n = 100$. But can we prove the formula to be reliable for every r, s and n?

Our proof that it is comes in two parts. First, we'll show that our general formula, $n/2 \times (r + s)$, is reducible to a special case,

$$n/2 \times (n + 1).$$

Then we'll use mathematical induction to prove that the special case holds for all n.

To see that $n/2 \times (r + s)$ reduces to the special case $n/2 \times (n + 1)$, we first notice that there is nothing special about the initial number in our series, r. In Gauss's original problem, the initial number was 81,297, but it could have been any number. In other words, instead of referring to this number by its normal numeral, there is no reason not to refer to it simply as our first number, or as 1. Next, since there is a constant interval between each pair of numbers in our series, we can also think of this interval as being a single unit. In Gauss's original problem, the interval was 198, and so his second number was 81,495. But just as we can think of 12 inches as 1 foot, and of 9,460,730,472,580.8 kilometres as 1 light year, we can think of 198 (or any other constant interval) as 1 unit. If it helps, we can give this new unit a name, say 1 ssuag ('Gauss' spelled backwards).

Gauss's original problem,

81,297	81,495	81,693	81,891	....	100,899
100,899	100,701	100,503	100,305	....	81,297
182,196	182,196	182,196	182,196	....	182,196

now looks very similar to the other version of the problem we considered, namely

1	2	3	4	5	...	98	99	100
100	99	98	97	96	...	3	2	1
101	101	101	101	101	...	101	101	101

In other words, r is now being referred to simply as 1, the first member in our series, and since we are adding 1 ssuag to each number in our series, the final number, s, is always going

---

MATHEMATICAL INDUCTION

To prove that a mathematical formula holds for every number (i.e., for all *n*), we need to prove both an *induction hypothesis* and an *induction step*:

    (i)   *Induction hypothesis.* Prove that the formula holds when $n = 1$.

    (ii) *Induction step.* Prove that *if* the formula holds for an arbitrary number, *n*, *then* it also holds for *n*'s successor, $n + 1$.

---

to be identical to the number of terms in our series, *n*, which in this case happens to be 100. Put in other words, in our original formula

$$n/2 \times (r + s),$$

the *r* can now be replaced with 1, and the *s* can be replaced with *n*, giving us $n/2 \times (1 + n)$ or

$$n/2 \times (n + 1).$$

Now, how can we prove that this rule holds for every value of *n*?

Mathematical induction is a method of proof that lets us prove that a formula holds for all values of *n*. Proofs using mathematical induction require us to prove two things: First, we need to show that our formula holds when $n = 1$. This is called the *basis of the induction* or the *induction hypothesis*. Second, we need to show that *if* our formula holds for an arbitrary number, *n*, *then* it also holds for *n*'s successor, $n + 1$. This is called the *induction step*. If both the induction hypothesis and the induction step are true, then our formula will hold for $n = 1$, for $n = 1 + 1$, for $n = (1 + 1) + 1$, and so on to infinity. In other words, our formula will hold for every *n*.

We begin with our induction hypothesis. Imagine that

$n = 1$. In this case there will be only a single number in our (now very short!) series: 1. Does our formula, $n/2 \times (n + 1)$, give us the correct sum of all the numbers in this series? In other words, does

$$n/2 \times (n + 1) = 1?$$

Substituting 1 for n, we get

$$1/2 \times (1 + 1) = 1$$

which is exactly what we need.

Now the induction step. Assuming that the formula $n/2 \times (n + 1)$ holds for an arbitrary n, does it also hold for $n + 1$? In other words, assuming that

(A) $\qquad 1 + 2 + 3 + \ldots + n = n/2 \times (n + 1)$

does our formula $n/2 \times (n + 1)$ give us the correct sum of all the numbers in a series with $n + 1$ members? In other words, is the following formula correct?

(B) $1 + 2 + 3 + \ldots + n + (n + 1) = (n + 1)/2 \times ((n + 1) + 1)$

To see that it is, simply add $(n + 1)$ to both sides of (A). This gives us

(C) $1 + 2 + 3 + \ldots + n + (n + 1) = [n/2 \times (n + 1)] + (n + 1)$
$$= [n \times (n + 1)/2] + (n + 1)$$
$$= [(n + 1)/2 \times n] + (n + 1)$$
$$= (n + 1)/2 \times (n + 2)$$
$$= (n + 1)/2 \times ((n + 1) + 1).$$

Since (C) is now the same as (B), it follows that our formula holds for all n.

***Proof by* reductio ad absurdum.** A second form of proof often used in mathematics is *reductio ad absurdum* or *indirect proof*. This is a form of proof in which an assumption is made, the assumption is shown to lead to a contradiction, and it is concluded that, because no contradiction can be true, the assumption that led to the contradiction must be false. One famous example of this type of proof comes from the ancient geometer Euclid.

Euclid asks us to consider whether the total number of prime numbers is finite or infinite. Recall that a prime number is any number (i.e., any of the natural or counting numbers 1, 2, 3, 4, 5, ...) whose only factors are 1 and itself. For example, 11 is prime since it has no factors other than 1 and 11. In other words, no (natural or counting) numbers other than 1 and 11 can be multiplied together to get 11. In contrast, 10 is not prime since it has factors in addition to 1 and itself, for example 2 and 5, since $2 \times 5 = 10$. A prime factor is any factor that is itself prime.

After identifying the first few primes as follows,

$$2, 3, 5, 7, 11, 13, 17, 19, 23, \ldots$$

It becomes natural to ask whether this series ever comes to an end. Is there a largest prime? Are there a finite or an infinite number of prime numbers? Euclid concludes that there must be an infinite number of prime numbers.[4] Here is his reasoning:

Begin by assuming, just for the sake of argument, that there is a final, largest prime – let's call it P. If so, we will be able to list the series of primes as follows:

$$2, 3, 5, 7, 11, 13, 17, 19, 23, \ldots, P.$$

Now, consider a new number, Q, which we define as follows:

$$Q = (2 \times 3 \times 5 \times 7 \times 11 \times 13 \times 17 \times 19 \times 23 \times \ldots \times P) + 1.$$

Reductio ad Absurdum or **Indirect Proof**

To prove that a proposition is true,

  (i) Assume its denial (or opposite).

  (ii) Show that this assumption is impossible, since it leads to a contradiction.

  (iii) Conclude that the assumption must therefore be false and, hence, that the original proposition is true.

Take a moment to think about Q. It is clear that Q cannot be prime since it is larger than the largest prime, P. But Q must be prime, since its only factors are one and itself.

To see this, try dividing Q by some number smaller than Q. If the number is less than or equal to P, then there will always be a remainder. (For example, if we divide Q by a prime factor such as 3, we will end up with a remainder of 1; and if we divide Q by a non-prime factor such as 6, we will also end up with a remainder since if we didn't, we wouldn't have had a remainder when we divided Q by one of its prime factors, such as 3.) Finally, if the number we use to divide Q is greater than P, then any factor we might discover will have to be prime or not prime. If prime, it will be a prime number larger than P, contrary to our assumption. If not prime, then it will have to have a prime factor larger than P (since otherwise we will have ended up with a remainder of 1), again contrary to our assumption.

It follows that there can be no largest prime, P, since, if there were, Q would be both prime and not prime, which is impossible. In other words, there must be an infinite number of primes.

Large numbers and scientific notation. Examples like the above remind us that in some disciplines we need to work with numbers that are very large or very small. For example, a mole is the amount of substance contained in a system having as many elemental entities as there are atoms in 12 grams of carbon-12. In other words, one mole of particles is approximately

602,214,000,000,000,000,000,000 particles.

In contrast, a Dalton is one twelfth of the mass of an isolated atom of carbon-12 at rest and in its ground state. In other words, 1 Dalton of mass is approximately

0.000,000,000,000,000,000,000,000,001,66 kg.

To avoid calculating with such cumbersome numbers, many disciplines require all numbers larger than 1,000 and smaller than 1/1,000 to be represented using scientific notation.

To translate a number such as

602,214,000,000,000,000,000,000

into scientific notation, place a decimal point after the first digit (in this case after the 6), count the number of places from the decimal point to the end of the number (in this case there will be 23), drop all the zeros at the end of the number, then write the number as

6.02214×10^{23} or 6.02214 E23.

(Here the E stands for 'exponent' and is often used on electronic calculators that are unable to display superscripts.)

For numbers less than one, the method is similar. To translate a number such as

0.000,000,000,000,000,000,000,000,001,66

into scientific notation, drop the initial zero and move the decimal point to immediately following the first significant digit (in this case after the 1), count the number of places from the decimal point to the beginning of the number (in this case there will be 27), drop all the initial zeros, then write the number as

$$1.66 \times 10^{-27} \text{ or } 1.66 \text{ E}{-}27.$$

Calculating with scientific notation is then no different from calculating with exponents more generally. To multiply two numbers in scientific notation, multiply the coefficients together and add the exponents. To divide two numbers in scientific notation, divide coefficients and subtract the exponents. To add or subtract two numbers in scientific notation, first express both numbers as the same power of 10, which will often involve changing the decimal place of the coefficient.

Calculators. Working with such large or small numbers of course is made easier through the use of calculators. There are two schools of thought about the use of electronic calculators in class and during exams. The first is that the use of calculators should be avoided while we are still learning the theory behind a mathematical result. In other words, working through a result or formula by hand helps us learn, understand and remember the underlying theory. The second is that avoiding the use of calculators encourages a lack of understanding of the power of machine calculation, something we need to know if we are to be comfortable working with almost all contemporary, real-world applications of mathematics. Since different instructors have different pedagogical goals, it is always a good idea to ask about your instructor's preferences at the start of each new course.

Calculators and computers can be especially valuable when they're used to extend our understanding, but not when they're used as a substitute for learning. When using a calculator or computer, it is always a useful exercise to ask yourself whether the answer given by the calculator seems to be

---

SCIENTIFIC NOTATION

5,000,000,000	five billion	5.0×10^9 or 5.0 E9
500,000,000	five hundred million	5.0×10^8 or 5.0 E8
50,000,000	fifty million	5.0×10^7 or 5.0 E7
5,000,000	five million	5.0×10^6 or 5.0 E6
500,000	five hundred thousand	5.0×10^5 or 5.0 E5
50,000	fifty thousand	5.0×10^4 or 5.0 E4
5,000	five thousand	5.0×10^3 or 5.0 E3
500	five hundred	5.0×10^2 or 5.0 E2
50	fifty	5.0×10^1 or 5.0 E1
5	five	5.0×10^0 or 5.0 E0
0.5	five tenths	5.0×10^{-1} or 5.0 E-1
0.05	five hundredths	5.0×10^{-2} or 5.0 E-2
0.005	five thousandths	5.0×10^{-3} or 5.0 E-3
0.000,5	five ten-thousandths	5.0×10^{-4} or 5.0 E-4
0.000,05	five hundred thousandths	5.0×10^{-5} or 5.0 E-5
0.000,005	five millionths	5.0×10^{-6} or 5.0 E-6
0.000,000,5	five ten-millionths	5.0×10^{-7} or 5.0 E-7
0.000,000,05	five hundred millionths	5.0×10^{-8} or 5.0 E-8
0.000,000,005	five billionths	5.0×10^{-9} or 5.0 E-9

---

roughly the right size. Estimating the approximate size of an answer (e.g., 4,257 x 4.071 ought to be a fraction more than 4,000 x 4, or a fraction more than 16,000) ensures that your basic understanding of the problem matches your ability to use the calculator. It also protects you against data-entry errors.

It is also important to know what type of calculators, if any, you will be permitted to use in your exams. Some instructors disallow the use of calculators during exams since modern programmable calculators have the capacity to store and retrieve so much information that it becomes impossible to check whether they contain study notes or other information that may compromise an examination. Once again, if you don't know or haven't been told, be sure to ask early in the term. This will let you practice solving problems throughout the term under the same conditions that will hold in your exams.

Statistical significance. When evaluating or reporting results that contain numbers, it is sometimes important to ascertain whether a number is likely to have occurred by chance. Numbers that are unlikely to have occurred by chance are said to be *statistically significant*. Since in many disciplines small variations between numbers are more likely to occur by chance than large ones, an often-used measure of statistical significance is *standard deviation*. Standard deviation is a measure of the variability of numbers within a data set or population. If numbers have low variation (i.e., if they all tend to be grouped together around a single mid-point or mean), they are said to have a low standard deviation, with a standard deviation of zero indicating that there is no variation at all. If they have high variation (i.e., if they tend to be spread over a large range of values), they are said to have a high standard deviation. More formally, we define the standard deviation as being equal to the square root of the arithmetic mean of the squares of a population's deviations from their arithmetic mean. A normal (or Gaussian) distribution is said to occur whenever data cluster around a mean or midpoint and the graph of the corresponding probability density function takes the shape of a *bell curve*. (If it helps, you can think of a probability density function as a real-valued function whose integral over any set gives the probability that a random variable has values in that set; if it doesn't help, don't.)

For example, when data are gathered, small differences often result from errors in measurement and other random variables. Researchers thus commonly report the standard deviation of experimental data, and only differences that fall well outside the standard deviation are assumed to be significant. Much the same happens in the case of polling data, in which standard deviation is used to help calculate the expected margin of error. Once again, only results falling well beyond the standard deviation are assumed to be significant.

Infinity. Another mathematical idea that has captured people's imagination for thousands of years is that of infinity. Among the first to consider the idea carefully was the Greek philosopher Aristotle. Among the questions Aristotle asked was whether we can count, not just ordinary objects such as books and buildings, but the total number of numbers.

Before answering this question, Aristotle distinguished between what he calls a *potential infinite* and an *actual infinite*. A series is *potentially infinite* whenever for every number, n, there is the possibility of there being a larger number, $n + 1$, along with the fact that there is no number larger than all such n, i.e. no number larger than all of the numbers in the series $n,\ n + 1,\ (n + 1) + 1,\ ...$. For example, given any distance, d, that we might travel, if there is potentially always a greater distance, $d + 1$, that we might travel in the future, and if the continued adding of 1s in this way exhausts all the possible ways of extending distance, then we can conclude that distance is potentially (but not actually) infinite. In contrast, an *actual infinite* is present whenever for every number, n, there is a larger number, $n + 1$, *and* the total number of numbers is larger than every one of these numbers. In other words, the total number of numbers is greater than every member of the series $n,\ n + 1,\ (n + 1) + 1,\ ...$.

If this seems confusing, think about it this way. One of the first series we're introduced to is the series

$$1, 2, 3, ...$$

Now ask yourself how many numbers are in this series. If your answer is that the series is always finite, even though it might always grow larger, say from n to $n + 1$ members, then

Aristotle would say that the series you've described would be finite but *potentially* infinite.

In contrast, if you answer that the three dots ("…") indicate that the series has an infinite number of members, then by "infinite" we must mean a number greater than every number in the series (since no number *in* the series gives the *total* number of numbers) and Aristotle would say that the series is *actually* infinite.

This distinction led Aristotle to ask whether an actual (as opposed to a merely potential) infinite might really exist. Aristotle explains one of his reasons for thinking this is impossible as follows:

> Number must be either infinite or finite. … Clearly it cannot be infinite; for infinite number is neither odd nor even, and the generation of numbers is always the generation either of an odd or of an even number.[5]

In other words, Aristotle reasoned as follows: It seems necessary that the total number of numbers must be either finite or infinite. But we know that the generation of each new natural number always results in a number that is either odd or even. So, it follows that every new finite number must be either odd or even. But the infinite, if it exists, is neither odd nor even, since if it were either, it too would be finite. Therefore, the infinite cannot be a number. Therefore, the total number of numbers cannot be infinite. Therefore, the total number of numbers must be finite, although it is always possible that it might be increased.

This is an interesting argument. If Aristotle is right, there's something contradictory about the very idea of a completed infinite series. If it were possible to complete such a series, the total number of members in the series would have to be both either odd or even *and* neither odd nor even, which would be impossible.

Although some people (including the Italian scientist Galileo Galilei and the Irish Bishop George Berkeley) remained puzzled by Aristotle's treatment of the infinite, the next major discovery about how to measure infinity didn't occur until over two thousand years later when the 19th-century German mathematician Georg Cantor came up with a way of thinking about the actual infinite and a way of counting the members of different sizes of infinite sets. Here is Cantor's argument that there is more than one size of infinity.[6]

First, recall that we distinguish between the natural (or counting) numbers (1, 2, 3, 4, 5, ...), the rational numbers (or fractions) that can be created using pairs of natural numbers (1/1, 1/2, 2/1, 2/2, 1/3, 3/1, 2/3, 3/2, 3/3, ...), and the real numbers (numbers that can be represented by infinite decimal expansions such as 0.187876559..., 179.743522..., *pi*, *e*, ..., etc.).

Next, consider all the real numbers between 0 and 1. If we can prove that there are more real numbers in this small interval than there are natural numbers, it follows immediately that there must be more real numbers (in total) than there are natural numbers (in total). In other words, the number of real numbers will be larger than the number of natural numbers. If we let **c** (from the word 'continuum') stand for the total number of real numbers and $\aleph_0$, or 'aleph-null,' stand for the total number of natural numbers, this will be the same as writing $\mathbf{c} > \aleph_0$.

To see that $\mathbf{c} > \aleph_0$, assume that the real numbers in the interval between 0 and 1 can be placed in a list (in no particular order) as follows:

(1) 0.85338773684 ...
(2) 0.15365433389 ...
(3) 0.42311854728 ...
(4) 0.92556722189 ...
(5) 0.35732871184 ...

⋮

Each real number in this interval is then represented by an infinite decimal expansion. Since we are assuming that these numbers can be listed in this way, we can associate with each real number in the list a natural (or counting) number. In other words, we can count the members of this list using the numbers (1), (2), (3), ... We can also use the *diagonal* of this list (i.e., the bolded, underlined numerals in the list) seen here

(1)   0.8̲5338773684 ...
(2)   0.15̲365433389 ...
(3)   0.423̲11854728 ...
(4)   0.9255̲6722189 ...
(5)   0.35732̲871184 ...
⋮

to help us create a new number. We do so as follows:

Begin by writing down 0 and a decimal point. Then write down the numerals from the above diagonal, i.e., the first numeral following the decimal point in the first number, the second numeral following the decimal point in the second number, the third numeral following the decimal point in the third number, and so on. The result will be the number d:

$$d = 0.85352 \ldots$$

Next, add 1 to each numeral following the decimal point (so that each 0 become 1, each 1 becomes 2, each 2 becomes 3, ..., each 8 becomes 9, and each 9 becomes 0). The result will be the new number r,

$$r = 0.96463 \ldots$$

Now, we know that r is a real number between 0 and 1; but we also know that it cannot correspond to any of the real numbers that appeared on our original (infinite) list. The reason we know this is that it differs from every real number on our list in at least one place:

The 1st digit of r is different from the first digit in (1)
The 2nd digit of r is different from the second digit in (2)
The 3rd digit of r is different from the third digit in (3)

$$\vdots$$

In other words, contrary to our original assumption, it is impossible to count all of the real numbers using just the natural (or counting) numbers since, whenever we try to do so, there will always be at least one number, such as r, left over. If the number of natural numbers is infinite, it follows that the number of real numbers must be larger than infinity. In yet other words, there must be more than one size of infinity. If we repeat this process over and over again, it looks like we soon will have an infinite number of different-sized infinite numbers.

Does this mean that Aristotle's argument that there could never be an actual infinite is mistaken? Most mathematicians, but not all, would probably say yes. Aristotle's argument assumes that the generation of each new number always results in a new number that is either odd or even. Put another way, he assumes that there is only one way to generate new numbers, namely by the adding of 1 to a previous number. This gives us the series

$$1, 1 + 1, (1 + 1) + 1, ((1 + 1) + 1) + 1, \dots .$$

In contrast, Cantor's argument assumes this isn't so, that there is more than just one way to generate new numbers and, hence, that there is a way of referring to an actual infinite that isn't self-contradictory. If this assumption is correct, then his proof shows that there is a way of generating new numbers larger than every member in the series

$$1, 1 + 1, (1 + 1) + 1, ((1 + 1) + 1) + 1, \dots .$$

If so, it follows that there will be an infinity of different-sized infinities.

Even so, Cantor's assumption seems to be just an assumption, perhaps one that is not so different than Aristotle's. If so, one is tempted to ask what evidence there might be that would support one assumption rather than the other. Answering questions like this turns out to require more than even the most detailed type of mechanical calculation. They also require creative thought, thought that is perhaps not so different than in other disciplines such as music.

Further reading

Artmann, Benno, *Euclid: The Creation of Mathematics*, New York: Springer, 1999

Barnes, Jonathan, *Aristotle: A Very Short Introduction*, New York: Oxford University Press, 2001

Beckman, Petr, *A History of Pi*, New York: Dorset Press, 1989

Boyer, Carl B., and Uta C. Merzbach, *A History of Mathematics*, New York: John Wiley & Sons, 1991

Clegg, Brian, *A Brief History of Infinity: The Quest to Think the Unthinkable*, London: Robinson, 2003

Dauben, Joseph W., *Georg Cantor: His Mathematics and Philosophy of the Infinite*, Boston: Harvard University Press, 1979

Franklin, James, and Albert Daoud, *Proof in Mathematics: An Introduction*, Quakers Hill, NSW: Quakers Hill Press, 1996

Gowers, Timothy, *Mathematics: A Very Short Introduction*, Oxford: Oxford Paperbacks, 2002

Hall, Tord, *Carl Friedrich Gauss: A Biography*, Cambridge (MA): MIT Press, 1970

Houston, Kevin, *How to Think Like a Mathematician*, Cambridge: Cambridge University Press, 2009

Paulos, John Allen, *Beyond Numeracy*, New York: Knopf, 1991

Paulos, John Allen, *Innumeracy*, New York: Hill and Wang, 1988

Rotman, Brian, and G.T. Kneebone, *The Theory of Sets and Transfinite Numbers*, London: Oldbourne, 1966

Wardhaugh, Benjamin, *Encounters with Euclid*, Princeton and Oxford: Princeton University Press, 2021

Chapter 7

Discover the Best
That Has Been Thought and Said

Alan Sokal is a professor of physics at New York University and a professor of mathematics at University College London. His research is primarily in the areas of combinatorics (a branch of finite set theory) and statistical mechanics (a branch of thermodynamics). In 1994, frustrated by what he perceived to be declining standards in some humanities and social-sciences disciplines, Sokal decided to write a paper liberally laced with nonsense and submit it to a journal known for its sympathy to postmodernism (the idea that the age of reason, or modernism, had ended). As Sokal explains, the paper was "structured around the silliest quotations I could find about mathematics and physics (and the philosophy of mathematics and physics) from some of the most prominent French and American intellectuals."[1] The result was an essay that intentionally contained "appeals to authority rather than logic to support arguments, unreadable prose, mistaken claims about scientific theories, and a general failure to give the scientific method its due."[2] The point was to see whether the journal would publish such a paper, despite its shortcomings.

Unfortunately, the editors were more than happy to oblige. Sokal's essay, entitled "Transgressing the Boundaries: Towards a Transformative Hermeneutics of Quantum Gravity," appeared in the 1996 Spring/Summer issue of *Social Text*, published by Duke University Press. Three weeks later Sokal revealed the hoax in another journal, *Lingua Franca*.

Sokal's hoax prompted a great deal of debate. Many believed that his experiment showed that standards in the social sciences are not as demanding as in the natural sciences. Others argued that *Social Text* was not a representative journal within cultural studies, or that cultural studies was not a representative discipline within the social sciences. Yet others said it had been unethical for Sokal to mislead the journal the way he had.

For his part, Sokal has been careful not to claim too much:

> From the mere fact of publication of my parody I think that not much can be deduced. It doesn't prove that the whole field of cultural studies, or cultural studies of science – much less sociology of science – is nonsense. Nor does it prove that the intellectual standards in these fields are generally lax. (This might be the case, but it would have to be established on other grounds.) It proves only that the editors of *one* rather marginal journal were derelict in their intellectual duty, by publishing an article on quantum physics that they admit they could not understand, without bothering to get an opinion from anyone knowledgeable in quantum physics, solely because it came from a "conveniently credentialed ally" (as *Social Text* co-editor Bruce Robbins later candidly admitted), flattered the editors' ideological preconceptions, and attacked their "enemies."[3]

Despite such comments, in many people's minds Sokal's hoax confirmed what they already believed: that work in the social sciences and humanities is not as objective or rigorous as in the natural and formal sciences. Were they right?

Snow's two cultures. In 1959, the English physicist and novelist C.P. Snow introduced the term the *two cultures*. Snow used the term to refer to the large gulf often thought to exist between the humanities and the sciences. As Snow put it, "I believe the intellectual life of the whole of western society is increasingly being split into two polar groups."[4] On the one hand are the literary intellectuals, on the other the scientists. Between the two, says Snow, lies "a gulf of mutual incomprehension – sometimes (particularly among the young) hostility and dislike, but most of all lack of understanding. They have a curious distorted image of each other. Their attitudes are so different that, even on the level of emotion, they can't find much common ground."[5] Not only do the two groups sometimes find it hard to speak to one another, and not only do they see the world in radically different ways, they also appear to have strikingly different goals and standards.

Since Snow's day, numerous other authors have commented on this division. Scientists have complained that humanists are ignorant, not just of the most basic mathematical and scientific concepts, but of even the most elementary scientific discoveries. Humanists have complained that scientists fail to appreciate even the most basic insights of literature, theatre and music and that, although they define their terms carefully when working in their own disciplines, they feel no similar obligation when talking about ethics or politics or economics. Others have asked whether there may be, not just two cultures, but three – the humanities, the natural sciences and the social sciences.[6]

Related to this debate are discussions about the ultimate purpose of a university education. As research focuses on more-and-more-specialized areas of investigation, many educational programs no longer take their mandate to be the education of 'the whole person.' At about the same time Snow was writing, University of Saskatchewan history professor Hilda Neatby effectively raised this concern when she wrote that she was "disturbed at the apparent indifference of the experts to the disappearance of the old-fashioned concept of the 'educated person.'"[7] In summary, Neatby found that many university programs no longer "attempt to exercise, train and discipline the mind,"[8] they no longer attempt to teach students that there is more to a good education than just the discovery of facts, dates and formulas, as important and interesting as these may be.

Snow sums up these various positions as follows:

> The non-scientists have a rooted impression that the scientists are shallowly optimistic, unaware of man's condition. On the other hand, the scientists believe that the literary intellectuals are totally lacking in foresight, peculiarly unconcerned with their brother men, in a deep sense anti-intellectual, anxious to restrict both art and thought to the existential moment.[9]

Kerr's multiversity. Is Snow right? Is there an unbridgeable gulf between the sciences and the humanities? Some people think so. Some even talk of the traditional university as having been replaced by a *multi*versity. The new term comes from a former president of the University of California, Clark Kerr.[10] According to Kerr, although the university was once "a single community" composed of "masters and students,"[11] it is now not one community but many. If Kerr is right, the traditional university has been replaced by "a whole series of communities and activities held together by a common name, a common governing board, and related purposes" – but no common essence.[12]

Kerr's multiversity has several features. First, it is divided into numerous separate groups: there is "the community of the undergraduate and the community of the graduate; the community of the humanist, the community of the social scientist, and the community of the scientist; the communities of the professional schools; the community of all the non-academic personnel; the community of the administrators."[13] Second, instead of having "a single 'soul' or purpose,"[14] these various groups have a variety of conflicting interests. The modern multiversity is thus "less an integrated and eternal spirit, and more a split and variable personality."[15] Third, Kerr's institution is neither completely a part of, nor fully separate from, contemporary society: it is modern yet medieval, technologically advanced yet still wedded to the book, not really private and yet not really public.[16] The result,

Faculties and Disciplines 1

The Arts & Humanities

Asian Studies – the study of the languages, literatures and cultures of the peoples of Asia

Classics – the study of the history, literature and physical remains of the ancient Western world, especially Greece and Rome

English – the study of the language, literatures and cultures of the English-speaking peoples

French – the study of the language, literatures and cultures of the French-speaking peoples

History – the study of the past, especially past events and movements in human affairs

Linguistics – the study of language, including sounds (phonetics) and systems of sounds (phonology), the forms of words (morphology) and of sentences (syntax), meanings (semantics), and how language is used (pragmatics)

Literature – the study of the written works of a culture, especially creative works in poetry, fiction and nonfiction

Literary Theory – the study of different approaches to reading and analyzing texts

Performing Arts – the study and practice of creative performance, including music, drama and dance

Philosophy – the study of the most general features of the world (metaphysics), of value (ethics, politics and aesthetics), of knowledge (epistemology), and of reason (logic)

Religious Studies – the study of religious belief and practice

Spanish – the study of the language, literatures and culture of the Spanish-speaking peoples

Visual Arts & Art History – the study and practice of creative expression through drawing, painting, printmaking and sculpture (the fine arts), filmmaking, photography and other media (the media arts), and interior design, industrial design, fashion design, graphic design and decorative art (the applied arts)

Faculties and Disciplines 2

The Formal Sciences

Computer Science – the study of the theory and practice of computation, especially algorithmic processes that create, describe and transform information

Mathematics – the study of the formal features of quantity (arithmetic), space (geometry), structure (algebra), chance (probability theory), change (calculus), functions (analysis) and infinity (set theory)

The Natural Sciences

Astronomy & Space Sciences – the study of the universe beyond the surface and atmosphere of the Earth

Biology & Life Sciences – the study of living organisms and living systems, and how they act in, and interact with, their environment

Chemistry – the study of the structure of, and interactions between, the elements, especially as they appear in organic matter (organic chemistry), inorganic matter (inorganic chemistry), living organisms (biochemistry) and physical systems (physical chemistry)

Earth Sciences – the study of the Earth, including the physical and biological properties of its lands (geology), seas (oceanography) and atmosphere (meteorology)

Physics – the study of matter and energy, especially their interaction in space and time

---

says Kerr, is an institution that "serves society almost slavishly – a society it also criticizes, sometimes unmercifully."[17] Fourth, although "Devoted to equality of opportunity, it is itself a class society."[18] It is open to everyone but committed to upholding objective standards of excellence that only a few can attain. Finally, says Kerr, "Its edges are fuzzy – it reaches out to alumni, legislators, farmers, businessmen, who are all related to one or more of these internal communities. As an institution, it looks far into the past and far into the future, and is often at odds with the present."[19] In sum, Kerr's multiversity is "pluralistic in several senses: in having several purposes, not one; in having several centres of power, not one; in serving several clienteles, not one."[20]

What are the consequences of such pluralism? According to Kerr, the main consequence is that, being so many things to so many people, today's multiversity "must, of necessity, be partially at war with itself."[21]

Is there an alternative to such a pessimistic view? To many within the university the answer is yes. Of course, there are differences between the natural sciences, the social sciences and the humanities, and of course professional and non-professional faculties serve different clienteles. Every university is and always has been connected to – and separate from – its broader society, and every university has, and always has had, multiple centres of power. Yet the modern university, in essence, remains a *uni*versity. It remains a single institution bound together by a single mission: *the production, promotion, preservation and application of knowledge* and, with it, the nurturing of the intellectual autonomy and intellectual community that is necessary to achieve these ends.

The essence of the university. Whether you have decided to study the bench sciences, the mathematical sciences, the social sciences, the humanities or the fine arts, whether you have enrolled in a professional faculty, an applied sciences faculty or a traditional arts and science faculty, whether you are a first-year undergraduate or a final-year doctoral student – in an important sense, none of this matters. None of these distinctions separates you from other members of the university.

Central to all university work is the belief that *knowledge matters*, that preserving and advancing knowledge is an important, worthwhile task, that it is important to have an institution committed to the dispassionate, disinterested investigation of "things and their forces" and "men and their ways."[22] It is this simple insight more than any other that unifies work done by universities around the world and across the centuries.

Faculties and Disciplines 3

The Social Sciences

Anthropology – the study of societies and cultures as they exist today (socio-cultural anthropology) and as they have existed in the past (archaeological anthropology), of language use and language change (linguistic anthropology), and human ecology and evolution (physical anthropology)

Archaeology – the study of human history and prehistory through the excavation and analysis of physical artifacts and other remains

Economics – the study of the creation and consumption of wealth and other scarce resources (labour, capital, environmental assets, etc.), as they affect individuals (micro-economics) and as they affect societies (macro-economics)

Geography – the study of large-scale patterns of human activity (human geography) and of how physical features of the Earth affect and are affected by such activity (physical geography)

Political Science – the study of political power, especially as it relates to the structures and processes of government

Psychology – the study of mind, brain and behaviour

Sociology – the study of social activity, especially as it relates to the development, structure and functioning of human societies

---

It is also worth noting that the original universities were more diverse – structurally, administratively and intellectually – than Kerr's comments might lead us to believe. Just as today, the original medieval institution was composed of multiple divisions or faculties. The initial four were arts, law, medicine and theology. Of these, the first was preparatory to the others, just as an undergraduate degree is preparatory to graduate or professional work today.[23] The original university was also diverse in its population, being one of the first truly international institutions, allowing scholars and students to move from region to region and country to country. Administratively, the early university also underwent numerous changes, just as today. As the historian Willis Rudy tells us, one of the most significant of these took place during the 13th century, when professors found it necessary to begin regularizing their fees:

> Previously, the masters had been somewhat haphazard in the fees that they charged for their services. Some, notably the monastic teachers of the early Middle Ages, had dispensed instruction *gratis*. But in the thirteenth century, the business of higher education became highly competitive and the supply of adequate church benefices or endowments was in increasingly short supply. As a result, the masters began to charge set fees for their instruction.[24]

Intellectually and pedagogically, there were also innovations. Although the principal method of instruction was the *lectio* (or lecture), medieval students were soon able to rent textbooks cheaply from *scriptoria* where, despite the lack of printing presses, non-illuminated manuscripts were beginning to be prepared in large quantities.[25]

Innovation also took place with the introduction of the *quaestiones disputatae* (or public disputation):

> Despite the ever-present lecturing, medieval higher education was not merely passive; it had a strong element of argumentativeness due to the disputation and its *pro et contra* technique. The disputation gave the medieval student a rare opportunity to express himself and perform in public in an oral debate wherein a student or master sought to maintain a proposition against another student or master. Abelard had pioneered in using this method with his famous work *Sic et Non (Yes and Its Opposite)*. The argument was supposed to follow faithfully the rules of logic incorporated in Aristotle's work, *Organon*. In other words, the thesis or *quaestio* (question) was to be explored by means of presenting a major premise and one or more minor premises, followed by a syllogism, statement of fallacies, and refutation of the opposing arguments.[26]

Faculties and Disciplines 4

The Professions

Agriculture & Food Sciences – the study of the production and consumption of food and related goods, including the practices of farming, ranching, food management and transportation.

Architecture – the study and practice of the design of buildings and other structures

Business – the study and practice of the production and trade of goods

Education – the study and practice of teaching and learning

Engineering – the study and practice of the design, construction and operation of engines, machines, materials, systems, and other physical structures and processes

Forestry & Environmental Studies – the study and practice of land and ocean management, especially as they relate to the sustainability of forests, fish stocks and other natural resources

Journalism & Communication – the study and practice of communication, including the conveying of news and information through newspapers, magazines, radio, television, the internet and other media

Law – the study and practice of the values, norms and rules having legal force in human societies, especially as they relate to contracts, torts and property (private law), government powers (public law), criminal offences (criminal law), business activities (corporate law), religious institutions (canon law), and relations between nations (international law)

Library & Information Sciences – the study and practice of the storing and retrieving of information

Medicine, Dentistry & Health Sciences – the study of health and illness, and the study and practice of the prevention, diagnosis and treatment of disease and injury

---

In other words, most of the features Kerr ascribes to the modern multiversity also apply to its medieval counterpart.[27] Of course, Kerr is right that the original university was largely built around a single purpose or animating principle, but this commitment to the preservation and expansion of knowledge –

something the medievals inherited from the ancient world[28] – remains the university's key unifying factor to this day.

Today's university. One complexity found in the modern university is the sheer number of academic disciplines most universities support. The grouping of these disciplines is not as easy or straightforward as might initially be assumed. Partly this is because of their complexity. Medicine alone has dozens of specializations ranging from anesthesiology (the administration of drugs designed to dull sensation) to urology (the medical care of urinary tracts), and dozens of sub-disciplines ranging from anatomy (the study of the physical structure of organisms) to toxicology (the study of the effects of drugs and poisons). Many of these specializations and sub-disciplines overlap with specializations and sub-disciplines in other areas. Because of this, it is often difficult to know where one sub-discipline or specialization ends and another begins.

Even developing definitions of individual disciplines and sub-disciplines can be a challenge. Partly this is because a great deal of scholarly work is constantly evolving. As new knowledge is discovered, the boundaries between disciplines often become blurred. The book in which Isaac Newton introduced his famous laws of motion was entitled *Philosophiae Naturalis Principia Mathematica,* or "Mathematical Principles of Natural Philosophy." Newton's reference to "Natural Philosophy" reminds us that many of today's disciplines, ranging from physics to psychology, initially originated as sub-disciplines of philosophy.

Sometimes researchers within even a single discipline will ask quite different questions and rely on quite different research methodologies. This, in turn, leads to different views about what is and is not essential within a discipline. Economics, for example, has traditionally been defined as the study of the creation and consumption of wealth. Today, many working economists find this definition too narrow. Partly this is because many of the mechanisms economists study turn out to be relevant to the study of, not just financial wealth but other goods as well. As a result, economics is now often said to concern itself with the measurement and distribution of resources in general, and of scarce resources in particular. Some economists even see their discipline as focusing, not just on the measurement and distribution of resources but on their allocation as well. In other words, some economists understand their discipline to involve a normative (or ethical) element. Economics (on this view) doesn't just study how scarce resources are *in fact* distributed. It also studies how scarce resources *should be* distributed. In response to this expanded definition – that economics is the study of how societies can and should allocate scarce resources – many traditional economists object. How resources *should* be allocated, they say, is a question of politics, not economics. (Hence the introduction of the 18th-century term "political economy.") Any attempt to define economics (in the narrower sense) in this expanded way must therefore be based on a confusion.

In psychology there is also a range of different suggestions about what is and is not essential to the discipline. Many psychologists are content to define psychology as the study of the mind. Others suggest that psychology is really the study of behaviour. (After all, it is difficult to look inside someone's head and see a mind. Although, perhaps even this may soon be possible.) According to this second view, whether working in abnormal psychology, developmental psychology, evolutionary psychology, educational psychology or any other sub-discipline, the only thing researchers can objectively study are people's (and sometimes animals') actions. If on the basis of these actions some researchers want to draw conclusions about the mind, they will be free to do so; but strictly speaking, psychology (according to this view) involves only the study of behaviour. Other psychologists – perhaps the majority – believe that since the mind is identical to the brain (or more precisely, to the brain together with the central nervous system, or even more precisely to functional states of the brain and central nervous system), it follows that psychology is really the study of the brain together with behaviour, or of states of the brain and central nervous system together with behaviour.

What is common among all these perspectives is the idea that objective evidence matters. Coming up with an interesting hypothesis, perhaps about the distribution of scarce resources or about the relation between brains and behaviour is one thing. Finding evidence to support our hypothesis is something else again.

The fallibility of man. Something else common, not just to all universities but to all human endeavor, is the fallibility of man. As Sokal's hoax reminds us, the advancement of knowledge is a nontrivial undertaking. The discovery of new knowledge is rarely easy. The preservation of old knowledge is never mechanical. In real-life contexts, it is always a challenge just to *get things right*.

Even so, it is a mistake to conclude that human fallibility implies the triumph of either skepticism or relativism. Just because something – a new cure for an old disease, a difficult translation of a foreign opera, a complex explanation for a persistent economic anomaly – isn't easy doesn't mean it is impossible. It also doesn't mean that some failed attempts aren't better than others.

It is also a mistake to conclude that work in science is somehow isolated from human fallibility in a way that work in other disciplines is not, or that unlike scientific research, work in other disciplines is just a matter of subjective preference. What Sokal's hoax shows is that work that gives preference to ideologically driven advocacy – rather than disinterested argumentation, experimentation, creativity or scholarship – is contrary to the very purpose of a university, regardless of one's discipline. The view that objective knowledge can never exist, or that all knowledge claims simply reflect power imbalances of various kinds, or that the selection of papers for publication in some disciplines but not others is just a matter of ideological preference, is simply mistaken. Work of high or low quality can be found in any discipline.

In 1912, the remains of *Eoanthropus dawsoni*, or Piltdown man, were found in a gravel pit at Piltdown, Sussex. For many years they were believed to provide an essential 'missing link' between modern humans and our primate ancestors. It wasn't until four decades later, in 1953, that paleontologists finally discovered the fraud. Using radiocarbon dating, they were able to show that the remains included parts of a modern human skull and a modern orangutan's jawbone.[29] To this day, no one is quite sure who initiated the hoax.

In Romania, when Nicolae Ceauşescu became General Secretary of the Romanian Communist Party and, later, President and head of state of Romania, he appointed his wife, Elena Ceauşescu, to be the country's Deputy Prime Minister. He and his government also began promoting the false claim that Elena was a world-famous chemistry researcher, even though the many publications that appeared under her name turned out to have been written by others. When the Romanian embassy in London tried to persuade various British academic institutions to recognize Elena's various scientific achievements, both the University of London and the Royal Society declined to do so. In 1989, the Ceauşescu dictatorship was overthrown and both Nicolae and Elena were publicly executed as part of the anti-communist uprisings that occurred throughout Europe that year. History's verdict on Elena's purported scientific achievements has been equally clear.

More recently, the respected journal *Physical Review Letters* published the results of work purporting to discover two new super-heavy elements. The work supposedly had been done at Lawrence Berkeley National Laboratory in California and involved bombarding small amounts of lead with intense beams of high-energy krypton ions using Berkeley's 88-inch cyclotron. Two years later, in 2001, a retraction was issued when researchers were unable to duplicate the findings.[30] The lead physicist on the project was removed shortly afterwards.

Something similar occurred in 2002 when a young scientist working at Bell Labs in New Jersey was fired for falsifying data that purportedly showed he had discovered a new superconductor supposedly made from plastic. His results had been published in several highly respected journals including *Science* and *Nature*.[31]

Such examples show that the natural sciences are not that much different from the social sciences or humanities, at least in this key respect: the advancement of knowledge requires, not just careful observation and sound reasoning. It also requires high standards of academic integrity on the part of both researchers and publishers alike.

The objectivity of knowledge. Where the arts and sciences sometimes can be said to differ is with regard to their *objectivity*, but even this difference is often misunderstood. Some academic work is *meant* to be subjective, in the sense that it is meant to prompt different feelings in different people. When a novelist writes about the challenges of war, this inevitably raises different memories in different readers. Depending on your age you might remember the Iraq War, the First Gulf War, the Vietnam War, the Korean War or even the Second World War. This subjectivity is part of what gives the novel its strength: the same words can be used to speak to different people in different contexts.

Even so, a great deal of objective work is carried out in the humanities, just as in the sciences. Just because a novel, say, gains part of its strength by being subjective, this doesn't mean that a disinterested party can't bring objective standards – standards independent of the particular beliefs and experiences of the person reporting them – to bear on how we understand or interpret the novel, or to its evaluation. Did it ramble? Was it contradictory? Did it succeed in achieving the (possibly subjective) goals it set for itself? Even the most subjective work can still be evaluated rigorously and fairly.

This idea that we are able to evaluate rigorously and fairly even the most subjective and controversial claims is central to the mission of the university. As with so many ideas, it has its roots in ancient Greece. As the Cambridge historian G.E.R. Lloyd tells us, two factors were of special importance when philosophers in the ancient world began the systematic study of nature. The first was that, when it comes to the evaluation of knowledge claims, no one has access to privileged, supernatural authorities. The second was that all evidence – whether based on observation, reason or something else – needs to be tested through open, public debate:

> In their very different spheres of activity, the philosopher Thales and the law-giver Solon may be said to have had a least two things in common. First, both disclaimed any supernatural authority for their own ideas, and secondly, both accepted the principles of free debate and of public access to the information on which a person or an idea should be judged. The essence of the Milesians' contribution was to introduce a new critical spirit into man's attitude to the world of nature, but this should be seen as a counterpart to, and offshoot of, the contemporary development of the practice of free debate and open discussion in the context of politics and law throughout the Greek world.[32]

These ideas were especially important in early Greek medicine. As Lloyd also tells us, "one of the chief battles that the Hippocratic physicians had to fight was to get it accepted that disease is a natural phenomenon, the effect of natural causes. Just as the Milesians had rejected the idea of divine interference in such domains as meteorology and astronomy, so too the doctors did in medicine."[33]

This question of objectivity – of the extent to which judgments can be justified independently of the particular preferences, experiences and circumstances of the observer – was also central to an important debate between the philosopher Socrates and the professional sophist Protagoras. According to Protagoras, the very idea of objective knowledge is an illusion. As he famously put it, "man is the measure of all things."[34] In other words, all knowledge is relative to the believer. All so-called knowledge is subjective. In his reply to Protagoras, Socrates famously pointed out that if all knowledge were subjective, it would follow that all of Protagoras' beliefs must also be subjective. And if so, then Protagoras must be "conceding the truth of the opinion of those who think him wrong."[35] In other words, since many people believe Protagoras' view to be mistaken, and since according to Protagoras all knowledge is relative to the believer, it follows that Protagoras must be "admitting the falsity of his own opinion"![36]

Today, just as in Socrates' day, there is debate over the significance of such arguments. For example, philosophy professor Mark Mercer is not so quick to dismiss Protagoras's view:

> Protagoras is concerned to present theses and to argue for them, and to hear and respond to criticism. It follows that any university should be proud to have Protagoras on its faculty. That Protagoras's doctrines are at odds with certain ideas about the nature and possibility of knowledge isn't to the point – Protagoras's own attitude toward his project and the rigour with which he attempts to carry it out, though, are to the point, and clearly mark him as a university person. (That his doctrines are false and, indeed, self-defeating is something for his academic colleagues to show him.)
>
> It's not objectivity that the academy presupposes, but rigour in argument (or in investigation generally), though the nature of argumentative rigour is itself a topic of investigation and dispute. Professors at a university are to be contrasted, not with thinkers who argue for relativistic views or against the idea that any beliefs can be objectively appraised, but rather with people for whom argument and investigation are foreign. A university person might *advocate* bursting into song in response to an objection; but a person who *actually* bursts into song isn't a university person. It's the person who doesn't debate who stands outside university culture.[37]

Famous Hoaxes

- *The Piltdown-man Hoax*, in which parts of a modern human skull and an orangutan's jawbone were planted as supposed evidence of an essential 'missing link' between modern man and his ancient primate ancestors. Uncovered in England in 1912, the remains were given the name *Eoanthropus dawsoni*. It took over forty years for the hoax to be discovered.

- *The Sokal Hoax*, in which Alan Sokal, a professor of physics at New York University, submitted a paper liberally laced with nonsense to a prominent cultural studies journal to see whether it would be accepted The paper was published in 1996, not because of its scholarly merits but because, according to Sokal, it flattered the editors' ideological preconceptions.

- *The Birds Aren't Real Hoax*, in which it was claimed that birds don't exist. Instead, it was said that what people see in the sky are small drones developed by the US government that recharge by resting on power wires and that are used to spy on ordinary Americans. The campaign, begun in 2017 by Peter McIndoe in Memphis, turned out to be a parody social movement with a purpose. The movement was designed to mock QAnon and other post-truth conspiracy theories, a Gen Z attempt to poke fun at misinformation with misinformation and lunacy with lunacy.

There is a great deal that is helpful and right about these observations – although one is tempted to ask what value "rigour in argument" could have unless Mercer means *objective* rigour in argument. Even so, universities have always been committed to more than just disinterested debate. At their best, they also seek to align themselves with what the English poet Matthew Arnold called "the best that has been thought and said."[38] In other words, part of what universities attempt to do is to identify and promote the best science, the best medicine, the best literature, the best music and the best philosophy. Having noticed the self-defeating aspect of Protagoras's view, it is unlikely that it could ever form part of our best theory of knowledge, despite Protagoras's other virtues.

Put another way, the assumption that beliefs can be justified, not on the basis of some private, privileged authority but on observation, reason and open, public debate, has important methodological consequences.[39] It means that there really can be genuinely objective ways of selecting between competing hypotheses. It means that things like public predictability matter more for the confirmation and falsification of knowledge claims than things like sacred texts and private hunches.

Once this view about the advancement of knowledge is accepted, it follows that many commonplace beliefs may be capable of being re-evaluated. For example, when the Athenians lost a major military campaign against Sicily in the midst of the Peloponnesian War,[40] one faction argued that the loss had been due to poor preparation on the part of the Athenians. Before blundering into battle, it should be incumbent on an army's commanders to reconnoiter their enemy's position, to discover how many troops they will be facing and to consider whether they will be able to withstand a protracted siege.

A second, quite different faction argued that the loss had been due, not to poor preparation, but to the displeasure of the gods. The morning the Athenian navy set sail for Sicily, Athenians woke to discover that many roadside statues of the god Hermes had been vandalized. Each statue had originally consisted of a small square post with a bust of the god's head on top and a large, carved phallus midway down the front. After a night of heavy drinking on the eve of their departure, many of the city's soldiers had vandalized the statues as they marched toward their ships, breaking off the statues' phalluses. Upon arriving in Sicily, the Athenian army was then badly defeated. One of their top generals, Alcibiades, even defected to Sparta. For many, the moral was clear. It is the gods who decide men's fortune. Little else matters.

Testing a Hypothesis

(Not just in science, but in any discipline)

1) Identify your subject.

2) Refine your concepts and define your terms.

3) Formulate your hypothesis.

4) Gather your evidence.

5) Evaluate your hypothesis.

Twenty-four hundred years later, similar questions of priority still occupy us. When it comes to the evaluation of knowledge claims, should we automatically dismiss naturalist explanations in favour of religious experience? Or should we automatically dismiss religious experience in favour of naturalist explanations? Should we assume that reason is always an essential corrective to fallible observation? Or that observation is a necessary corrective to fallible reason? When it comes to understanding the origins of human behaviour, should we automatically assume that nature trumps nurture? Or that nurture trumps nature?

Here is a recent example raised by the respected Canadian neuro-psychologist, Doreen Kimura:

> [S]ome writers insist that ability differences between men and women must be considered experientially determined [i.e., determined by nurture] unless we can demonstrate unequivocally that they are not. For example, "I impose the highest standards of *proof* ... on claims about biological inequality." (Fausto-Sterling 1992) This is surely a very strange approach. It implies that we may not entertain biological explanations of human behavior until we have ruled out all plausible socialization mechanisms. To illustrate how strange this viewpoint is, we might turn the argument around and say we will not accept a difference between the sexes as environmentally influenced unless we can rule out the possibility that

the differences are congenital [i.e., determined by nature]. This is as logically acceptable as the first position, and equally flawed. The aim of scientific research is not (or should not be) to uphold or deny any particular social or political ideology. Rather, the aim in science must be to find the truest explanation we can; that is, the explanation that best fits all the current facts, regardless of current dogma.[41]

In the absence of conclusive evidence one way or another, should we assume that different cognitive abilities between men and women are primarily a function of socialization? Or of biology? Of nature? Or of nurture? If men underperform women in language acquisition, or if women underperform men in mathematics, should we assume that this is primarily a function of social pressure and systemic discrimination? Or of differences in brain chemistry?

As tempting as it may be to come down on one side or the other, it is a simple mistake to think that one approach is somehow intrinsically more privileged than the other. As Kimura points out, the error of thinking that such differences must result from socialization probably comes from confusing the concept

of equal treatment before the law – the societal application of the idea that 'all men are created equal' – with the claim that all people are in fact equal. People are not born equal in strength, health, temperament, or intelligence. This is simply a fact of life no sensible person can deny.[42]

Similarly, the error of thinking that such differences must result from differences in biology probably comes from confusing the idea of genetic influence with genetic determinism. Thus, rather than assuming that nature always trumps nurture or that nurture always trumps nature, today's best researchers, just as in centuries past, accept that genuine advances in knowledge result from our use of reason, observation, and free and open debate, rather than from some single form of privileged authority.[43]

No sin but ignorance. Why did Sokal's hoax provoke such widespread debate among scientists and humanists alike? The answer seems to be that, regardless of one's discipline, most people recognize the value of clear, objective, publicly testable standards of academic achievement. Research and scholarship require us to do more than simply give voice to private beliefs and prejudices.[44] They require that we listen to all sides (an important principle, not just in science but in law), that we evaluate hypotheses carefully and rigorously, and that we pay attention to evidence rather than simply accept beliefs because they are appealing or popular. Whether it is the economist wanting to discover the causes of inflation, the geographer wanting to map the movements of an ancient people, or the psychiatrist wanting to understand the efficacy of a new drug, the underlying methodology remains the same. Contrary to what Snow and Kerr suggest, it is this commitment to publicly testable standards of investigation and achievement that binds together different disciplines within the university.

Of course, debate continues – as it should – over the nature of such standards. One view is that all standards are political. For example, when comparing the differences between scientific theories and non-scientific narratives, the French literary theorist Jean-François Lyotard concludes that neither is more fundamental or more valuable than the other.[45] Ultimately, says Lyotard, all standards are political:

> Take any civil law as an example: it states that a given category of citizens must perform a specific kind of action. Legitimation is the process by which a legislator is authorized to promulgate such a law as a norm. Now take the example of a scientific statement: it is subject to the rule that a statement must fulfill a given set of conditions in order to be accepted as scientific. ... The parallel may appear forced. But as we will see, it is not. The question of the legitimacy of science has been indissociably linked to that of the legitimation of the legislator since the time of Plato.[46]

134

In other words, like Protagoras, Lyotard believes that so-called objective knowledge is ultimately a myth. What one group understands to be objective, another group will take to be subjective. On this view, being 'objective' simply means having wide social acceptance. In Lyotard's words, "knowledge and power are simply two sides of the same question."[47] And as a result, "all we can do is gaze in wonderment at the diversity of discursive species, just as we do at the diversity of plant or animal species."[48]

Of course, once again, we need to ask, in the midst of all this wonderment, whether there is going to be an objective standard for what constitutes wide social acceptance, and whether the "diversity of discursive species" Lyotard refers to should be thought of as an objectively existing diversity. We should also ask whether it is going to be an objective fact that knowledge and power are simply two sides of the same coin. For surely, on Lyotard's view, he will want to claim that it is an objective fact that political lobbying and scientific investigation are simply two sides to the same coin. For if not, the rest of us will also be right to conclude that his view is mistaken.

An alternative suggestion to Lyotard's is the view that objective standards can be found independently of any subjective beliefs or preferences individuals may have. If this doesn't seem obvious, ask yourself why a university theatre company decides to perform one theatrical work rather than another. Is it simply because one work is likely to be more popular, or to draw a larger box office, than the other? (And even here, we're surely entitled to ask whether it is thought that one work is going to be *objectively* more popular.) Or is it because we hope to learn something more important from the one than the other? Similarly, why do we choose to study one social issue (say the movement for the abolition of slavery) rather than another (say the collecting of trading cards)? Is it because one simply satisfies our subjective preferences in a way the other does not? Or is it because one is of more consequence, of greater importance, than the other? As the

American author William Henry puts it, on this view it is simply a brute fact that some ideas

> are better than others, some values more enduring, some works of art more universal. Some cultures, though we dare not say it, are more accomplished than others and therefore more worthy of study. Every corner of the human race may have something to contribute. That does not mean that all contributions are equal.[49]

On this view, what distinguishes scientific accomplishment from mere speculation is the lasting insight it gives people about the world around us. What distinguishes classical literature, history, music, art and philosophy from more transient achievements is simply their intrinsic value, the fact that they are grounded in the natural world and in human nature in a way that is independent of any subjective beliefs we may have. If Henry is right, those who tell us that they know for a fact that there is no knowledge and there are no facts are simply mistaken.

Which view is correct? In his play *The Jew of Malta,* Shakespeare's contemporary Christopher Marlowe reminds his audience that since the time of the Enlightenment many have believed that knowledge holds the key to human flourishing.[50] As the Senecan ghost Machiavel confidently announces at the opening of the play, "there is no sinne but Ignorance."[51] Improved health, improved food supplies, improved housing and improved security all result from advances in knowledge. By refusing to learn, we sin against ourselves and against our fellow man. This, too, is a Greek idea, since it was Plato who tells us that the highest good is the cultivation of the intellect[52] and that it is only out of ignorance that we do evil.[53]

Even so, the fact that it is Marlowe's unscrupulous Machiavelli character speaking these lines gives us pause. Here too, we are reminded that there has long been disagreement over the value of knowledge. Just as knowledge gives us the power to cure disease and learn from the past, it also gives us the power to wage war and destroy our environment.

Knowledge alone, without a desire to do what's right, has often been thought more a detriment than a benefit.

Perhaps the most famous advocate of this latter view is the author of the book of *Genesis*. In *Genesis* we read the story of how the serpent tempted Adam and Eve to eat the forbidden fruit from the tree of knowledge, and how doing so not only opened their eyes but also led to their expulsion from the Garden of Eden.[54] Similar themes have been prominent in much of Western literature – for example in the stories of Prometheus, Faustus and Frankenstein, among others. Each serves to remind us that prohibitions on at least some types of knowledge have often been thought necessary.[55]

The view we accept will affect dramatically how we chose to understand and structure the modern university.

Further reading

Flexner, *Universities: American, English, German*, New York: Oxford University Press, 1930

Goodall, Amanda H., *Socrates in the Boardroom: Why Research Universities Should Be Led by Top Scholars*, Princeton: Princeton University Press, 2009

Gross, Paul R., and Norman Levitt, *Higher Superstition: The Academic Left and Its Quarrels with Science*, Baltimore: Johns Hopkins University Press, 1994

Haack, Susan, *Defending Science – Within Reason*, New York: Prometheus Books, 2007

Haack, Susan, *Putting Philosophy to Work: Essays on Science, Religion, Law, Literature, and Life*, New York: Prometheus Books, 2008

Heath, Joseph, *Enlightenment 2.0*, New York: HarperCollins, 2014

Kagan, Jerome, *The Three Cultures: Natural Sciences, Social Sciences, and the Humanities in the 21st Century*, New York: Cambridge University Press, 2009

Kerr, Clark, *The Uses of the University*, 5th edn, Boston: Harvard University Press, 2001

Lingua Franca, *The Sokal Hoax: The Sham that Shook the Academy*, Lincoln, London: University of Nebraska Press, 2000

Minogue, Kenneth, *The Concept of a University*, London: Transaction Publishers. 2005

Newman, John Henry, *The Idea of a University*, New York: Longmans Green & Co., 1947

Pinker, Steven, *Enlightenment Now: The Case for Reason, Science, Humanism and Progress*, New York: Viking, 2018

Pinker, Steven, *Rationality: What It Is, Why It Seems Scarce, Why It Matters*, New York: Viking, 2021

Rauch, Jonathan, *The Constitution of Knowledge: A Defense of Truth*, Washington, DC: Brookings, 2021

Shattuck, Roger, *Forbidden Knowledge*, San Diego, New York, London: A Harvest Book / Harcourt Brace & Company, 1997

Snow, C.P., *The Two Cultures and the Scientific Revolution: The Rede Lecture, 1959*, New York: Cambridge University Press, 1959

Sokal, Alan, *Beyond the Hoax: Science, Philosophy and Culture*, Oxford: Oxford University Press, 2008

Sokal, Alan, and Jean Bricmont, *Fashionable Nonsense: Postmodern Intellectuals' Abuse of Science*, New York: Picador, 1998; published originally as *Impostures Intellectuelles*, Paris: Editions Odile Jacob, 1997

Stove, David, *Scientific Irrationalism: Origins of a Postmodern Cult*, New Brunswick (NJ), London: Transaction Publishers, 2001; published originally as *Popper and After: Four Modern Irrationalists*, Oxford: Pergamon, 1982

Weiner, Joseph S., *The Piltdown Forgery: The Classic Account of the Most Famous and Successful Hoax in Science*, Oxford: Oxford University Press, 2003

Youngson, Robert M., *Scientific Blunders: A Brief History of How Wrong Scientists Can Sometimes Be,* London: Robinson, 1998

Chapter 8

Beware the Fribling, Fumbling Keepers of the Age

Should university researchers be free to investigate *anything*? In their lectures, should university instructors be able to talk about any subjects they think important and relevant? Should students be given unrestricted access to everything that has been thought and said? Or should we return to the days when librarians held the keys to locked cabinets used to store the heretical texts listed in the *Index librorum prohibitorum* (the *Index of Prohibited Books*)?

Throughout history, attempts have been made to prohibit, not just various kinds of publication but various kinds of teaching and learning. Socrates was put to death for corrupting the youth with his unorthodox ideas.[1] Galileo was summoned to appear before the Inquisition, placed under house arrest and forced to recant his heretical heliocentric views.[2] In 1896, the entire Economics Department at Kansas State Agricultural College – the precursor of today's Kansas State University – was dismissed for refusing to accept a "populist version of economic theory."[3] In 1940, Judge John McGeehan of the New York Supreme Court found the philosopher Bertrand Russell to be "morally unfit" to teach at City College New York, just ten years before he was to receive his Nobel Prize for Literature.[4]

To shield students from a variety of curse words, the editors at Ballantine Books carefully excised some 75 separate sections of Ray Bradbury's famous novel, *Fahrenheit 451*.[5] Ironically, the novel tells the story of a dystopian society in which reading is outlawed and 'firemen' – Bradbury's euphemism for book burners – are hired to destroy libraries of books for the good of humanity. The omissions weren't repaired until students wrote to Bradbury to tell him about the irony. Not surprisingly, Bradbury was less than pleased to learn of these unauthorized deletions. As he tells his readers,

> The real world is the playing ground for each and every group, to make or unmake laws. But the tip of the nose of my book or stories or poems is where their rights end and my territorial imperatives begin, run and rule. If Mormons do not like my plays, let them write their own. If the Irish hate my Dublin stories, let them rent typewriters. If teachers and grammar school editors find my jawbreaker sentences shatter their mushmilk teeth, let them eat stale cake dunked in weak tea of their own ungodly manufacture.[6]

Similar prohibitions of various kinds continue to be the subject of controversy even today. In some parts of the world women are barred from attending school or university[7] and students and professors of both sexes can be imprisoned or even executed for studying forbidden material.[8] At many North American universities, student clubs advocating unpopular political views have been banned.[9] But as much as some people might think otherwise, intolerance is not an academic virtue.

Loyalty oaths. In 1948, the former Soviet Union made it illegal to criticize the views of the President of the Soviet Academy of Agricultural Sciences, Trofim Lysenko. Hundreds of scientists were fired from their jobs. Many others were imprisoned. In the years that followed, the uncritical acceptance of Lysenko's crack-pot theories led, not just to the steady deterioration of crop yields in the Soviet Union and China but to eventual, wide-spread, deadly famine.[10]

In the West, loyalty oaths of various kinds have sometimes been used to try to enforce uniformity of thought and teaching. On April 12, 1950, the University of California Board of Regents passed a regulation requiring all professors to sign a declaration affirming that they were not members of the Communist Party. Thirty-one faculty members were fired for refusing to sign the oath. Two years later the California State Supreme Court ruled in favour of those who had been fired and ordered the university to reinstate them.[11] Ironically, just a few years earlier, numerous prominent academics – including Albert Einstein – had written letters protesting the "oath of loyalty to the Fascist system" that had been in place in Italy during the Second World War.[12] One problem with all such oaths is that they make it difficult for people affiliated with the university – whether students, faculty or alumni – to benefit from hearing opposite points of view.

Examples like these illustrate the importance of academic freedom. If they are to be free to learn, students need to be free to ask questions about any subject they think important. If they are to be free to advance knowledge, professors need to be able to follow the evidence wherever it might lead, to pursue their research however they see fit. Where it exists, academic freedom is what protects students and faculty alike from being forced to accept any kind of political, religious or scientific party line. Academic freedom is what makes possible the free exchange of ideas of all kinds, something that is necessary for the advancement of knowledge, the main focus of any university.

Academic freedom. At its core, academic freedom is based on a profound respect for people's ability to think for themselves. What academic freedom does is ensure that people are given the opportunity to think and reason independently of all pressures other than those of evidence and argument. What academic freedom doesn't do is insulate people and their pet theories from criticism (which at times can be intense), hurt feelings or failing grades. Academic freedom allows us all to consider counterintuitive ideas free from the threat of institutional reprisal and discrimination, not free from the rigour of academic criticism.

For the institution, academic freedom gives universities the independence they need to establish academic programs as they see fit. For the individual, academic freedom gives students and scholars the right to investigate topics they find to be of interest and to have their work evaluated solely on the basis of academic (rather than non-academic) criteria.

Once governments gain the power to require universities to advance one political or religious view rather than another, or universities gain the power to require faculty to accept one scientific theory rather than another, or educators gain the power to require students to believe one historical account rather than another, academic freedom will be lost. Once we begin incorporating political or religious tests into student grading, or into academic hiring, the academic mission of the university will be compromised. Once a university takes an official position on substantive matters of fact (other than those needed to carry out its mission), its reputation as a place for disinterested investigation and debate will be gone. If a university or the people speaking on its behalf become partisans in the on-going social, religious, legal, scientific, historical or public-policy debates of their day, public trust in the objectivity of university teaching and research will inevitably be diminished.

Academic freedom also gives students and professors the freedom to criticize their universities whenever they think it is important to do so. In Canada, when Professor Tomáš Hudlický – one of Brock University's most prominent and accomplished chemists – expressed his concerns about various hiring practices within his field, *Angewandte Chemie* (the prestigious German chemistry journal in which he published his comments) withdrew his article. Because of his observation that equity, diversity and inclusion policies may sometimes "have influenced hiring practices to the point where a candidate's inclusion in one of the preferred social groups may override his or her qualifications," his university publicly reprimanded him for advancing views that the university concluded might be "alarming to students and others."[13] As the Canadian Association of University Teachers (CAUT) observed, Professor Hudlický's published comments discussed "what he considers to be the major drivers of change in the profession over the past 30 years. In his opinion, these include new scientific technologies, the emergence of online journals, the corporatization of universities, the diversity of the workforce, and the training and mentoring of new professionals." In CAUT's opinion, the university's statements reprimanding Hudlický, were "a clear violation" of the university's obligation to uphold academic freedom. "By publicly attacking Professor Hudlický, without even the courtesy of consulting with him beforehand, the University administration has failed to respect and defend his academic freedom. Actions such as these threaten to have a profound chilling effect across the institution."[14] As Hudlický himself has warned, "The witch hunt is on."[15]

Academic responsibility. To avoid misunderstanding, it is worth emphasizing that academic freedom does not imply that all ideas are of equal value or that all theories are of equal importance. Just because someone is free to suggest an idea doesn't mean it should be accepted. Most unpopular ideas are unpopular for a reason. Innovation simply for innovation's sake is rarely a good thing. Even so, the freedom to consider unorthodox alternatives is an essential part of evaluating competing knowledge claims. As Charles Darwin tells us, "Without speculation there is no good and original observation."[16] If knowledge is to advance, students and professors need to be free to suggest alternatives to even the most widely held theories and beliefs, and to test them according to the best evidence available.

Academic Freedom

Academic freedom is the freedom scholars, researchers, artists and academics have to pursue the truth unencumbered by non-academic interference. It protects professors, students and alumni from having to accept any form of 'party line.' It gives members of the university the right to advance unpopular ideas free from the threat of discrimination or reprisal, whether from government officials or university administrators, and gives them the right *to* have their work evaluated on purely academic (rather than non-academic) grounds. Academic freedom is what gives universities and their members the independence they need to carry out their work.

Underlying academic freedom is a purely instrumental purpose. Freedom of inquiry is an essential condition for the advancement of knowledge, the main mission of any university. It follows that not only are members of the university *free* to evaluate one another's ideas according to purely academic (rather than non-academic) criteria, they are *required* to do so. In short, with academic freedom comes the responsibility of evaluating ideas on their merits. With academic freedom comes the responsibility of pursuing the truth, of allowing ourselves to be schooled by nature, rather than by popular opinion.

At its core, academic freedom is based on a simple but profound respect for people's ability to think for themselves. Academic freedom is what makes a university inclusive. Academic freedom ensures that people are given the opportunity to think and reason independently of all pressures other than those of evidence and argument. It allows students and professors alike to consider counterintuitive ideas free from the threat of coercion, not free from the threat of criticism.

Put another way, if students and faculty have the right to have their work evaluated solely on the basis of academic (rather than non-academic) criteria, this creates an obligation for those of us working and studying in universities to evaluate ideas and theories solely on their merits. Students and faculty alike need to be committed to the ideal of following the evidence wherever it may lead. Mathematicians need to be promoted on the basis of how well they do mathematics, not because of their political beliefs. Historians need to be hired on the basis of how well they write history, not because they happen to be married to people who already work at the university or because they happen to fit some desired social profile. Students need to be graded on the basis of how well they've mastered their subjects, not on the basis of what high school they attended or how much time they've put into an assignment.[17] It is by focusing solely on academic rather than non-academic considerations that knowledge advances.

As the British historian Conrad Russell reminds us, academic freedom also has important parallels to the autonomy of the legal profession. Academic freedom is the freedom that academics have to test received wisdom. It is the freedom they have to suggest new ideas and unpopular opinions. In other words,

> It is the freedom to follow a line of research where it leads, Regardless of the consequences, and the corresponding freedom to teach the truth as we see it, with suitable acknowledgement of views which differ from our own. This is as essential to academics as it is to lawyers to be able to say: *fiat iustitia: ruat caelum* [let justice be done though the heavens fall]. Without the basic principle, the whole system would have no *raison d'être*. The use of having judges depends entirely on the willingness of the public to believe that their judgements represent the law as they see it: were this to be otherwise, contempt of court would become the normal state of affairs. Any judge who listens to private ministerial whispers, saying: 'Of course I understand there's a case against us, but it would be *very inconvenient* if you said so now', risks destroying the whole public acceptance of the legal system.[18]

As Russell also writes, academic freedom also has parallels to the medical profession:

> Doctors, for example, have the Hippocratic oath, and it is to be hoped, if Government were to require them to do things which contradict that oath, that they would refuse their consent. They would certainly be poor doctors if they did not. Academics have no formal equivalent of the Hippocratic oath, yet they too have professional values, and are no use to

society if they give them up. ... An academic who listens to pleas of convenience before publishing his research risks calling in doubt the whole of his determination to find the truth. If academic research is not devoted to finding the truth, it is a form of propaganda, and not necessarily to be preferred to other forms, much cheaper and perhaps more persuasive. Academic research is a laborious, expensive and time-consuming way of investigating problems. It can only be justified on the ground that those who undertake it have been trained to put the attempt to get it right above all other considerations whatsoever.[19]

In short, anyone who goes to the time, trouble and expense of establishing a university needs to be assured that they are getting what they pay for. Historians, economists, linguists, foresters, psychologists, classicists, surgeons, anthropologists, cartographers, ethicists, agronomists, political scientists and others all need to be able to give their considered opinions without fear of reprimand or of being fired every time they say or publish something with which someone in a position of power might disagree.

This does not mean that academic work is beyond criticism, any more than is the work of a doctor or lawyer, or of a pilot, engineer or actuary. Instead, what it means is that if, say, we want to hold a pilot accountable for how he flies his plane – for his choice of velocity, altitude or runway approach – then in all likelihood we will need to rely on the judgment of other qualified pilots.[20] Neither the government nor anyone else will have the competence to do this. If, for example, the government were to pass a law requiring pilots to fly at a particular speed to save fuel, it may unwittingly place not only the pilot but also his plane and passengers at risk. The same is true of attempts to regulate the work of historians, economists, linguists, and all the rest.

"But," someone might reply, "surely this is wrong. I may not be qualified to fly a plane. But if a pilot crashes his plane with the loss of all life on board, I'm certainly qualified to conclude that he can't have been a very good pilot." This kind of objection is helpful since it shows exactly why non-experts shouldn't rush to judgment about issues that require expert knowledge. It may turn out that, far from being a bad pilot, the pilot in this case was an exemplary pilot. It may turn out that, not only was the accident caused by some factor entirely beyond the pilot's control, it was only through Herculean efforts on the pilot's part that he was able to crash the plane in an unpopulated, rather than a populated, area. In the absence of expert investigation, this is something that most of us simply aren't qualified to judge. It is for this reason that protection from outside (or even internal) non-academic interference is necessary if we want universities to fulfill their mandate.

Of course, protection from outside *interference* does not mean protection from outside *criticism*. Universities almost by definition are places in which non-experts are not just free to question the views of experts but encouraged to do so. What academic freedom does is protect experts and non-experts alike from having judgments imposed upon them for non-academic reasons. Not only does this mean that governments must play no role in deciding academic questions, it means that university administrators must play no such role either.

The flat-Earth test. Is academic freedom really so important? Do we really need to provide institutional protection to flat-Earth advocates, religious fundamentalists[21] and holocaust deniers? Isn't there sufficient consensus on some issues to say that they have been resolved once and for all?

Academic freedom doesn't commit universities to defending every crackpot idea or failed theory advanced throughout history. Many issues have been resolved and will remain so. Eratosthenes' calculation of the circumference of the Earth in the 3rd century BCE was sufficient to settle the question of the (approximate, non-relative) shape of the Earth some 2,200 years before the first photographs of our planet were taken from space.[22] Fundamentalist theories suggesting that the world is only 6,000 years old continue to lack convincing evidence and explanatory power.[23] The Holocaust remains one of the best-documented examples of barbarism in human history.[24] Any applicant for a university lectureship who offered weak or tenuous evidence in favour of such implausible views isn't likely to be hired, simply on grounds of academic incompetence.

Students and Academic Freedom

Academic freedom for students includes their

- freedom to study, to do research, and to produce and perform creative works in the programs of their choice

- right to freedom of expression, both inside and outside the class-room

- right to freedom of association, including the freedom to invite visiting speakers to campus

- right to publish freely in student newspapers, websites and elsewhere

- right to have their work evaluated solely on academic grounds, without regard to extraneous factors such as political or religious belief, place of origin, sexual orientation, etc.

- right to criticize their university.

Academic freedom does not mean that students are free to set their own course or program requirements, or that a student's work is incapable of being evaluated on the basis of academic criteria.

With a student's academic freedom comes the responsibility

- to learn as much as possible in one's program of studies, and

- to evaluate ideas and theories on the basis of evidence

Even so, failing to advocate a theory is not the same as prohibiting its discussion. Allowing students the freedom to question even such well-established facts does little harm and usually does much good. Dogmatically and uncritically accepting false propositions or incoherent theories offers the student few if any academic advantages. Dogmatically and uncritically accepting true propositions and theories is little better. In contrast, having the freedom to ask whether mathematical and scientific truths are simply subjective social constructions, or why the fossil record has gaps, or what kinds of evidence we have about the Holocaust remains an indispensable component of any good education.

The same is true for the advancement of knowledge more generally. Being able to test dominant theories against less well-supported conjectures is as necessary to intellectual progress as good libraries and good laboratories. Academic freedom is what gives students, scholars and universities the autonomy they need to carry out their work. If governments or other powerful forces were free to decide what can and cannot be taught or researched, it would become significantly harder for knowledge to advance. In some countries, university autonomy is so great it is even illegal for police or the military to enter a university campus without permission from the university's rector or president.[25] In others, not only do universities have policies specifically designed to protect academic freedom, independent associations and societies actively check to ensure that governments, universities and the media all live up to their obligations.[26]

Academic freedom is also what gives universities the power to set their own curricula. Unlike high schools and other teaching institutions that have their curricula set by governments or other non-academic bodies, universities decide for themselves which ideas are worth pursuing and which are not. Having the freedom to establish a university's curriculum solely on academic (rather than political or religious) grounds is important. People in universities have the power to help shape debates on controversial topics. What they bring to such debates is their disinterestedness. Is racial profiling an effective way to reduce terrorism? Was the latest economic crash brought about by too little, or too much, government intervention? Is religious conflict or the competition for scarce energy resources the more likely cause of contemporary warfare? It is because universities are able to pursue independent research on any number of such topics that they are able to contribute to the common good.

Inevitably, controversial ideas sometimes lead to conflict. When Socrates began encouraging his fellow citizens to examine their lives and beliefs, Meletus and Socrates' other accusers became so annoyed that they charged him with corrupting the young. His execution raised in dramatic form the question of how society can both benefit from *and* protect itself from controversial ideas. As the Canadian philosopher Graeme Hunter writes,

> Not until the late Middle Ages was a solution found, but it was worth waiting for. The ingenious invention for ending the repression of important ideas was the University.
>
> University was to be a place set apart from political strife, in which opinions on every topic could be dispassionately considered, not simply as opinions, but as possible truths. Students were invited to participate in an ongoing struggle to show which opinions merely resembled truths and which, if any, were the genuine article. University was for tough-minded people who would track down what is true through study and argument. It was intended for the kind of person who cares about being right. Universities were keen on students who could graduate, for the term "graduation" originally meant not simply leaving university with a degree, but taking a step up the mind's ladder. It meant self-improvement.
>
> University held out no promise of advancement in wealth or power, though the ones who studied there often did advance in those ways. But the institution was dedicated to the proposition that you could improve yourself in a meaningful way by learning to think. Students and faculty alike were expected to put aside the cliché opinions they arrived with and acquire from years of academic struggle resilient, tough minds, able to spot shoddy reasoning in others and avoid it themselves. [27]

How can we continue to benefit from the advantages of university life? How can we protect ourselves from returning to the days of Socrates, when people might be shouted down or arrested or banished or executed, simply for their options? Here, too, Hunter's insights are helpful:

> The greatest calamity that can befall a university is for it to be politicized, that is, for it to be infiltrated with people in love with ideology and indoctrination. Such people are lovers of power, not of truth, and they cling to any opinion they suppose will advance their power, detesting anything that would impede it. If the fashionable opinions they hope to exploit for their advantage are put in question, they move to shut the discussion down. A university that acts in that way becomes a docile purveyor of government or industry propaganda. When rumour of an idea reaches its ears, it calls security. But controversial ideas are like controversial people. Make them unwelcome enough and eventually they stop coming around. A stale quiet descends on the academy and makes you wonder what it's for.[28]

It may seem quaint to discover that Lewis Carroll's *Adventures in Wonderland* was once banned because of the way the book anthropomorphized animals, or that D.H. Lawrence's *Lady Chatterley's Lover* was once banned because of its supposed obscenity. It may seem outré to learn that the American government tried to stop publication of the *Pentagon Papers* because of the risk publication posed to the outcome of the Vietnam War. But every new generation has its own shibboleths and taboos. For some, decades after Salman Rushdie's *Satanic Verses* was first published it remains important to try to ban the book because of its purported blasphemy against Islam. Others want to remove Mark Twain's *The Adventures of Huckleberry Finn* from university reading lists because it contains a hurtful word. But without access to *Mein Kampf* as well as *Schindler's List*, without being able to read the *Times of London* as well as the *People's Daily*, it is impossible to discover and think about the full breadth of human activity. Without access to all that has been written and said, it is impossible for a university to do its job.

Organizations Championing Academic Freedom

Campus Freedom Index (CFI)
campusfreedomindex.ca

Foundation for Individual Rights in Education (FIRE)
thefire.org

National Association of Scholars (NAS)
www.nas.org

Society for Academic Freedom and Scholarship (SAFS)
safs.ca

Beware the "fribling, fumbling keepers of the age." Through-out history, the desire for free and open debate has often led to change. Scholars unwelcome at Oxford founded the University of Cambridge.[29] Advocates of Italian humanism moved to the private and semi-private academies of Florence, Venice, Milan, Rome and Naples rather than stay in the religiously intolerant universities of their day.[30] In France, the rise of humanism was met with such fierce opposition in the Sorbonne that humanist scholars lobbied King Francis I to establish the new Collège de France, something he did in 1530.[31]

Many of the Western world's first scientists found it easier to establish their own learned societies – the Royal Society of London, the Académie des Sciences of Paris, the Accademia del Cimento of Florence – than to become involved with mainstream universities.[32] At Oxford and Cambridge, religious tests for admission were not removed until the second half of the 19th century. During the 20th century, numerous 'think tanks' were established independently of state-funded colleges and universities, sometimes more from political necessity than choice.

Of course, it is one thing to fail to protect someone's freedom. It is another to participate actively in its suppression. In 1681, the English playwright Nathaniel Lee published his play, *Lucius Junius Brutus*. In the Epilogue he bitterly attacks the "fribling, fumbling keepers of the age," and the judges "whose only business is to damn," who shut down the play after just three nights.[33] According to the censors, some of Lee's dialogue may have reflected poorly on King Charles II. As a result, it became their duty to protect the public and end the play's run. How far have we come since 1681?

During the 1960s, students led a series of demonstrations and disturbances that regularly interfered with work done at universities throughout the Western world. As one student leader explained through a bullhorn at Columbia University in 1968, "Our reason for closing down Fayerweather Hall is to call attention to the unconscionable violence in Vietnam, the police state in Harlem, and the intolerable oppression by the United States in Latin America."[34] Regardless of whether one agreed or disagreed with such concerns, it is important to recognize that the methods chosen were clearly anti-intellectual. They were clearly intended to impinge upon the rights of those working and studying in the university to go about their academic business. As the American philosopher Sidney Hook commented at the time, "Like all revolutionaries, convinced that they are fighting for values of transcendent importance, they are prepared to sacrifice the principles of academic freedom, which they tend to regard merely as a redoubt of professional privilege."[35]

More recently, it has sometimes been universities themselves that have attempted to restrict the speech of their students. In 2002, a student studying law at Harvard joined several of his classmates in posting his class notes on the internet so other students could benefit from them. The notes contained language that some people found offensive. The resulting complaints led to the introduction of a proposed speech code designed to prohibit members of the law-school community from voicing racially insensitive remarks.[36] The problem with all such codes is that they restrict the free-speech rights of the very people who most need to be able to debate these issues freely and openly.

In 2005, the University of British Columbia adopted a Mission Statement stating that all of its graduates would "value diversity" and "acknowledge their obligations as global citizens."[37] The Mission Statement was more symbolic than real, since no one was required to make such acknowledge-ments publicly. Even so, it made it more difficult for students and faculty who may have wanted to question such values to do so. The University's corresponding Vision Statement, stating that it was the purpose of the University to "promote the values of a civil and sustainable society," was also inconsistent with the province's *University Act,* since the act explicitly required the university to be "non-political in principle."[38] This requirement, it may be worth noting, does not mean that individual students and faculty members are prohibited from advocating political or religious views. Instead, just the reverse: it is *because* the university is not allowed to take a formal position on such matters that students, faculty and alumni become free to express their views on such subjects without constraint. In other words, being a member of a university does not commit one to a particular political or religious point of view. Instead, it commits one only to the sincere academic investigation of such issues. Perhaps for this reason, both university statements were repealed in 2009.

In 2008, the University of Calgary decided to prevent students from viewing a much-publicized anti-abortion display, going so far as to charge some of its own students with trespassing after they set up large colour photographs of aborted fetuses. The display had been erected numerous times previously without incident, as had other potentially offensive displays by other student groups, including displays showing the consequences of spousal abuse, the effects of laboratory testing on animals, and the effects of torture on religious minorities around the world. The university took no action while reporters were present, but administrators later asked that court summonses be delivered privately to students at their homes without the glare of media attention, hardly the action of an institution whose primary mandate is to advance free and open debate on a wide variety of important issues.[39]

In 2009, Yale University Press refused to allow publication of several controversial images in a book it had contracted to publish entitled *The Cartoons that Shook the World*.[40] The author of the book, a professor at Brandeis University, wanted to discuss the infamous 2005 Danish cartoons that many Muslims found blasphemous. Published originally in the Danish newspaper *Jyllands-Posten*, one of the cartoons depicted Muhammad wearing a turban in the shape of a bomb. Another showed him telling a line of recently deceased martyrs that they should stop their violence since heaven had run out of virgins. Infamously, the cartoons sparked anti-Western riots in several parts of the world. Embassies were attacked, property was destroyed and people were killed.[41] (Of course, in many other parts of the world, their publication was met with admirable tolerance.) In 2020, violence was still being felt when a teacher in Paris was killed for showing similar cartoons to his history class.

The cartoons also prompted the Iranian newspaper *Hamshahri* to hold a Holocaust-cartoon contest so people in the West would understand just how offended some in the Arab world felt by the original cartoons. One of the cartoons from the contest showed Adolf Hitler in bed with one of the most famous victims of the holocaust, Anne Frank. "Write this one in your diary, Anne," says Hitler after they have just had sex. But as *New York Times* columnist David Brooks wrote, the Hitler cartoon failed to have its desired effect: "You want us to know how you feel. … But I still don't know how you feel. I still don't feel as if I should burn embassies or behead people or call on God or bin Laden to exterminate my foes. I still don't feel your rage. I don't feel threatened by a sophomoric cartoon, even one as tasteless as that one."[42]

Despite all this debate, or perhaps because of it, instead of publishing *The Cartoons that Shook the World* as originally agreed, Yale University Press took it upon itself to publish only a bowdlerized version. Not only did the book not include any of the original twelve Danish drawings, all other controversial images were omitted as well.[43] "What's next?" we might ask ourselves. "Is Yale going to stop publishing anatomy textbooks that contain photographs of – gasp! – the human body, since some people find such images offensive?" Yale's self-censorship has led to speculation that the university was more interested in placating prominent Muslim donors than it was in encouraging unfettered scholarly debate. It also led New York commentator Roger Kimball to suggest that Yale's famous motto *Lux et Veritas* (*Light and Truth*) should be exchanged for the more appropriate *Timiditas et Deditio* (*Cowardice and Surrender*).[44] What is certain is that the actions of the university stand in stark contrast to the words of one of its own former presidents, Benno Schmidt. According to Schmidt,

> I take a completely different view of what a university is …
> It's not a place, first and foremost, that is about the inculcation of thought [and] habits of mind that I might agree are correct and constructive.
>
> The university has a fundamental mission which is to search for the truth. And a university is a place where people have to have the right to speak the unspeakable and think the unthinkable and challenge the unchallengeable.[45]

And, one might add, publish the unpublishable.

Further reading

Ben-Porath, Sigal R., *Free Speech on Campus*, Philadelphia: University of Pennsylvania Press, 2017

Chemerinsky, Erwin and Howard Gillman, *Free Speech on Campus*, New Haven: Yale University Press, 2017

Doumani, Beshara, *Academic Freedom after September 11*, New York: Zone Books, 2006

Downs, Donald Alexander, *Free Speech and Liberal Education: A Plea for Intellectual Diversity and Tolerance,* Washington, DC: Cato Institute, 2020

Downs, Donald Alexander, *Restoring Free Speech and Liberty on Campus*, New York: Cambridge University Press, 2005

Fish, Stanley, *Save the World on Your Own Time*, Oxford: Oxford University Press, 2008

Furedi, Frank, *On Tolerance: A Defence of Moral Independence*, London: Bloomsbury Academic, 2013

Furedi, Frank, *What's Happened to the University? A Sociological Exploration of its Infantilisation*, London: Routledge, 2017

Gerstmann, Evan, and Matthew J. Streb, *Academic Freedom at the Dawn of a New Century: How Terrorism, Governments and Culture Wars Impact Free Speech*, Stanford: Stanford University Press, 2006

Hamilton, Neil, *Zealotry and Academic Freedom: A Legal and Historical Perspective,* New Brunswick (NJ), London: Transaction, 1998

Hook, Sidney, *Academic Freedom and Academic Anarchy*, New York: Cowles Book Co., 1970

Hook, Sidney, *In Defense of Academic Freedom*, New York: Pegasus, 1971

Horn, Michiel, *Academic Freedom in Canada: A History*, Toronto, Buffalo, London: University of Toronto Press, 1999

Kirk, Russell, *Academic Freedom: An Essay in Definition*, Chicago: H. Regnery Co., 1955

Lukianoff, Greg and Jonathan Haidt (2018), *The Coddling of the American Mind: How Good Intentions and Bad Ideas are Setting Up a Generation for Failure*, New York: Penguin Press

MacIver, Robert M., *Academic Freedom in Our Time*, New York: Columbia University Press, 1955

Nelson, Cary, *No University is an Island: Saving Academic Freedom*, New York: New York University Press, 2010

Oakeshott, Michael, *The Voice of Liberal Learning: Michael Oakeshott on Education*, Timothy Fuller (ed.), New Haven: Yale University Press, 1989

O'Neil, Robert M., *Academic Freedom in the Wired World: Political Extremism, Corporate Power, and the University*, Cambridge (MA): Harvard University Press, 2008

Russell, Conrad, *Academic Freedom*, London, New York: Routledge, 1993

Taleb, Nassim, *Antifragile: Things that Gain from Disorder,* New York: Random House, 2012

Taleb, Nassim, *Skin in the Game*, New York: Random House, 2018

Whittington, Keith E., *Speak Freely: Why Universities Must Defend Free Speech*, Princeton: Princeton University Press, 2018

Williams, Joanna, *Academic Freedom in an Age of Conformity: Confronting the Fear of Knowledge*, London: Palgrave Macmillan, 2016

Chapter 9

Inoculate Yourself Against Ergophobia

ॐ ॐ

Regardless of when or where you attend university, some things never change. One of these things is that sometimes, just sometimes, students will find their professors out of touch and boring, and professors will find their students inattentive and unprepared. Whether your university is centuries old or brand new, whether it is a large public institution or a small private one, whether you eat at High Table or in the local cafeteria – none of this matters. At some point, attending lectures will become a chore, and giving them will seem like drudgery.

After graduating from Yale University, James Gamble Rogers designed many of his university's most handsome neo-Gothic buildings. Among his most noticed sculptures are two stone carvings that decorate entrances to the Yale Law School. They illustrate this point perfectly. Above the door used by professors is a frieze showing an enthusiastic professor lecturing to a group of bored, sleepy students. Above the door used by the students is a different carving, one in which enthusiastic students, hungry for knowledge, face an uncaring professor, and a teaching assistant who sits behind him interested only in his own work. It is hard to say either carving is completely unrepresentative.

None of us is born lazy. Well, at least that is what my grandmother, the indomitable troglodyte Lulu, used to tell me.

(It would be interesting to see if a cognitive psychologist could figure out some way to test her hypothesis.) But regardless, how can we avoid feeling that it is no longer worth our time and trouble to pick up a book or memorize a formula? In short, how can we inoculate ourselves against ergophobia, the fear of hard work?

One way is to form a study group. At the very least, this will let you share your misery with others. Another is to find a way to make the work more interesting. This sounds hard but really isn't. It is often no harder than reminding ourselves that we take pleasure from discovering new ideas, from learning new facts, from reading new works of fiction. When we get tired of writing essays and lab reports, sometimes it helps to read something that has given us pleasure in the past. Re-reading a passage from a novel or an interesting news report or an old email from home can sometimes remind us of the pleasure we get from being able to write down our own thoughts in language that others will understand and enjoy. Knowing that other people can write interesting prose gives us confidence that this is something that we, too, should be able to do.

John von Neumann was one of the many academics who emigrated from Germany in the lead-up to the Second World War. In 1933, he resigned his position in Germany and became one of the original six mathematicians appointed to positions at the newly formed Institute for Advanced Study in Princeton, a position he held for the rest of his life. Today he is remembered as one of the greatest mathematicians of the 20th century.

Even so, according to legend his housekeeper found him a little odd: "Oh, he seems like an okay person," she is reported to have said, "except for being a little strange in some ways. All day he sits at his desk and scribbles, scribbles, scribbles. Then, at the end of the day, he takes the sheets of paper he's scribbled on, scrunches them all up, and throws them in the trash can."[1]

This probably isn't entirely fair. Academic work of any kind requires a large amount of solitary effort. It also means having to face failed attempts and dead ends. To persevere in the face of such odds requires genuine dedication. But if you enjoy the work, and realize that even the dead ends and failures can lead to increased knowledge, the work isn't as tedious as it might seem to an outsider.

Lectures. What makes one set of lectures successful and another not? Often the answer is simply good two-way communication. Most professors admit that their best lectures – the ones they prepare with the greatest effort and deliver with the most enthusiasm – are the ones in which students ask the most questions. Knowing that students are interested in what they have to say is a great incentive to get their lectures right.

For their part, students often agree. Knowing that a professor is willing to answer questions and meet students halfway gives them an incentive to work harder and come to lectures prepared. Many graduates also admit that learning to ask questions during their undergraduate lectures was one of the most valuable parts of their education. Overcoming shyness, learning to craft questions that will be of interest to others as well as themselves, speaking with a clear voice in front of a group – all are skills worth developing. None comes naturally. So, if you find yourself taking a course from a less-than-stimulating lecturer, here are a few suggestions about what to do.

First, *come to class prepared*. Lectures are rarely boring if you prepare beforehand. Not only will you understand more of what's going on, you'll find it easier to engage both the material and the lecturer. Some lectures are crafted in such a way that they only make sense once the textbook or other course materials have been read. If so, it is doubly important to read your course materials beforehand. Some courses also have regular homework exercises. Don't fall behind. If you do, make an appointment to see your professor so you can ask about how to get caught up.

Second, *ask questions.* Before going to each lecture, make a list of the questions you'd like answered. If no one else asks them, make sure you do. Every time you ask a question, other students will be grateful you did. Asking questions also helps point your professor towards topics you find interesting.

PREPARING FOR LECTURES

- Ask your instructor for a course syllabus so you can come to class prepared.

- Review your assigned readings (or other course materials) *before* each lecture.

- Review your assigned readings (or other course materials) again *after* each lecture.

- If lecturers are covering material too quickly or too slowly, take a moment to let them know.

- If a lecturer speaks unclearly, or is consistently late for lectures, or consistently slow returning assignments, take a moment to let your faculty advisor or department head know.

- If you're unsure, ask!

Sometimes professors lecture at too high or too low a level of difficulty. If they do, make sure you tell them. Ask them to go through the material more slowly or more quickly. Most lecturers sincerely want to help their students and are pleased to receive this kind of feedback.

Third, *don't underestimate your abilities.* In class, professors often ask students whether they would like previously covered material to be reviewed a second time. Just as often, students are uncertain about whether they should respond. "If no one else is asking the professor to review this material," students often think, "I guess everyone understands it except me." This is a mistake. If something in the textbook or in a previous lecture is unclear, ask your professor to go over it one more time. Other students will be glad you did.

Finally, if a lecturer is genuinely bad, take the time to meet with your faculty advisor or department head. Be polite, but don't hesitate to explain why you think improvements need to be made. Also, don't wait until the end of term. If a lecturer isn't speaking clearly, or is regularly showing up late for class, or isn't returning student work in a timely way, take a moment to inform your university.

Libraries. The most famous library of the ancient world was the Royal Library at Alexandria, Egypt. For over two thousand years it has served as a prototype for other important libraries, perhaps not as a strict blueprint, but certainly as an inspiration. Today it is probably impossible to tell which of the many stories about the library are true and which are apocryphal but, whether true or not, they indicate the enormous prominence the library had in the minds of historians, both during its existence and for centuries afterwards. Founded during Egypt's Ptolemaic period, the library is sometimes said to have contained close to a million scrolls, with some 200,000 of them apparently being given to Cleopatra as a wedding gift from Mark Antony. It is also said that under Ptolemy III, a law was passed requiring visitors to Alexandria to temporarily surrender all written materials in their possession so they could be copied during the owner's stay in the city. Whether true or not, it is clear that the library was one of the ancient world's most important centres of learning.

Today, libraries not only house huge collections of books, journals, papers, maps, tapes, films and archival materials, they also serve as access points to even larger collections of online information that are sometimes available publicly and sometimes only to university subscribers. If you are new to a university, it is important to take a tour of your new library. Even if you think you'll likely be accessing most of your research materials online, it still pays to discover how the library works and where to go if you have questions.

Librarians are often the most under-utilized resource within a university. If you go to them for help, they can often locate a source for you within seconds. Librarians are like search engines on steroids. Be sure to take advantage of what they know. Many libraries offer free, short seminars designed to introduce students to their online holdings. Others give guided tours of their physical collections. Learning to do research in a library will give you a variety of important, transferable skills. Learning to do work in one area also helps you do well in other, unrelated areas, both while you are a student and afterwards.

LIBRARY RESEARCH

- Ask your instructor or teaching assistant how to search for peer-reviewed articles in your discipline.
- Read widely to *develop* your thesis.
- Read narrowly to defend your thesis.
- Document all sources and give references for all quotations.
- If you're unsure, ask!

Laboratories. The pleasure many people find in making a new discovery is genuine and often long lasting. As a result, lab work and fieldwork are a highlight of many people's time at university. Time spent in the field or in a laboratory can be energizing and fun, but it also can have risks. Most labs have a set of rules (including safety rules), a dress code, and guidelines for cleaning up. Make sure you familiarize yourself with them all before you begin work.

One of the great advantages of the modern university is the ready access students have to labs. This hasn't always been the case. From the time of the rise of modern science in the early 1500s until late in the 19th century, almost all experiments took place in private laboratories, either at the homes of wealthy amateur scientists or in the college rooms of university professors. According to one account, any assistant researchers who might have been hired would have been

relatively unskilled – for instance Newton's poor eyesight led him to employ others to describe the results of his optical work to him. But, astonishingly, helping an acknowledged master of experimentation was the only way open to a student physicist to receive any teaching in experimental techniques whatsoever. Indeed, such knowledge was actively discouraged by some academics, such as the great Cambridge mathematician Dr. Isaac Todhunter, who said: "Experimentation is unnecessary for the student. The student should be prepared to accept whatever the master told him."[2]

LABORATORY RESEARCH

- Follow all recommended safety procedures.
- Follow all recommended hygiene procedures.
- Follow all recommended administrative procedures.
- Never work in a lab alone.
- Be considerate of others with whom you share the lab.
- Act responsibly.
- If you're unsure, ask!

Things started to change in the 19th century when universities began to gather scientists together and encouraged them to share experimental data with one another, and with their students. They also began to build recognizably modern laboratories. One of the first was at the University of Glasgow in Scotland. There, in the 1840s,

William Thompson, later Lord Kelvin, "took over an old wine cellar in his predecessor's house ... threw out the bins, installed a water supply and a sink, and called the room a physical laboratory." Many students were taught in this laboratory and some remarkable work was produced, but still the student worked only as the Professor's assistant, not on any organised course, and only a few students could be accommodated in this way.[3]

Not long after Kelvin's time, both Oxford and Cambridge realized the need to establish larger, more student-friendly facilities. By 1872 Oxford had completed the Clarendon Laboratory, funded through a donation by Edward Hyde, the 1st Earl of Clarendon, and by 1874 Cambridge had established the Cavendish Laboratory, funded through a donation by William Cavendish, the Seventh Duke of Devonshire.

Today, laboratory work is fundamental to almost all programs of study in the sciences, whether in traditional disciplines such as chemistry and physics or in newer disciplines such as psychology or cognitive science. As computing power has grown, the role of computers has also become more central, not only for recording data, but also for creating many of the conditions required for experimentation itself. Whether the experiment involves a particle accelerator or a vacuum chamber, a wet lab or flume tank, the line between traditional experiment and computer simulation is becoming more and more difficult to draw. Regardless of their discipline, students working in laboratories or in the field are well advised to include enough coursework in computer science to be able to take advantage of the latest developments in computing technology.

How to make studying more enjoyable. So how can we make academic work more enjoyable? First, never study while watching TV or while listening to music or while downloading a podcast. Students who say, "I work better with my ear buds in" are mistaken – it simply isn't true. Find a quiet place to review your course materials before each lecture and then again afterwards. If your course has study exercises or lab assignments, complete them and hand them in on time. Don't fall behind. If you do fall behind, make an appointment to see your professor or teaching assistant to ask about how to get caught up.

Whenever possible, it is also a good idea to join a study group, or to form one if you can't find one you want to join. In the group, discuss your course readings and assignments. After your assignments have been submitted and graded, make sure you pick them up and review them. At the end of every term, professors always have to throw out assignments that have been graded but never picked up. Reviewing your assignments after they have been graded is one of the best ways to discover what expectations your instructor has about future work. Occasionally a difficult question may be repeated on a later assignment or exam so students are given a chance to show that they have learned from their earlier mistakes. Don't miss a second opportunity to get the answer right.

When studying, also try to take pleasure from being exposed to new ideas. A good university education will not only introduce you to a wide range of ideas. It will teach you how to evaluate competing claims critically. It will teach you to follow the evidence wherever it may lead. One of the best lessons you can learn is that simply wanting an idea or theory to be true doesn't make it so. This is as true in economics, history and political science as it is in chemistry, biology and mathematics. As James Baldwin, the first professor of Logic and Metaphysics at the University of Toronto noted in his 1890 inaugural lecture, "Facts are sacred." They lead to where they will. Do they interfere with our views of life? Then our views of life are wrong. Do they conflict with authority? Then authority must go ... .[4]

Don't be surprised if it turns out that some questions have unexpected answers. Do theories about the indeterminacy of translation show that no language can ever be fully and accurately translated into another? Does Darwinism imply that there are no independent ethical truths, that ethics is just one survival mechanism among many? Do theories of computing show there are some things that can never be computed, even in principle? Such questions are worth considering even if they don't have clear and immediate answers.

Studying is also always easier if you have attended lectures. If you've understood a lecture, it will be easier to figure out which parts of the lecture were important and which weren't. If you haven't understood the lecture, making a list of questions will help focus your discussion when you meet with your friends or your teaching assistant or your professor.

STUDY TIPS

- Study regularly – don't leave things until the last minute.

- Don't study in front of the TV or computer – people who say "I work better with my earbuds in" are mistaken.

- Join a study group – or form one if you can't find one you want to join.

- After they've been graded, pick up and review previous assignments and quizzes.

- If you have questions, meet with your professors, teaching assistants or other advisors – there's no shame in admitting you don't know something.

- When things get tough, don't give up.

- Remember: studying is important, but studying can't replace attending lectures, and attending lectures can't replace studying.

One difference between high school and university is that most university professors don't take attendance. Deciding whether to attend lectures is up to each individual student. Sometimes it can be tempting to skip a class. This usually doesn't work out well. Catching up is always harder than you might think. Part of doing well at university is discovering how to understand topics that don't come easily to you. If you have attended lectures and made a good-faith attempt to read your textbook, this will give you something concrete to discuss with your professor. Rather than just saying "I'm lost," it is always easier to approach a professor about a specific lecture topic or book chapter or assignment.

BOOKS AND LIBRARIES

Books

AbeBooks
abebooks.com

Google Books
books.google.com

Project Gutenberg
gutenberg.org

ViaLibri
vialibri.net

WorldCat
worldcat.org

National Libraries

Australia – National Library of Australia
www.nla.gov.au

Canada – Library & Archives Canada
www.bac-lac.gc.ca/eng/

France – Bibliothèque nationale de France
bnf.fr

United Kingdom – British Library
bl.uk

United States – Library of Congress
www.loc.gov

Remember, too, that university professors were also once students just like you. Most professors enjoy meeting students and enjoy talking about academic questions, even those that are not a part of the curriculum. While at university, take advantage of what your professors and teaching assistants know. Knock on their office doors. Send them an email. Pick their brains. At the same time, remember that they are ordinary Human beings who are also capable of bias and error. Whenever it is a choice between trusting your professor and trusting evidence you can check directly, always side with the evidence you can check directly.

Using the internet. When Johannes Gutenberg invented moveable type in Germany in the mid-15th century, people soon came to recognize the power of his new printing press. Gutenberg's invention meant that ideas and opinions – both true and false – could be widely circulated in very short order. As a result, initiatives of various kinds were undertaken to try to ensure that the power of the press wasn't abused. One of the most famous was the British Licensing Order of 1643. This order required all publications to be cleared (or licensed) by a censor prior to publication. It was in response to this order that John Milton wrote his famous tract against censorship, *Areopagitica*, and it was because of the arguments of people like John Milton, John Locke and John Stuart Mill that governments throughout the Western world soon gave up the vain hope of censorship.[5]

Even more than Gutenberg's press, today's internet gives all of us the power to make public our views on any number of issues. Knowing this, it is important to ask your librarian, instructor or teaching assistant which internet sites are most reliable for your particular project or discipline. Don't assume that just because something is on the internet it has to be true. Always check the reliability of your sources.

It is also helpful to remember that there is an important difference between work that has been peer-reviewed and work that has not. Researchers don't get their work published in peer-reviewed journals because they are friends with the editor or because they can afford to purchase the space. Articles published in peer-reviewed journals and books published by reputable academic presses – whether online or on a shelf in the library – have all been reviewed by experts.

This doesn't guarantee that they will be free from error – nothing can do that – but it helps.

NATIONAL BUREAUS OF STATISTICS

Australia – Australian Bureau of Statistics
abs.gov.au

Canada – Statistics Canada
statcan.gc.ca

United Kingdom – UK National Statistics
www.statistics.gov.uk

United States – US Bureau of Labor Statistics
bls.gov

International – OECD StatExtracts
stats.oecd.org

Preparing for exams. Examinations are most stressful when students are poorly prepared. The best advice about exams, therefore, is to study regularly throughout the term. Don't leave things until the last minute. If you've mastered your course materials, an exam can seem more like an opportunity to show off rather than a time to discover what you don't know.

Many universities have specific guidelines about examinations, but here are a few that are helpful to follow regardless of which university you're attending:

Try not to be late. Many universities allow students to enter an examination only during the first 30 minutes. They also don't allow students to leave until after at least 30 minutes have passed. Of course, it is better to arrive on time.

Come prepared. How much time will you be given? Is the exam closed book or open book? Will you be allowed to use a calculator? Do you have an extra pen? If the exam is online, are you in a quiet room where you won't be disturbed? Have you set aside enough time? If the exam is in a room you have never been to before, do you know how to find it and how long it will take to get there?

Don't forget your name. Remember to write your name and student number on all answer sheets you submit. Take your student card to the exam in case the invigilator or proctor asks to see it.

UNIVERSITY NEWS

Arts & Letters Daiky
aldaily.com

Chronicle of Higher Education
chronicle.com

Science News
sciencenews.org

University World News
universityworldnews.com

Be polite. Before you begin, turn off your phone and any other electronic devices you may have with you. Place all notes, textbooks and other study aids out of sight. Don't make noise or do things that will inconvenience other students.

Relax. Take a deep breath and relax. Review any instructions given to you by the examiner. Don't worry about what others are doing; focus instead on your own work.

Budget your time. Before you begin writing, read through the entire examination carefully. Answer the easy questions first. Divide the time remaining between the remaining questions. Complete your examination within the time allowed.

Write neatly. Answer all questions in ink. Write your answers neatly so they will be easy for your grader to read. If you write something that you later decide you don't want your grader to read, just place a line through it.

ARTS & SCIENCES

Asian Studies – Association for Asian Studies
www.asianstudies.org

Classics – Perseus Digital Library
www.perseus.tufts.edu

English – Luminarium
www.luminarium.org

French – Radio France Internationale
www.rfi.fr

History – Best of History
www.besthistorysites.net

Chemistry – American Chemical Society
www.acs.org

Earth Sciences – Google Earth
google.com/earth

Physics – Physics News
www.physnews.com

Aim high. During your time at university there will be ups and downs. In one course you may receive a grade lower than you were expecting. In another you may receive a grade higher than you were expecting. Throughout it all, just do your best. Instead of trying to complete your homework or research in the shortest time possible, set aside the same amount of time for independent work each day. On days when you finish early, use the extra time to do extra work.

To get into university, most students have had to be at or near the top of their high-school classes. Upon arriving at university, they often discover that they are now among many other, equally talented people and they, like most people, are now receiving more average grades. For some, this can be disappointing. For others, it becomes an incentive to read more and study harder. This is fine, but remember that the *real* opportunity of attending university is the chance to be exposed to new ideas, to explore new concepts, to think about things you might not have a chance to think about later in life. The four years it takes to complete a degree may seem like a long time, but looking back decades later, what many people often regret most is the course they didn't take.

SOCIAL SCIENCES

Anthropology – Anthropology.net
anthropology.net

Archaeology – Archaeology
www.archaeology.org

Economics – American Economic Association
www.vanderbilt.edu/AEA

Geography – National Geographic
www.nationalgeographic.com

Political Science – Political Resources
www.politicalresources.net

Psychology – Encyclopedia of Psychology
www.psychology.org

Sociology – American Sociological Association
www.asanet.org

While listening to lectures or reading an article online, take pleasure in the joy of discovery. If your grades aren't as high as you might hope, don't retreat to only 'safe' courses. Ask yourself what it is you genuinely want to learn and then set regular and realistic goals for yourself. Remember that the pleasure that comes from discovering something new, whether through work done in the library or the laboratory, can be genuine and invigorating, regardless of your grades.

PROFESSIONS

Agriculture & Food Sciences – Agriculture Institute of Canada
www.aic.ca

Architecture – World Architecture
www.worldarchitecture.org

Business – Financial Times
www.ft.com

Education – Education in the News
www.educationnews.org

Engineering – Engineers without Borders
www.ewb-international.org

Forestry & Environmental Studies – World Forestry Center
www.worldforestrycenter.org

Journalism & Communication – Poynter Online
www.poynter.org

Law – World Legal Information Institute
www.worldlii.org

Library & Information Sciences – International Federation of Library
Associations and Institutions
www.ifla.org

Medicine, Dentistry & Health Sciences – National Library of Medicine
www.nlm.nih.gov

In the courses you decide to take, don't be satisfied with doing the bare minimum. Make it a point of pride to try to improve. If you put in extra effort, you'll find it eventually pays off. Even more importantly, be sure to attend lectures in subjects you genuinely want to learn. Don't be satisfied taking courses that cover material you could learn yourself, even if you think you need a few 'easy courses' to help boost your GPA. Graduate schools and professional schools know which courses are easy and which are not and, when it comes time to evaluate applications, they take these facts into account. Choose courses that will introduce you to ideas you would otherwise find inaccessible. You don't need to pay someone to teach you how to surf the web.

Finally, when things get tough, don't give up. Usually, the people who know the most in a class are the people who ask the most questions. There's no shame in admitting you don't know something. If you have questions, meet with your professor or teaching assistant. It is their job to help you. If you need more help, many student associations have lists of peer tutors who, for a fee, will be willing to review material with you. It can also be encouraging to remember that even the greatest authors, musicians, artists, scientists and scholars were once students exactly like you. Take pride in the fact that you are part of a scholarly tradition going back centuries. If you value learning, and if you're willing to put in the work, you'll do just fine.

Further reading

Beasley, David, *How to Use a Research Library*, New York: Oxford University Press, 1988

Baird, D.C., *Experimentation: An Introduction to Measurement Theory and Experiment Design*, Englewood Cliffs (NJ): Prentice-Hall, Inc., 1962

Brower, Kenneth, *The Starship and the Canoe*, London: Whizzard Press, and New York: Holt, Rinehart, Winston, 1978

Canfora, Luciano, *The Vanished Library: A Wonder of the Ancient World*, Berkeley, Los Angeles, London: University of California Press, 1992

Carey, Stephen S., *A Beginner's Guide to Scientific Method*, 3rd edn, Belmont (CA): Wadsworth Publishing Company, 2003

Casson, Lionel, *Libraries in the Ancient World*, New Haven (CT): Yale University Press, 2002

Cohen, Harlan, *The Naked Roommate: And 107 Other Issues You Might Run into in College*, 3rd edn, Naperville (IL): Sourcebooks, 2009

Cryer, Pat, *The Research Student's Guide to Success*, 3rd edn, New York: McGraw Hill, 2006

De Laubier, Guillaume, and Jacques Bosser, *The Most Beautiful Libraries in the World*, New York: Harry N. Abrams, Inc., 2003

Dyson, Freeman, J., *Disturbing the Universe*, New York: Harper & Row, 1979

Ellis, Dave, *Becoming A Master Student*, 12th edn, Boston: Houghton-Mifflin, 2009

Finney, D.J., *An Introduction to the Theory of Experimental Design*, Chicago: University of Chicago Press, 1976

Flores, Kathy Ochoa, *What Every ESL Student Should Know: A Guide to College and University Academic Success*, Ann Arbor: University of Michigan Press, 2008

Franklin, James, *What Science Knows, and How It Knows It*, New York, London: Encounter Books, 2009

Hicks, Charles R., and Kenneth V. Turner, *Fundamental Concepts in the Design of Experiments*, 5th edn, New York: Oxford University Press, 1999

Kornhauser, Arthur W., *How to Study: Suggestions for High-School and College Students,* 3rd edn, Chicago: University of Chicago Press, 1993

Lepore, Ernie, and Sarah-Jane Leslie, *What Every College Student Should Know: How to Find the Best Teachers and Learn the Most from Them*, New Brunswick (NJ): Rutgers University Press, 2002

May, Matthew E., *In Pursuit of Elegance: Why the Best Ideas have Something Missing*, New York: Broadway Books, 2009

Nist-Olejnik, Sherrie L., and Jodi Patrick Holschuh, *College Rules! How to Study, Survive and Succeed in College*, 2nd edn, Berkeley (CA): Ten Speed Press, 2007

Roberts, Andrew, *The Thinking Student's Guide to College: 75 Tips for Getting a Better Education*, Chicago: University of Chicago Press, 2010

Rumsey, Sally, *How to Find Information: A Guide for Researchers*, 2nd edn, New York: McGraw Hill, 2008

Trumble, Kelly, *The Library of Alexandria*, New York: Clarion Books, 2003

Worek, Micahel, *Nobel: A Century of Prize Winners*, Toronto, Buffalo, New York: Firefly Books Ltd, 2008

Chapter 10

Be Honest

৩৯ ৵৶

Would you want to fly in an airplane designed by an engineer who cheated on his exams? Would you hire an accountant to prepare your tax return if you knew she lied to get her job? Would you trust doctors who falsified their grades so they could graduate from medical school? For most of us, to ask these questions is to answer them. We also know that since *our* reputations are no less important than those of other people, it follows that none of us should want to misrepresent ourselves or our work.[1]

Academic misconduct strikes at the heart of the academic enterprise. If someone – a faculty member, a research assistant, a student – can't be trusted to present his work honestly, why should we hire him? Why should we trust what he has to say?

All academic work, from the most objective calculation to the most subjective judgment, requires the honest reporting of results. It requires that we honestly say what we think we have reason to believe, not what we think someone else wants to hear. Here is how one scientist puts it when discussing the concept of measurement: "Quite plainly – are people going to believe your measurement or not? It is clear that only your professional reputation can instill confidence in other people."[2]

Helpful Advice

- Don't buy anything from someone who's out of breath!
- Don't spit into the wind!
- Don't believe what you read on a bathroom wall!
- Don't spend money before you have it!
- Don't join more clubs than classes!
- Don't spend your book money on beer!
- Don't sleep with anyone who can't remember your name!
- Don't post anything on the internet you don't want your grand-children to see!

And don't believe people who tell you cheaters never get caught

---

If this is true in science, it is also true in other disciplines. Whether you work in economics or political science, in history or medicine, there are few things as important as your reputation for honesty.

Academic misconduct. Academic misconduct comes in a variety of forms. One of the most common is *plagiarism* – taking credit for work that is not one's own. (The word comes from the Latin word *plagiare*, meaning 'to steal' or 'to kidnap.') Of course, different types of publications have different conventions for citing sources. Readers of newspapers don't expect to find footnotes at the bottom of each article. Authors of book reviews don't usually give the kind of detailed citations commonly found in more scholarly work. Even so, if you mention facts or ideas in your writing that you think your readers might be curious about, it is always a good idea to reference your source. If you quote the words of another author, it is normally important to include a credit of some kind. Cheating on an exam and falsifying data in a lab report are other familiar types of proscribed behaviour. If you're uncertain about what's permissible and what's not, it is easy to find out. Don't be shy. Just ask your professor or teaching assistant.

Different universities approach the issue of academic misconduct in different ways. Some use sophisticated computer software to ensure that written work hasn't been plagiarized and that essays haven't been purchased from online essay banks. (Some software, such as the WriteCheck feature at www.turnitin.com/products/writecheck, even allows students to check their own work to ensure that they haven't accidentally included uncited material.) Other universities search classrooms and restrooms to ensure that notes can't be consulted during an exam. Some use multiple examination sheets so students sitting side by side during an exam aren't asked the same questions. Almost all ensure that invigilators are present to proctor examinations.

Some institutions take a different approach. In return for pledging to uphold an honour code, students at some colleges and universities need not have their exams proctored. Students who break the honour code are often asked to leave the university. At Stanford University, for example, a common penalty for students who break the honour code not only includes temporary suspension from the university, but also 40 hours of community service.[3] Some research shows that such codes have been effective in reducing cheating.[4]

Instituting an honour code has additional advantages. Before signing the code, students are reminded about the benefits of doing their own work and about the harms that come from cheating. The story of one unfortunate student serves as an illustration. Convinced that academic work wasn't relevant to his goal of becoming a police officer, and knowing he had difficulty with writing, he purchased his essays from an online essay bank. He was never caught. After graduation, he succeeded in becoming a police officer. Unfortunately, what he failed to realize is that police work involves more than just driving a police car and issuing tickets. An essential part of the job involves writing reports – reports that need to stand up in court if convictions are to be obtained. In this case, because his

---

STANFORD UNIVERSITY HONOR CODE

The Stanford University Honor Code was written by students in 1921 and is still used today. It outlines student, faculty and university expectations for "establishing and maintaining the highest standards in academic work."

Honor Code

(a) The Honor Code is an undertaking of the students, individually and collectively:

1. That they will not give or receive aid in examinations; that they will not give or receive unpermitted aid in class work, in the preparation of reports, or in any other work that is to be used by the instructor as the basis of grading;
2. That they will do their share and take an active part in seeing to it that others as well as themselves uphold the spirit and letter of the Honor Code.

(b) The faculty on its part manifests its confidence in the honor of its students by refraining from proctoring examinations and from taking unusual and unreasonable precautions to prevent the forms of dishonesty mentioned above. The faculty will also avoid, as far as practicable, academic procedures that create temptations to violate the Honor Code.

(c) While the faculty alone has the right and obligation to set academic requirements, the students and faculty will work together to establish optimal conditions for honorable academic work

(From The Stanford University Office of Judicial Affairs,
at honorcode.stanford.edu.)

---

writing skills were so poor, he was fired after less than a year on the job. Sadly, had he taken advantage of the opportunity given to him as an undergraduate and asked for help to improve his writing, he likely would still be working in a career he obviously loved.[5]

It is also important to know that people who have outsourced their homework to online writing services have sometimes received more than they bargained for. Once they have your name and credit card information, some online writing services continue to charge a monthly "subscription fee", without your permission and whether you want it or not. And if their customers stop payment, the service then threatens to inform their university of the service they have been receiving. [6] It is a despicable, corrupt practice that can only lead to unhappiness.

Cheating can also have other unwelcome consequences. An investigation into plagiarism in a physics department in Virginia led to the dismissal of 45 students and to the revocation of three graduate degrees.[7] In British Columbia, 44 students were suspended for purchasing solutions to an economics assignment. Since the solutions had been advertised as being 'custom designed' for each student, students believed their chances of being caught were minimal. They were wrong.[8] At a school of dentistry in Indiana, 46 students were disciplined and nine students were expelled for hacking into a password-protected computer file in an attempt to review test materials prior to an exam.[9] In Britain, 234 medical school applicants included in their application exactly the same anecdote about how they first became interested in medicine. All had copied the anecdote from the same site on the internet. None were successful.[10]

The penalty for academic misconduct varies from institution to institution. Students may be placed on probation. They may be required to re-submit work, to complete new, additional work, or to meet regularly with a faculty advisor to discuss their academic progress. Disciplinary hearings may be held and findings may be recorded in a student's file or on a student's permanent transcript. Repeat offenders may be asked to leave their university. In Britain, 143 students were expelled from 93 universities in just one year, all for academic misconduct.[11] It should go without saying that, after working so hard to get into university, students are well advised not to throw away their careers by making such an elementary error of judgment. Employers (and others) need to have confidence in the quality of your university's degrees. Every time

---

PROHIBITED ACTIONS

The following actions are not allowed:

- *Consulting* books, notes, calculators or other sources of information without permission during an examination.
- *Consulting* another student's answer sheet during an examination.
- *Showing* your answer sheet to another student during an examination.
- *Talking* to another student during an examination.
- *Failure to follow* the instructions of a proctor or invigilator during an examination.
- *Submitting* academic work done by someone else as if it were your own.
- *Submitting* the same academic work for credit in multiple courses.
- *Collaborating* on assignments in which collaboration is not permitted.
- *Accepting credit* for a group assignment in which you have not done your fair share.
- *Revising and resubmitting* academic work for re-grading without permission.
- *Fabricating or falsifying* data gathered in the laboratory or in the field.
- *Plagiarizing* someone else's words, ideas or data in an essay or assignment.
- *Sabotaging* the work of others.
- *Falsifying* grades, transcripts or letters of reference.

---

someone cheats at your university, this lowers the reputation of your degree.

It is worth noting that students who are caught cheating on an exam often receive a grade of zero. This is because cheating on even a single question throws into doubt the integrity of the entire exam. Separate from the academic evaluation of a piece of work is the issue of penalties. Grades are used to report a student's degree of academic knowledge. In contrast, penalties are imposed as consequence for academic misconduct. However, just as grades can never be used as rewards – a student who does valuable volunteer work as a campus tour guide or as a special-needs tutor can't be rewarded by being given a higher grade in mathematics – reductions in grades can never be used as penalties. Even so, the penalties that are imposed – academic probations, course and program suspensions, university expulsions – can often be of greater consequence than merely failing an exam.

Group work and internet access present special challenges. There is nothing wrong – and a lot right! – with studying together. For most of us, this is one of the best ways to learn. Even so, there is a difference between studying together and completing assignments together. Assignments for credit should not be completed together unless you have permission to do so from your instructor. This doesn't mean you can't ask your friends, librarians and teaching assistants about what to read, where to find information, or how, in general, to solve the kinds of problems you have been assigned. It is always helpful – and allowed! – to ask a friend to look over a draft of your essay and to give you some advice before you hand it in. But it is important to remember that there is a difference between asking a friend to help you understand the basic concepts of a course, and copying and submitting someone else's answer as if it were your own.

One way to keep this distinction clear is as follows: getting advice from friends and teaching assistants helps us learn in a way cheating does not. Asking a friend for advice, like looking something up in a textbook, helps us internalize new information. It teaches us something we previously didn't know. It teaches us some fact that is important or how to approach a new type of problem successfully. Asking for this kind of help is to be encouraged. In contrast, if a student simply copies someone else's solution and submits it as if it were his own, it is unlikely he will have learned anything at all.

Using information found on the internet can also be problematic. In one study conducted by Donald McCabe at Rutgers University, it was found that many students mistakenly believe that information found on the internet is automatically in the public domain and so needn't be referenced.[12] This is a mistake. Most information found on the internet (including class notes posted by your instructor) remains protected by copyright. This means it can't be re-published or re-posted without permission from the copyright holder. Regardless of whether information is in the public domain or not, quotations still need to be referenced. In other words, even material no longer protected by copyright (and so capable of being reprinted in its entirety without permission) still needs to be properly attributed to its original author. As a general rule, if you include someone else's words or data in what you write, you're normally required to explain, in a formal citation or just in your own words, where you found them.

It doesn't follow from any of this that students should be fearful of discussing their work with others. Almost all academic work builds on the work of others, so it always helps to discuss your work with others. Students who avoid writing about other people's ideas simply because they're afraid they may be accused of plagiarism place themselves at a tremendous disadvantage. It is much better to report the views of others as you understand them and, in a sentence or a footnote, explain where it was that you found the information you did. If you do this honestly, you will never have anything to fear.

In any case, if you're unsure about what is and is not permissible, just make an appointment to see your instructor or teaching assistant and ask.

Faculty misconduct. Just like students, professors need to maintain high standards of scholarly integrity. Almost all make it a point of professional pride to meet or exceed these standards. Most have had years of academic and professional training. Most colleges and universities also have mechanisms of regular peer review to ensure that, in those rare cases where misconduct does occur, it is discovered and dealt with quickly.[13]

All university instructors have an obligation to teach with integrity, to grade their students' work solely on the basis of its academic merit, and to honour the confidentiality of student records and letters of reference. If you ever have a question about why some material has or has not been included in a course, or about why you have received the grade you did, make an appointment to meet with your instructor and ask. If your instructor is consistently late for lectures or consistently slow returning assignments and you don't feel you can raise the issue directly with him or her, take a moment to contact your faculty advisor or department head.

Each year, professors are required to report their academic work to their university. When doing so, they list the teaching, research and administrative service they have completed and, just like students, professors need to be honest in making these reports.[14] Between 1998 and 2005, several medical professors failed to disclose that they were not the sole authors of some 26 scientific papers published in 18 different journals. Upon investigation, it turned out that large sections of the papers had been ghost written by employees of a large, multi-national pharmaceutical company. Many of the papers promoted products marketed by the company. The discovery prompted calls for greater transparency about the influence corporations sometimes have on university research.[15]

In all such cases, professors who falsify their research data,[16] who are found guilty of plagiarism,[17] or who fail to meet basic standards teaching and scholarship[18] can be demoted, barred from teaching or removed from their positions.[19]

WHEN TO INCLUDE A REFERENCE

A great deal of learning comes from being exposed to the words and ideas of others. In academic writing, you can show that you have read or consulted other people's words and ideas by including a reference:

- *Quotations* – If you include someone else's *words* in your academic work, place them inside quotation marks or offset them in the text and then reference your source.

- *Citations* – If you include someone else's *ideas* or *data* in your academic work, or if you mention *facts* in your academic work that you think your reader might like to check but not know how to follow up, reference your source.

- *Bibliographies* – If you read someone else's work and it provides helpful *background information* to your academic work that you think others might like to read, reference your sources in a Bibliography, References, or Further Reading section.

If you are unsure about what to reference, or about how much group work is permitted when working on assignments, be sure to ask your professor or teaching assistant.

Administrative misconduct. University administrators may seem far removed from the day-to-day lives of students, but they too have obligations and responsibilities that can affect a student's time at university. Although rare, administrative misconduct can have far-reaching consequences. In 1995, the U.S. National Institutes of Health found that a university in Virginia violated regulations governing the use of human subjects in experiments. As a result, the university had to suspend 35 medical and psychological studies, disrupting the work of students and faculty alike.[20] In Atlanta, the president of Morris Brown College pleaded guilty to charges relating to a financial-aid scheme that fraudulently obtained millions of dollars in federal student loans and grants, leaving many students in financial need.[21] In Philadelphia, Temple University was accused of misrepresenting information about student scores on the Graduate Management Admission Test to boost the university's MBA ranking in *U.S. News & World Report*. The university did not admit guilt but agreed to pay $700,000 to settle the complaint.[22]

University administrators also overstep their authority whenever they try to tell professors what may and may not be taught in the classroom, something that has become more common in recent years than one might expect.[23] One worry is that what some people see as free and vigorous debate, others can find offensive or intimidating. As a result, some university administrators have taken it upon themselves to try to limit comments that might be interpreted as being disrespectful or unpopular. For example, a comment by a sociology professor at the University of Ottawa about the importance of honesty in relationships was thought by some in his class to imply intolerance of certain sexual preferences. As a result, the professor was formally reprimanded by his university, despite the fact that no investigation was held, no students other than the complainants were interviewed, and no consideration was given to the academic benefits that come from having professors speak frankly and honestly about topics they are required to teach and research. Equally troubling was the fact that the university acknowledged there was no evidence of any form of harassment or discrimination. As cultural studies professor John Fekete writes,

> This leaves only speech, and the *perception* of speech. Anyone who has seen student notes on lectures or student performance in assignments and exams knows well that these are not a reliable index much of the time of what material has actually been presented. The dean, however, makes much of the fact that *some* students "perceived some of [the professor's] classroom comments as insensitive, offensive, and/or indicative of intolerance on [his] part" – especially the expression of personal opinions or asides … Ought [the professor] to have known that an aside would produce a small minority perception of offence? Perhaps. Should he have refrained from making the aside? His choice. Should his

asides be subject to dispute? Of course. Should they be forbidden? Definitely not. Such a prohibition offends academic principles, freedom of speech, and also the entitlement of other students who do find [his comments] educationally stimulating to have access to his uncensored teaching.[24]

The main problem with such censorship and the subjective criteria on which it is based is that this makes discussion of controversial issues much more difficult. Censorship of this kind overlooks the fact that conflicting opinion is an inevitable and necessary part of intellectual debate, for students and faculty alike. As the historian Michiel Horn puts it, "Universities are not repositories of approved ideas and attitudes; they do not exist primarily to make people feel intellectually or emotionally 'at home.' And although civility is important, academics owe a loyalty to something more important yet; they must commit themselves to the search for knowledge and truth *as they see it.*"[25]

Just as this is true for faculty, it is equally true for students. Professors can and should be reprimanded for refusing to allow students the opportunity to express their opinions, or for not allowing them to investigate theories that may be unpopular or controversial. But just as students should be free to express their opinions, so should professors. No professor should be reprimanded for honestly expressing an opinion relevant to his or her research or teaching.[26] To do so destroys the freedom necessary for both students and professors to carry out their work. As Horn tells us, advocates of academic freedom are therefore correct to remind us that

> disinterested inquiry and comment are essential if a society is not to become intellectually and ideologically hidebound. Most working people cannot afford to assume a stance of disinterest. Whether they are self-employed or employees, the need to earn a living usually takes precedence over the inclination to indulge their curiosity, to challenge authority or received wisdom, or to state the truth about some subject as

they see it. Without academic freedom, only the independently wealthy or those unconcerned about their financial or professional prospects would be able to pursue research of unpredictable duration and uncertain payoff or to make public comments that might prove unwelcome.[27]

Giving universities such a high degree of independence is not without risk. Some students and faculty will want to use their lack of external accountability, not to advance disinterested research, but to advocate partisan points of view. This is something that needs to be guarded against. As the Stanford economist Thomas Sowell reminds us, "Not only have intellectuals been insulated from material consequences, they have often enjoyed immunity from even a loss of reputation after having been demonstrably wrong. ... In short, constraints which apply to people in most other fields do not apply even approximately equally to intellectuals. It would be surprising if this did not lead to different behavior."[28]

It is for this reason that universities have a responsibility to protect themselves from undue politicization. Students need to be protected from professors whose grading practices may be politically or religiously biased. Professors need to be protected from tenure and promotion committees that focus on factors other than the academic quality of their work. Departments and faculties have to be protected from the overzealous influence of outside parties.

University administrators need to guard against giving preferential treatment to some political groups at the expense of others.[29] They also need to guard against allowing themselves to become co-opted for non-academic purposes. Despite their best intentions, people who argue that it is the university's job to stimulate the economy, or to produce good citizens, or to strengthen national identity are all mistaken. These are often important and desirable by-products of what universities do, but unlike the production, promotion, preservation and application of knowledge, it is not the university's mission to advance other social goods, regardless of how desirable they may be.

Honesty and Friendship. Being honest in one's academic work has clear academic benefits. If you are honest with yourself about what you do and do not understand, this will give you the courage to ask your professor or teaching assistant to review difficult material with you. But being honest has other important benefits as well.

Marcus Tullius Cicero is remembered today as one of the greatest orators of the ancient Western world. During his lifetime, his political impact was at times significant, at times marginal; but over the centuries his writings have never ceased being influential. His innumerable letters, many of which were written to his friend Atticus, have had an especially lasting impact, introducing centuries of scholars and school children alike to the history and values of ancient Rome.

Among Cicero's most interesting writings is his book, *De Amicitia* (*On Friendship*). In it, Cicero argues that friendship is based more than anything else on honesty. His reasoning is straightforward: true friendship comes only with trust, and trust comes only with honesty. Put another way, Cicero (like many others in the ancient Greek and Roman world) believed that the main cause of evil was ignorance. And since friendship can never be based on evil, friendship requires the honest sharing of ideas, beliefs and values.

According to this view, true and lasting friendships are formed, not as a result of need, but as a result of honest character,[30] and when a friendship ends, it will be because of the weakness of character of one or both of the former friends.[31] Friends will do almost anything for one another, but friendship never requires a friend to do an immoral act, since acting immorally destroys a person's character and, with it, the friendship.[32] It is also true that friendships are necessary for everyone. They are an essential part of what it means to be human and to live a good life.[33] As Cicero tells us, the one thing in human experience about whose advantage all men with one voice agree, is friendship; even virtue itself is regarded with contempt by many and is said to be mere pretence and display; many disdain riches, because they are content with little and take delight in meager fare and plain dress; political honours, too, for which some have a burning desire – how many so despise them that they believe nothing more empty and nothing more inane! Likewise other things, which seem to some to be worthy of admiration, are by many thought to be of no value at all. But concerning friendship, all, to a man, think the same thing: those who have devoted themselves to public life; those who find their joy in science and philosophy; those who manage their own business free from public cares; and, finally, those who are wholly given up to sensual pleasures – all believe that without friendship life is no life at all.[34]

It is surely one of the great benefits of university life that it is while at university that so many true and lasting friendships are formed.

Further reading

Bercuson, David, Robert Bothwell and J.L. Granatstein, *Petrified Campus: The Crisis in Canada's Universities*, Toronto: Random House of Canada, 1997

Bloom, Allan, *The Closing of the American Mind: How Higher Education Has Failed Democracy and Impoverished the Souls of Today's Students*, New York: Simon & Schuster, 1987

Decoo, Wilfried, *Crisis on Campus: Confronting Academic Misconduct*, Cambridge (MA): MIT Press, 2002

Horowitz, David, *Indoctrination U: The Left's War against Academic Freedom*, New York: Encounter Books, 2007

Kimball, Roger, *Tenured Radicals: How Politics has Corrupted Our Higher Education*, New York: Harper Collins Publishers, 1990

Kors, Alan Charles, and Harvey A. Silverglate, *The Shadow University: The Betrayal of Liberty on America's Campuses*, New York: Harper Collins, 1998

Lipson, Charles, *Doing Honest Work in College: How to Prepare Citations, Avoid Plagiarism and Achieve Real Academic Success*, 2nd edn, Chicago: University of Chicago Press, 2008

Loney, Martin, *The Pursuit of Division: Race, Gender, and Preferential Hiring in Canada*, Montreal, Kingston, London, Buffalo: McGill-Queen's University Press, 1998

Thomas, Andrew Peyton, *The People v. Harvard Law: How America's Oldest Law School Turned Its Back on Free Speech*, New York: Encounter Books, 2005

Chapter 11

Have Fun

Here's a nice little proof to give your physics professor if you don't know the answer to an exam question.

From physics, we know that

$$Work = Power \times Time.$$

From the famous scientist and statesman Francis Bacon, we also know that *scientia et remendou humana in idem remendous* or, as it is usually translated, "Knowledge is power,"[1] and from the diplomat and inventor Benjamin Franklin we know that "Time is money."[2]

Substituting Knowledge for Power and Money for Time we get

$$Work = Knowledge \times Money.$$

Solving for Money, we then get

$$Money = Work / Knowledge.$$

In other words, regardless of how little we work, Money will approach infinity as Knowledge approaches zero. In short, the less you know, the more you'll make!

While not wanting to endorse this 'proof' outright, it is true that there is more to university life than just studying and attending lectures. For most of us, there are few times in life when we'll have greater opportunity to make new friends and have fun. For most of us, too, university is hardly a time of moderation. It is a time when we push ourselves to the limit – in sports, in our studies, in our attempts to achieve as much as we can in the time we have. So, it is worth pausing for a moment to think about one of the oldest pieces of advice ever offered: *Nothing in excess*.[3] This ancient advice is a warning, not just about too much drinking or too much partying, but also about too much studying. As the Greek philosopher Aristotle, put it, in all things it helps to aim for "the Golden Mean," the right balance (or mean) between various extremes.[4] So after a long week of hard work, how will you choose to fill your spare time?

Pranks. Some pranks are just plain, good fun. For example, there was the time engineering students put a giant propeller beanie on the Great Dome of the Engineering Library at the Massachusetts Institute of Technology. (Later they did the same with a giant R2-D2 head from Star Wars, and then later with a giant breast.[5]) There was also the time students placed a 60-pound pumpkin on the tip of the spire of Cornell University's 173-foot-tall McGraw tower,[6] and the time students in the U.K. entered a contest sponsored by the Donside Paper Company that required contestants to "tell a lie convincingly." Their entry took the form of a letter printed on Donside letterhead and mailed to their potential competitors telling them that, regrettably, the contest had been cancelled. (They won.[7]) There was the time students from the California Institute of Technology, frustrated at their lack of representation in the annual New Year's Day Rose Bowl game, arranged to have hundreds of unsuspecting spectators hold up flip-cards spelling out the name CALTECH live on national television.[8] In Vancouver, engineering students at the University of British Columbia placed a Volkswagen Beetle on top of the University's 121-foot-tall Ladner Clock Tower. Not to be outdone, their classmates a few years later hung a second Volkswagen from the city's famous Lion's Gate Bridge. A few years after that, in February of 2001, residents of San Francisco woke up to see yet another UBC Volkswagen dangling from beneath the Golden Gate Bridge.[9]

Of course, some pranks are not worth emulating. Percy Shelley is remembered today as one of England's most influential 19th-century Romantic poets, but his time at Oxford was not especially successful, either academically or socially. After entering the university in October, 1810 Shelley spent his days doing almost anything other than attending lectures. He wrote to strangers using a pseudonym in the hopes of engaging them in religious discussion. He carried around a pair of duelling pistols and threatened to kill a dog that had ripped his favourite coat. His experiments with electricity and various types of acid drove his friends and tutors to distraction. Although he tells us that he avoided the typical undergraduate activities of his day – wine, horses, the prize ring and the cock pit – to concentrate on his writing, the explicit, sexual content of some of his poems wasn't well received. He toyed with the idea of suicide. After five months he was expelled on the ground that his writings, which included a pamphlet entitled *The Necessity of Atheism*, were incompatible with the university's admission oath, although one can't help but wonder whether, from the point of view of his long-suffering College tutors, any excuse for expulsion might have been a good one. Offered the chance to remain at University College on condition that he recant his atheism, he refused. Four months later he married a sixteen-year-old schoolgirl named Harriet Westbrook whom he had impregnated. Not long afterwards, he abandoned Harriet to run off with the daughter of William Godwin and Mary Wollstonecraft, the woman we remember today as Mary Shelley, the author of the novel *Frankenstein*.[10]

Other undergraduate activities have had more lasting consequences. For example, have you ever wondered why the fine print on contest applications often limits the number of entries to one per customer? The reason is that in 1975, students at Caltech wrote a computer program designed to run on their college's IBM System 370 mainframe computer. Over a three-day period, it generated 1.2 million completed contest application forms. McDonald's had encouraged customers to enter their contest "as often as you wish." Prizes included a new car, a year's worth of groceries and plenty of McDonald's gift certificates. Although the cost of using the computer was about $500, the students won the car – which they donated to the United Way – as well as many of the other prizes. Their donation helped mollify the enormous media criticism they received accusing them of having won unfairly. Ever since then, McDonald's and other sweepstakes sponsors have been careful to limit contest applications to one per customer.[11]

Alcohol. The ancient Greeks wrote a lot about alcohol. Homer writes about how Odysseus uses strong drink to outfox the dangerous Cyclops and about his long journey home over the "wine-dark sea" following the Trojan War.[12] Euripides tells the story of how the god Dionysus punishes King Pentheus for refusing to worship the god by pouring the required libations.[13] Aristophanes tells us how, with help from Lampito the Spartan, Lysistrata convinces the women of Greece to withhold sex from their husbands to force an end to the Peloponnesian War, and how the women swear their solemn oath over a bowl of wine.[14] Plato recounts the most famous drinking party in history, telling us how Socrates and Alcibiades argued over the nature of love while drinking cups of wine.[15]

Alexander Nazaryan, who teaches English at the Brooklyn Latin School in New York, sums up how many people feel when they read such stories and how they relate to the modern student's experience:

> I admire how open the Greeks were about the role of alcohol in their society (unsurprising, perhaps, for a people whose highest ideal was "the examined life"). In modern times, it

seems we readily migrate to the extremes, either abusing alcohol or treating it as if it doesn't exist, without acknowledging a healthy middle ground. As a constant conduit between the realms of adulthood and innocence, I find this particularly troublesome because too many young adults will discover drinking in a rowdy fraternity or a bar that doesn't care much about whom it serves. Surely, there must be something for them between "Animal House" and the Anti-Saloon League.[16]

Nazaryan, like Aristotle, is likely correct: when using alcohol there needs to be a middle ground, a Golden Mean. Too much drink has led to uncountable tragedies: the destruction of a promising career because of alcoholism, the death of a loved one because of drunk driving, the end of a promising friendship because of boorish behaviour brought on by a night of drinking.

The same freedom students have in other areas applies here as well. Just as students are free to choose their own programs of study, they are also free to decide when and how much to drink, whom to socialize with and what risks they want to take. Perhaps there was once a time when universities acted *in loco parentis* ('in place of parents') by regulating and overseeing students' social activities, but today it is almost universally agreed that, unlike high-school students, university students have reached a stage in life where they have the maturity to make their own decisions, not only about alcohol but about other social activities as well. In other words, the same independence and maturity that serves us so well when it comes to making decisions about which courses to take, what to research in the lab and what to read in the library, also serves us well when it comes time to make decisions about how much to drink and where and when to socialize. Exercising your own good judgment, rather than simply going along with the crowd, usually makes good sense.

Interestingly, there is a great deal of academic work still to be done about alcoholism and about addiction more generally. Is there a scientific difference between desire and addiction? Is there a measurable distinction between ordinary weakness of will and a medical disease? Should the law distinguish between a driver's impaired ability when the impairment is brought about by alcohol addiction and when it is brought about by other types of disease? Can historians studying the failure of Prohibition in the early 20th century help politicians as they struggle to make sense of the failure of the War on Drugs in the 21st century? For anyone wanting to work in these areas, there is still a large amount of (controlled!) research that needs to be done.

EIGHT WAYS TO AVOID ACCIDENTS WHILE DRIVING

1. *Always* leave three seconds between you and the vehicle in front of you.

2. *Always* signal *and* shoulder check before changing lanes or turning.

3. *Never* use a cell phone (or ear buds, or a shaver, or a hair dryer) while driving.

4. *Never* run a yellow light.

5. *Never* speed.

6. *Never* drive when drowsy.

7. *Never* drive high.

8. *And never* drink and drive.

Sex. It is interesting to note that a great deal of the history of the world is largely incomprehensible without taking into account the availability or unavailability of birth control.[17] Prohibitions on pre-marital relations, the educational, professional and social division of the sexes, the institution of marriage and many other social practices all arose in part to help young men and women, and their families, guard against the social, financial and psychological challenges of unplanned pregnancies. To think that citizens of the ancient or medieval worlds, or even of the modern world up until the early or mid-20th century, somehow failed their social obligations because they refused to permit men and women identical social roles is one of the great misconceptions of the modern age. Put another way, it is not at all surprising that the manufacturing of effective condoms and the discovery of a safe and effective birth control pill have resulted in some of the most widespread social changes in human history.

Here, too, the role of knowledge is central. As in so many other areas, there has always been a division between those who believe that increased knowledge about sex leads to an increased risk of unplanned pregnancies and those, in contrast, who believe that increased knowledge is the best safeguard we have against the spread of disease and other social harms. Here, too, there have been tremendous changes, at least in the West, in less than a century. As the commentator Alan Wood reminds us, these changes in outlook have been so dramatic that "few people now even realize the nature of the old ideas."[18] As Wood reminds us, few people today have any lingering knowledge or recollection of a past in which

> sexual ignorance was deliberately fostered, so that a boy might think the changes of puberty were signs of some dreadful disease, a girl might marry without knowing anything of what lay ahead of her on her bridal night; where women were taught to look on sex, not as a source of joy, but of painful matrimonial duty; where prudery went to the extent of covering the legs of pianos in draperies; where artificial mystery evoked morbid curiosity, and where humbug went hand in hand with unhappiness.[19]

Today there is not a university anywhere in the Western world where reliable information about sexually transmitted diseases, pregnancy and other sexual matters is not freely and openly available to anyone who inquires.

It is also easy to understand why, in those parts of the world in which ignorance is still deliberately fostered, efforts are made to suppress statistics about sexually transmitted disease, about unwanted pregnancies and about abortions. It is impossible to make such information public without also educating people about the nature of sexual relations and without initiating free and open debate on a wide range of social experiences and phenomena.

Just as in other areas, it is important to remember that some sources of information about sex are more reliable than others. It is shocking to my troglodyte heart, I know, but it turns out that not everything posted on the internet is true. Sex has long been recognized as a natural need for most people. In some ways, the appetite for intimacy is no different than the appetite for food and drink. But sexual relations are also among the most complex of human relations, intimately tied to many of our deepest emotions. To think that sex can be trivialized by disassociating it from serious emotions and feelings of affection is inevitably a mistake. Of course, someone might say "It is different for me," and it might be; but then again it might also turn out that a complete stranger has left you a million dollars in his will. This, too, might be true, but I wouldn't plan on it.

Video games. The main worry many people have about video games is not that they are addictive (they can be), not that they often include violent and explicit imagery (some do), and not that they are sold unrated (many still are but this is changing). Rather, the main worry many people have is that video games often serve as a form of anti-social retreat, a way of plugging into a private world of make-believe, having few if any connections to the day-to-day world of real people and real events.

Video games can give users certain advantages. Players often have improved visual-motor skills, increased ability to concentrate (at least on some things), and improved peripheral vision.[20] But unlike traditional games (card games, board games, table games, sporting matches) that require social interaction between players, or between players and fans, video games give users unrivaled opportunity to isolate themselves from family, friends and strangers. Even those games that involve other players (online poker, for example) do so through such strong electronic filters that the human element becomes significantly diminished. Like the widespread availability of television in the 1950s and 1960s, the widespread availability of video games has had unpredictable social consequences.

Here, too, there are unrivaled opportunities for research. Does video gaming decrease people's social skills? Does it decrease people's understanding of real-world cause and effect? Does it increase people's ability to operate certain types of computer software: flight simulators, medical diagnostic software, programs designed to edit films and television programs? Does being able to operate modern electronic military equipment (bomb diffusion robots, Air Force drones, spyware of various kinds) as if it were simply a video game increase or decrease people's ability to function ethically and humanely?[21] These are just a few of the questions we don't yet know how to answer and that were not even being asked a generation ago.

Was Aristotle right that "man is by nature a political animal,"[22] that he is essentially "a social being,"[23] and that anyone who has no need of society, "must be either a beast or a god"[24]? If so, it is perhaps not surprising that in his *Nicomachean Ethics*, he devotes more room to discussing friendship than any other topic. If he is right that the social instinct is something implanted into us all, then it is a small wonder that we take great pleasure from being with others. University is one of the places in which we are given the opportunity to make new friends. It is most often through these relationships that we learn to laugh at the world around us, as well as at ourselves.

Further reading

Austin, John, *Prank University: The Ultimate Guide to College's Greatest Tradition*, New York: Three Rivers Press, 2006

Cicero, Marcus Tullius, *Selected Political Speeches*, London: Penguin Classics, 1969

Cicero, Marcus Tullius, *Selected Works*, London: Penguin Classics, 1960

Enright, D.J., *The Oxford Book of Friendship*, New York: Oxford University Press, 1992

Jillette, Penn, *Penn & Teller's How to Play in Traffic*, New York: Boulevard Books, 1997

Luftig, Victor, *Seeing Together: Friendship between the Sexes in English Writing from Mill To Woolf*, Stanford: Stanford University Press, 1993

Northcutt, Wendy, *The Darwin Awards: Evolution in Action*, New York: Dutton Adult, 2000

Price, A.W., *Love and Friendship in Plato and Aristotle*, Oxford: Clarendon Press, 1990

Rawson, Beryl, *The Politics of Friendship: Pompey and Cicero*, Sydney: Sydney University Press, 1978

Reuben, David, *Everything You always Wanted to Know about Sex but Were Afraid to Ask*, 2nd edn, New York: Harper Collins, 1999

Steinberg, Neil, *If at All Possible, Involve a Cow: The Book of College Pranks*, New York: St Martin's Press, 1992

Chapter 12

Remember the Past, Look to the Future

Not everyone looks forward to graduation day. Some of us who graduated long ago still have nightmares about the exam we failed or the essay we never completed. Some of us who haven't returned to our universities in decades still worry about bumping into an old boyfriend or girlfriend – the one we'd rather not have to introduce to a less-than-understanding spouse, let alone to children who may be curious about events that took place long before they were born. For many people, attending graduation also means having to buy a new suit or a new dress and, once there, the ceremony will be just so, well, *ceremonial*.

So, when graduation day approaches, it is often the student's job to remind family and friends just how much it will mean to have them attend the ceremony. It also doesn't hurt to brush up on some of the admittedly arcane traditions associated with this ancient rite of passage.

Good manners matter, but mostly you're meant to have fun.
Graduation ceremonies (also called Congregation, Commencement and Convocation ceremonies) can sometimes seem rather stuffy, but they're not meant to be. Graduation marks the completion of a student's formal education, but it is also meant to be a time of celebration, a time when new graduates can say thank you to friends and family members who have encour-

aged and supported them over the years. Graduation is meant to be a time when students can share a few jokes, and when parents can relax and take some justifiable pride in their children's accomplishments.

Parents no doubt will remember a day not that long ago when the government told them that their child was now qualified to operate a motor vehicle, even though they knew in their hearts that the apple of their eye wasn't qualified to operate a coat hanger. That day is now long past. The young men and women who graduate from university today are intelligent, hardworking and passionate about their values. In the past few years, they've matured and achieved a lot. It is natural to want to take a moment to mark their success.

Knowing a little Latin never hurts. Since their traditions go back centuries, even the youngest of universities are ancient institutions. As a result, it never hurts to know a little Latin. The phrase *alma mater* is Latin for "nourishing mother." Hence a graduate is referred to as an *alumnus* – literally a child or nursling of his *alma mater*. The plural of *alumnus* is *alumni*. Among the politically correct, the distinction is sometimes made between the male *alumnus*/*alumni* and the female *alumna*/*alumnae*. For most of us this is just pedantry. Most graduates, men and women alike, are usually pleased to be referred to simply as *alumni*.

It is also worth noting that during the ceremony, degrees are usually awarded in order of seniority. Before the bachelor's degrees will come the master's degrees, before the master's degrees will come the doctoral degrees, and before the doctoral degrees will come the degrees granted *honoris causa* ("for the sake of honour"), or in recognition of achievements that have been important for society generally. Many people rightly enjoy the recognition that comes with receiving an honorary degree; but like any good host, the university will insist that it is the recipients of honorary degrees who honour the university with their presence, not vice-versa.

Upon receipt of their degrees, graduates become members of the *universitas magistrorum et scholarium* – the universal community of teachers and scholars. Knowing any more Latin than this isn't called for and among polite people is just seen as showing off.[1]

Deciphering those mysterious letters. Although university degrees were originally granted in the language of Virgil, in English-language universities it is now almost universal to refer to them by their English abbreviations. For example, a Bachelor of Arts degree is generally referred to as a BA, rather than as an *artium baccalaureus* (or an AB). A Bachelor of Science degree is generally referred to as a BSc, rather than as a *scientiae baccalaureus* (or an SB). There are exceptions. Harvard University, the oldest university in the United States, has never seen the need to change and still awards AB and SB degrees. Canada's oldest university, l'Université Laval, like other French-speaking universities, awards its degrees in French.

It is also worth noting that regardless of their field of study, most people who carry out advanced research receive a Doctor of Philosophy degree (a *philosophiae doctor* degree or PhD). This can be confusing until it is remembered that the word *philosophy* originally referred, not to one discipline among many, but to all organized knowledge.

Medical practitioners receive an MD (or *medicinae doctor*) degree. Perhaps being jealous of this, many law schools have abandoned the traditional LLB (or *legum baccalaureus*) degree in favour of a JD (or *juris doctor*) degree. As a result, some lawyers now ask to be referred to as "doctor," even though they haven't done the research required to obtain a PhD. Genuine doctoral degree holders humor them in this practice.

You can't tell the players without a scorecard. The different coloured hoods and gowns worn at graduation indicate which degrees graduates have earned. To help you decipher the

SOME TRADITIONAL DEGREES

BA, AB	Bachelor of Arts	*artium baccalaureus*
BSc, BS, SB	Bachelor of Science	*scientiae baccalaureus*
MA, AM	Master of Arts	*magister artium*
MSc, MS, SM	Master of Science	*magister scientiae*
PhD	Doctor of Philosophy	*philosophiae doctor*
BD	Bachelor of Divinity	*divinitatis baccalaureus*
MDiv	Master of Divinity	*magister divinitatis*
DD	Doctor of Divinity	*divinitatis doctor*
LLB	Bachelor of Laws	*legum baccalaureus*
LLM	Master of Laws	*magister legum*
LLD	Doctor of Laws	*legum doctor*
BLitt, LittB	Bachelor of Letters	*litterarum baccalaureus*
MLitt, LittM	Master of Letters	*magister litterarum*
DLitt, LittD	Doctor of Letters	*litterarum doctor*
MD, DM	Doctor of Medicine	*medicinae doctor*
BPhil, PhB	Bachelor of Philosophy	*philosophiae baccalaureus*
MPhil	Master of Philosophy	*magister philosophiae*
DPhil	Doctor of Philosophy	*philosophiae doctor*

An abbreviation for a degree followed by the letters *hc* (e.g., DLitt. *hc*) indicates that the degree has been granted *honoris causa,* or "for the sake of honour."

colours, most graduation programs include a section on academic regalia.[2] Since faculty members come from a variety of universities, and since each university has its own system of colours – no member of the Black Hawks wants to wear a Red Wings uniform – the information in your program will apply only to the hoods and gowns worn by the graduates of your home university. Even so, it is often fun to compare the different hoods, gowns and hats from around the world.

The Marshall of the ceremony is usually the person carrying the mace, a huge, ornate club that symbolizes the authority of the university, although sometimes this job is assigned to a younger, more junior official called the 'mace-bearer.' There will also be ushers whose job is to answer your questions.

Talking to the president. Sometimes graduates will want to introduce their parents to their favourite professors. Admittedly this can be risky. As students will have learned over the past few years, some professors can be notoriously quirky. Even so, most parents understand that some members of the chattering class are easier to talk to than others and no harm will be done.

One thing to remember is that even though teaching is now finished for the year, it is usually a mistake to ask your professors whether they are enjoying being 'off for the summer.' Since teaching comprises only two-fifths of an ordinary faculty member's workload (the other three-fifths consist of research and administrative service), most faculty members hate being confused with high-school teachers. Of course, the occasional game of poke-the-bear-with-a-stick can have its own rewards, especially if you find yourself stuck in a hot receiving line with nothing to drink.

Graduation is also one of the few times most of us get to rub shoulders with university presidents, visiting dignitaries, honorary degree holders and other high muckety-mucks. You may have already discovered that members of the university administration come in a variety of shapes and sizes: assistant department heads, department heads, associate deans, deans, associate vice-presidents, vice-presidents, the provost, the president (who may also be called the rector, or principal, or vice-chancellor), and the chancellor. The position of chancellor, like that of the Queen, is largely honorific. The president (think CEO) is responsible for the overall operation of the university. No one quite knows what a provost does, but everyone agrees it's important.

Despite all these ranks and titles, there is really only one *faux pas* worth avoiding while speaking to members of the university administration. This is the mistake of thinking that people holding administrative ranks are somehow higher in authority than those holding academic ranks.

SOME CONTEMPORARY BACHELOR DEGREES

BAcc	Bachelor of Accounting
BAg	Bachelor of Agriculture
BAM	Bachelor of Applied Mathematics
BASc, BAS	Bachelor of Applied Science
BArch	Bachelor of Architecture
BB	Bachelor of Business
BBA	Bachelor of Business Administration
BBioChem	Bachelor of Biochemistry
BChem	Bachelor of Chemistry
BCL	Bachelor of Canon Law
BCL	Bachelor of Civil Law
BCom	Bachelor of Commerce
BCS	Bachelor of Computer Science
BDS	Bachelor of Dental Science
BDS	Bachelor of Dental Surgery
BEd	Bachelor of Education
BE, BEng	Bachelor of Engineering
BChE, BChEng	Bachelor of Chemical Engineering
BCE, BCEng	Bachelor of Civil Engineering
BEE, BEEng	Bachelor of Electrical Engineering
BEnD	Bachelor of Environmental Design
BFA	Bachelor of Fine Art
BF	Bachelor of Forestry
BSF	Bachelor of Science in Forestry
BHSc	Bachelor of Health Science
BHK	Bachelor of Human Kinetics
BJ	Bachelor of Journalism
BLS	Bachelor of Liberal Studies
BMath	Bachelor of Mathematics
BMS	Bachelor of Marine Science
BM	Bachelor of Medicine
BMLSc	Bachelor of Medical Laboratory Science
BMW	Bachelor of Midwifery
BMus, BM	Bachelor of Music
BNurs, BN	Bachelor of Nursing
BPharm, PharmB	Bachelor of Pharmacy
BPhys	Bachelor of Physics
BSN	Bachelor of Science in Nursing
BSW	Bachelor of Social Work
BVetMed, BVM	Bachelor of Veterinary Medicine

SOME CONTEMPORARY MASTER DEGREES

MET	Master of Educational Technology
MASc, MAS	Master of Applied Science
MArch	Master of Architecture
MAS	Master of Archival Studies
MBA	Master of Business Administration
MCS	Master of Computer Science
MEd	Master of Education
ME, MEng	Master of Engineering
MChE, MChEng	Master of Chemical Engineering
MCE, MCEng	Master of Civil Engineering
MEE, MEEng	Master of Electrical Engineering
MEnvSci	Master of Environmental Science
MFA	Master of Fine Art
MFS	Master of Food Science
MF	Master of Forestry
MHSc	Master of Health Science
MHA	Master of Health Administration
MHA	Master of Hospital Administration
MHK	Master of Human Kinetics
MJ	Master of Journalism
MJur	Master of Jurisprudence
MLA	Master of Landscape Architecture
ALM	Master of Liberal Arts
MLS	Master of Library Science
MLIS	Master of Library Information Studies
MM	Master of Management
MMS	Master of Marine Science
MMath	Master of Mathematics
MMus, MM	Master of Music
MME	Master of Music Education
MNurs, MN	Master of Nursing
MOT	Master of Occupational Therapy
MPT	Master of Physical Therapy
MPharm, PharmM	Master of Pharmacy
MPlan	Master of Planning
MPH	Master of Public Health
MRSc	Master of Rehabilitation Science
MSW	Master of Social Work
MSS	Master of Software Systems
MVetMed, MVM	Master of Veterinary Medicine

Naturally enough, the president will think it is the president who runs the university. But faculty members passionately disagree, since no member of the university administration has the power to tell professors what they can or can't teach or publish. In other words, professors believe that, just like the custodial staff, it is the president's job to see that the chalk is in the classroom. Presidents will often admit as much when they tell you that running a university is a lot like running a cemetery: there are lots of people under you, but not many of them are listening.

When shaking hands with professors and presidents alike, it is easy to avoid becoming embroiled in this dispute simply by focusing your attention on your fellow graduates, all of whom, everyone will agree, are resplendent.

That pesky issue of academic freedom. Almost inevitably, just before graduation a student or faculty member will say or do something controversial. It will make the papers and everyone will agree that a line was crossed that shouldn't have been. Everyone, that is, except the person responsible, along with his or her supporters. This, as we all know, is the cost of academic freedom. To the university's media-relations officer, this is often small consolation.

Of more consolation is the fact that this same freedom extends, not just to professors and students, but to guests and alumni of the university as well. So, if Professor Brown has said something foolish, no one will be offended if, while attending graduation, your guests prominently announce that Professor Brown's views are nonsense. In fact, more likely than not, Professor Brown would be pleased to have them track him down so he can discuss the issue with them over coffee.

Degrees versus diplomas. Depending on their program of study, some students receive degrees. Others receive diplomas.

It is a mistake to confuse the two. For example, don't call the piece of paper given to a BA or BSc graduate a diploma. It is a degree.

SOME CONTEMPORARY DOCTORAL DEGREES

DASc, DAS	Doctor of Applied Science
DA, DArts, ArtD	Doctor of Arts
DBA	Doctor of Business Administration
DCL	Doctor of Canon Law, Doctor of Civil Law
DDS	Doctor of Dental Science
DDS	Doctor of Dental Surgery
DMD	Doctor of Dental Medicine
DEd, EdD	Doctor of Education
DEng	Doctor of Engineering
LHD	Doctor of Humane Letters
JSD, SJD	Doctor of Juridical Science
Drjur	Doctor juris
JD	Doctor of Law
JSD, SJD	Doctor of Juridical Science
DLS	Doctor of Library Science
DMS	Doctor of Medical Science
DMus, MusD	Doctor of Music
DMA	Doctor of Musical Arts
OD	Doctor of Optometry
DPharm, PharmD	Doctor of Pharmacy
DPH	Doctor of Public Health
DSc, ScD, DrSc, SD	Doctor of Science
SScD, SocSciDoc	Doctor of Social Science
DSW	Doctor of Social Work
DUniv	Doctor of the University
DVetMed, DVM	Doctor of Veterinary Medicine

Programs of study leading to diplomas are usually shorter than those leading to degrees. In some universities, the recipients of diplomas wear a stole (a sort of ceremonial scarf) rather than a hood. Technically, a person receiving a diploma rather than a degree is a *diplomate* rather than a *graduate*, a distinction now on the verge of being lost.

In Scotland, the first degree awarded in the arts and humanities is still usually an MA (a Master of Arts degree), a practice dating back to the days when the awarding of a degree in a subject entitled one to teach (or become a *master* of) that subject. In Europe, practice also varies. Many European universities offer a Licentiate as their first degree, although since the signing of the Sorbonne Declaration in 1998 and the Bologna Declaration in 1999,[3] in which agreement was reached to begin the process of harmonizing many European degrees, this has become less common. Some universities also still follow the tradition of granting a general degree after three years of study and an Honours degree after four. Others offer only four-year degrees, but bestow Honours on students who have completed a more demanding program of study.

"I admit you." The most common misunderstanding about graduation is the assumption that, having been members of a university for several years, students cease this membership upon graduation. In fact, exactly the opposite is true. Students study *to become* members of their university. It is only upon graduation that they are invited to take up this membership.[4] This is the meaning of the chancellor's phrase "I admit you," said at every graduation ceremony.[5]

Upon admission to membership in the university, a student ceases to be a *graduand* (someone who has completed the requirements for graduation but who has not yet taken up membership in the university) and becomes a *graduate*. It is also at this point that new graduates are entitled to write the letters signifying their new status (BA, BSc, etc.) following their names.

As members of a university, graduates also gain the responsibility of participating in the oversight of their institution through bodies such as the university Senate and the university Alumni Association. As is only proper, only those who participate are allowed the privilege of complaining.

Gifts are always welcome. New graduates may sometimes be hesitant to admit it, but it is always nice to receive a gift on graduation day. An inscribed book or a new pen will serve as a cherished and lasting memento. A watch or piece of jewelry will often grow in importance over the decades. A new computer might help give a new graduate a head-start in his or her chosen career. But if someone is uncertain about what to give that special person who hasn't yet landed his or her first real job, it also never hurts to be reminded of the old slogan, flowers are nice, but money is better.

Further reading

Albom, Mitch, *Tuesdays with Morrie*, New York: Random House, 1997

Bray, Tara, *Why Won't the Landlord Take Visa? The Princeton Review's Crash Course to Life after Graduation*, New York: Princeton Review, 2001

Cobban, A.B., *The Medieval Universities: Their Development and Organization*, London: Methuen & Co. Ltd, 1975

Jordan, Louis and David E. Sparks, *Medieval Universities, Our Academic Origins*, South Bend (IN): University of Norte Dame Press, 1987

Klassen, Thomas R. and John A. Dwyer, *How to Succeed at University (and Get a Great Job!)*, Vancouver: UBC Press, 2015

Meyer, Ingrid, *Your Own Two Feet (and How to Stand on Them): Surviving and Thriving after Graduation*, New York: St Martin's Press, 2000

Pausch, Rancy, and Jeffrey Zaslow, *The Last Lecture*, Scranton (PA): Hyperion Books, 2008

Pedersen, Olaf, *The First Universities: Studium Generale and the Origins of University Education in Europe*, Cambridge: Cambridge University Press, 1998

Rudy, Willis, *The Universities of Europe, 1100-1914: A History*, London, Toronto: Associated University Presses, 1984

Smith, Hugh, *Academic Dress and Insignia of the World*, 3 vols, Cape Town: A.A. Balkema, 1970

Acknowledgements

As the British Prime Minister Benjamin Disraeli once said, "I feel a very unusual sensation. If it is not indigestion, I think it must be gratitude."[1]

In my case, the gratitude I feel makes it necessary for me to extend a sincere and affectionate thank you to all my students. Over many decades, you have made teaching a pleasure. You have also made it easy to remember just how invigorating life at university can be for young and old alike.

I thank you all.

A. Troglodyte

References and Sources

When referencing sources in footnotes, endnotes or side notes, academic authors have an obligation to ensure that readers are given sufficient information to identify the exact sources an author has used. However, deciding when to include a reference and what kind of information to include is often not as mechanical as one might hope. The reason is simple: different contexts have different conventions for referencing. Readers of newspaper and magazine articles, for example, don't expect to be presented with long lists of footnotes. (What readers of newspaper and magazine articles – and even well-respected online blogs and columns – *do* expect is that the information they are reading will be accurate.) The writers of book reviews, literary essays and other forms of *belle lettres* are similarly not expected to provide the same kinds of detailed citations and references found in academic writing. Politicians, business leaders, judges and other office holders are sometimes required to release materials over their names, even omitting mention of a document's actual author, since convention (or law) dictates that it is their office, rather than the author, that is to take responsibility for the content of what is being said.

As a general rule, academic writing is different. Academic writing requires facts and quotations to be referenced whenever authors believe that their readers may want to check the original source but not know how to do so. This requires authors to give some thought to who their readers are likely to be. Will they be students wanting guidance about important underlying assumptions? Or will they be established scholars only interested in evaluating a paper's more controversial claims? Will they already be familiar with the technical terminology being used? Or will they want to be introduced to important basic concepts and background information? The birth and death dates of a famous historical figure, for example, normally don't need to be cited (even if an author hasn't committed them to memory and needs to look them up before reporting them) since it is common knowledge that such dates can be checked in almost any encyclopedia. In contrast, if there is controversy over such dates and you believe your reader might like to know why you have selected one date rather than another, then a citation will be helpful. Since what counts as common knowledge varies from context to context and from discipline to discipline, and if you are unsure about what needs to be referenced, it is often a good idea to check with your professor or teaching assistant.

Good references give your work credibility. They help strengthen your argument by showing readers where to find additional, confirming information. In undergraduate essays especially, instructors often look more for sound judgment than original argument. Picking reliable citations is one way of demonstrating sound judgment.

Whether a reader will want to know the source of a quotation will also depend on its importance. The very first quotation appearing in the final sentence of the fourth paragraph of the Preface of this book, for example, was not referenced since it is difficult to imagine someone wanting to know exactly who made this passing comment or when. Even so, if there is a chance that a reader might like to have further details about the sources of such remarks, it never hurts to include a reference. (Now that you're curious, the speaker was Dr Joan Bryans of the Department of Philosophy at Thompson Rivers University in British Columbia, Canada.) Similarly, the quotations from Francis Bacon and Benjamin Franklin on the first page of Chapter Eleven normally wouldn't need to be referenced. Because they are quotations they need to be accurate, but writers don't normally need to include references when recounting amusing anecdotes. (Who else but an academic would interrupt a joke with a footnote!) In this case, the references have been included only because, knowing how curious some students are, it seems possible that some readers may be interested in following up one or the other of these two quotations, or in citing them themselves in some other context.

When deciding whether to reference a quotation, it helps to know the difference between primary and secondary sources. *Primary sources* are sources of information (books, articles, recordings, archival materials, artifacts or interview subjects) that are closest to the person, idea, theory, period or object being discussed. *Secondary sources* are sources of information that repeat, discuss or build on primary sources. Say you want to repeat Francis Bacon's comment that knowledge is power. In many contexts (for example, in a newspaper article or book review), there will be no need to include a reference. Even in some academic contexts, because the comment is so famous most readers will recognize that it can be checked in most standard dictionaries of quotations or in almost any reliable encyclopedia. In other contexts (for example, in an essay for your history professor), it likely will be sufficient to cite the secondary source where you first learned of the quotation (for example, the first page of Chapter 11 of this book). In yet other contexts (e.g., your master's thesis on 17th–century British politics), you'll likely need to remind your readers that this English phrase is really a translation from the original Latin and that it can be checked by consulting volume 14 of *The Works of Francis Bacon*, edited by Basil Montagu, London: William Pickering, 1831, p. 31.

It also helps to familiarize yourself with your discipline's main referencing conventions. Some sources – for example, plays and poems written by Shakespeare, books written by classic authors such as Plato and Aristotle, the books of the *Bible* and documents such as the *Declaration of Independence* – are so famous they are often referenced using only a series of numbers (sometimes combined with letters) common to all scholarly printings of these works. These numbers allow readers to consult a quotation or citation without having to find the same edition or translation used by the author. In the case of works written by Aristotle, for example, the numbers referenced are called 'Bekker numbers,' after the editor of the first complete works of Aristotle published in the modern period, August Immanuel Bekker. In the case of works written by Plato and Plutarch, the numbers are called 'Stephanus numbers,' after the first modern editions of these works edited by Henricus Stephanus. Similar conventions are used for numerous other works in disciplines as diverse as English, Classics, Philosophy, Mathematics, Medicine and Law.

In this book, references are regularly given in both formats. A reference such as "Aristotle, *Nicomachean Ethics*, 1174b21" refers the reader to a specific line (line 21) in section 1174b of Aristotle's book *Nicomachean Ethics*. This reference is followed by a second reference such as "*The Complete Works of Aristotle*, vol. 2, edited by Jonathan Barnes, Princeton: Princeton University Press, 1984, p. 1857" which gives the page number (1857) of the specific English translation quoted or cited. As a general rule, if you're uncertain about which format to use, or whether to include a reference or not, it never hurts to err on the side of caution and ask your professor or teaching assistant for guidance.

Notes

† *Nullius in verba* is the motto of the Royal Society of London, the oldest of today's many scientific societies. The motto means "On the word of no one" or, as my students might say, "Don't take anyone's word for it." The motto is meant to remind us that it is important not to take things for granted. Before reaching a decision on any matter, large or small, it is helpful to take the time to consider the evidence on both sides of the issue, and then to make up our own minds.

For anyone studying at college or university, aphorisms like this are worth remembering, even if the Latin might be a little off-putting. Once ubiquitous within the university, Latin is now assumed by many to be little more than a modern-day anachronism, something that can be ignored without causing disadvantage to one's future career or fortune.

As a troglodyte, I see things a little differently. Colleges and universities still use Latin for mottos like this to remind us of our history and, in doing so, to pay respect to those who have come before us. Troglodytes also believe that having never been introduced to Latin is a little like having never been introduced to one's parents, something that naturally turns out to be a source of significant sadness.

Preface

1 The word "Preface" comes from the Latin verb *praefari*, meaning "to say beforehand." It means the same as "Prolegomenon," from the Greek verb *prolegein*, but "Preface" is

now almost universally preferred since it's easier to spell. It would be fun to discover whether this nod to practicality helps explain why Roman roads were straighter than Greek roads, and why Greek culture eventually came to be dominated by Rome. But given our other obligations, such investigations will have to wait until another day.

[2] John Maynard Keynes, *The General Theory of Employment, Interest and Money* (1936), New Delhi: Atlantic, 2008, p. 351. Keynes' reference to "Practical men" and "Madmen in authority," rather than to "Practical people" and "Mad people in authority," may strike some readers as rather antiquated. Since he wrote these words almost a century ago, this shouldn't be surprising. Throughout this book I have made no attempt to update or sanitize other people's language. I have no desire to pretend they have written anything other than what they wrote. As my editors, colleagues and students so kindly remind me, this is exactly what one might expect from a troglodyte.

Chapter 1 – Be Curious

[1] James McAuley, "Comment, By Way of Prologue," *Quadrant*, 1 (1957), no. 1, p. 4.

[2] For a helpful introduction to events following the Cold War, interested readers might like to consult Richard K. Betts, *Conflict after the Cold War*, 3rd edn, New York, Toronto: Pearson Longman, 2008.

For discussion about the recent resurgence of religion, see John Micklethwait and Adrian Wooldridge, *God Is Back: How the Global Revival of Faith is Changing the World*, London: Allen Lane, 2009, and Hugh Heclo and Wilfred M. McClay, *Religion Returns to the Public Square: Faith and Policy in America*, Washington: Woodrow Wilson Center Press, and Baltimore: Johns Hopkins University Press, 2003.

For criticism of this re-emergence, see Ayaan Hirsi Ali, *Heretic: Why Islam Needs a Reformation Now*, New York:

Harper Collins, 2015; Richard Dawkins, *The God Delusion*, New York: Bantam Press, 2006; Sam Harris, *Letter to a Christian Nation*, New York: Knopf, 2006; Christopher Hitchens, *God Is not Great: How Religion Poisons Everything*, Toronto: McClelland & Stuart, 2008; and Joan Konner, *The Atheist's Bible*, New York: Echo, 2007.

For discussion of recent developments in the arts, see Roger Kimball's trilogy of books: *Experiments Against Reality: The Fate of Culture in the Postmodern Era,* Chicago: Ivan R. Dee, 2000; *Art's Prospect: A Challenge of Tradition in an Age of Celebrity*, Chicago: Ivan R. Dee, 2004; and *The Rape of the Masters: How Political Correctness Sabotages Art*, New York: Encounter Books, 2005.

For information about population growth, see Lloyd T. Evans, *Feeding the Ten Billion*, Cambridge: Cambridge University Press, 1998, and Jeffrey K. McKee, *Sparing Nature: The Conflict between Human Population Growth and Earth's Diversity*, New Brunswick (NJ): Rutgers University Press, 2004.

For helpful summaries of 20th-century developments in civil rights, see Peter B. Levy, *Let Freedom Ring: A Documentary History of the Modern Civil Rights Movement*, New York: Praeger, 1992, and Nelson Mandela, *Long Walk to Freedom: The Autobiography of Nelson Mandela*, Boston: Little, Brown and Co., 1994.

[3] The James Webb Space Telescope, developed by the National Aeronautics and Space Administration (NASA) in coordination with the European Space Agency (ESA) and the Canadian Space Agency (CSA), was launched in 2021 and represents the next generation of space telescopes.

[4] For information about the Human Genome Project and related issues, see Matt Ridley, *Genome: The Autobiography of a Species in 23 Chapters*, New York: Perennial / Harper Collins, 1999, and Daniel J. Kevles, *The Code of Codes: Scientific and Social Issues in the Human Genome Project*, Cambridge (MA): Harvard University Press, 1992.

For interesting discussion about developments in the computer industry, see Paul E. Ceruzzi, *A History of Modern Computing*, London, Cambridge (MA): MIT Press, 2003, and Reed E. Hundt, *You Say You Want a Revolution: A Story of Information Age Politics*, New Haven: Yale University Press, 2000.

For discussion of the many connections between developments in information technology and politics, see Marcus Franda, *Launching into Cyberspace: Internet Development and Politics in Five World Regions*, Boulder, Colorado: Lynne Rienner Publishers, 2001, and Mark J. Lacy, and Peter Wilkin, *Global Politics in the Information Age*, Manchester (UK), New York: Manchester University Press, 2005.

For introductions to recent developments in astronomy, see Robert Zimmerman, *The Universe in a Mirror: The Saga of the Hubble Telescope and the Visionaries Who Built It*, Princeton: Princeton University Press, 2008, and Jay Barbree and Martin Caidin, *A Journey through Time: Exploring the Universe with the Hubble Space Telescope*, New York: Viking Press, 1995.

[5] William A. Henry, *In Defense of Elitism*, New York, London, Toronto, Sydney, Auckland: Anchor Books / Doubleday, 1994, p. 154.

[6] University graduates, on average, do earn more than others. People who graduate with a bachelor's degree often earn about one-and-a-half to two times as much over their lifetimes as people who have only high school diplomas. With a higher degree – a graduate degree or a professional degree – university graduates have the potential to make three or more times as much as they might otherwise.

For example, see Jennifer Cheeseman Day and Eric C. Newburger, "The Big Payoff: Educational Attainment and Synthetic Estimates of Work-Life Earnings," *Current Population Reports* (Special Studies, P23-210), Washington (DC): U.S. Department of Commerce, Economics and Statistics Administration / U.S. Census Bureau, 2002, figure 1, p. 2, available at www.census.gov/prod/2002pubs/p23-210.pdf.

It is also worth noting that studies like this (that attempt to estimate the economic value of a university education) also show just how difficult statistical research can be. Although it is relatively easy to compare the income levels of people who have a university education with the income levels of people who don't, determining whether these differences are due to education or to some other factor is not easy. For example, if people who elect to go to university turn out to be the kind of people who would have a higher earning potential independently of the education they receive, it becomes unclear whether such studies succeed in isolating the cause of the greater income levels, or whether they merely succeed in pointing to a correlation between greater education and greater income.

[7] Caroline Bird, *The Case against College*, New York: D. McKay Co., 1975, part 2; but see too Murray Baker, *The Debt-Free Graduate: How to Survive College or University without Going Broke,* rev. edn, Toronto: Harper Collins Publishers, 1998.

[8] Bertrand Russell, *What I Believe*, Second Impression (Revised), London: Kegan Paul, Rench, Trubner & Co. Ltd, 1925, pp. 28-29.

[9] Stephen Hawking, "Introduction," in I. Bernard Cohen, *A Guide to the Principia Mathematica*, London: The Folio Society, 2008, p. xi.

[10] Or at least he wasn't talking *only* about such pleasures. See not only Socrates' famous comment about the unexamined life in Plato's *Apology* at 38a, in Plato, *Euthyphro, Apology, Crito, Phaedo, Phaedrus* (Loeb Classical Library, *Plato I*), translated by Harold North Fowler, London: William Heinemann Ltd, and Cambridge (MA): Harvard University Press, 1943,

pp. 132, 133, but also the rest of Socrates' discussion in the *Apology* about what is and isn't valuable in life.

[11] Matthew Arnold, quoted in Roger Kimball, *Tenured Radicals: How Politics has Corrupted Our Higher Education*, New York: Harper Collins Publishers, 1990, p. 4.

[12] Bloom, Allan, *The Closing of the American Mind: How Higher Education Has Failed Democracy and Impoverished the Souls of Today's Students*, New York: Simon & Schuster, 1987, p. 336. Cf. Fareed Zakaria, *In Defense of a Liberal Education*, New York: W.W. Norton & Company, 2015.

[13] Mark Mercer, "In Defense of Liberal Learning and Intellectual Community," *C2C: Ideas that Lead*, 14 December 2016, c2cjournal.ca/2016/12/the-values-that-universities-forgot.

[14] For example, see Michael B. Stoff, Jonathan F. Fanton and R. Hal Williams, *The Manhattan Project: A Documentary Introduction to the Atomic Age*, Philadelphia: Temple University Press, 1991.

[15] John F. Kennedy, "Special Message to the Congress on Urgent National Needs," Joint Session of Congress, 25 May 1961, John F. Kennedy Presidential Library and Museum, Boston, available at www.jfklibrary.org/Historical+Resources/ Archives/Reference+Desk/Speeches.

[16] Thierry Bardini, *Bootstrapping: Douglas Engelbart, Coevolution, and the Origins of Personal Computing*, Stanford: Stanford University Press, 2000.

[17] Judith Philipps Otto, "DARPA Revolutionizes Prosthetics: How and Why?" The O&P Edge, November 2007, at www.oandp.com/articles/2007-11_01.asp. Additional DARPA program information can be found at www.darpa.mil/dso/thrus ts/bio/restbio_tech/revprost.

[18] Recently, I have been told by some of my students that there are places on the internet (I was told I should search for the sites YouTube, Facebook, Flickr, Reddit, Instagram, MySpace

and Twitter, I believe) that encourage the free exchange of information simply for its own sake. Being a troglodyte, I have to admit that I have no first-hand knowledge of any of these sites. Even so, venues in which people are able to share words and ideas, music and videos simply for their own sake, without any expectation of financial benefit or academic credit, have the potential to be of great benefit to everyone. I am encouraged to learn of their existence. I hope they turn out to be successful!

[19] Kurt Lewin, *Field Theory in Social Science: Selected Theoretical Papers*, New York: Harper and Row, 1964, p. 169.

[20] Quoted in N. Sukumar Gowda, *Learning and the Learner: Insights into the Processes of Learning and Teaching*, 2nd edn, Delhi: PHI Learning Private Limited, 2015, p. 177.

[21] See Edmond Halley, "The True Theory of the Tides, Extracted from that Admired Treatise of Mr Isaac Newton," *Philosophical Transactions*, 19 (1696), p. 445 ff., and Michael S. Reidy, *Tides of History: Ocean Science and Her Majesty's Navy*, Chicago: University of Chicago Press, 2008.

[22] Marie Curie, *The Discovery of Radium: Address by Madame M. Curie at Vassar College, May 14, 1921* (Ellen S. Richards Monographs No. 2), Poughkeepsie (NY): Vassar College, 1921, p. 2.

[23] Robert Fulford, "The Anti-racism Boom," *The National Post*, 03 April 2010, p. A15. In this context, you might like to read Richard, L. Epstein, *The Pocket Guide to Critical Thinking*, 4th edn, Socorro, NM: Advanced Reasoning Forum, 2011.

[24] T.H. Huxley, "A Liberal Education and Where to Find It" (1886), in *Science and Education* (Collected Essays, vol. 3), London: Macmillan and Co., 1893, pp. 81-2.

[25] T.H. Huxley, "A Liberal Education and Where to Find It" (1886), in *Science and Education* (Collected Essays, vol. 3), London: Macmillan and Co., 1893, p. 83.

Chapter 2 – Be Brave

[1] Bertrand Russell, *The Autobiography of Bertrand Russell: 1872-1914* (vol. 1), Boston, Toronto: Little Brown and Company, 1967, p. 73.

[2] Bertrand Russell, *The Autobiography of Bertrand Russell: 1872-1914* (vol. 1), Boston, Toronto: Little Brown and Company, 1967, pp. 73-4.

[3] Although the question itself is most commonly associated with the German astronomer Heinrich Olbers, it has been of interest to numerous other astronomers over the centuries, including Johannes Kepler and Edmond Halley.

[4] My thanks go to Lorne Whitehead for these data.

[5] The following discussion largely follows that given in Paul S. Wesson, "The Real Reason the Night Sky is Dark: Correcting a Myth in Astronomy Teaching," *Journal of the British Astronomical Association*, 99 (1989), no. 1, pp. 10-13.

[6] Charles H. Lineweaver, and Tamara M. Davis, "Misconceptions about the Big Bang: Baffled by the Expansion of the Universe? You're not Alone. Even Astronomers Frequently Get It Wrong," *Scientific American*, March 2005, available at www.scientificamerican.com/article.cfm?id=misconceptions-about-the-2005-03.

[7] Paul S. Wesson, "The Real Reason the Night Sky is Dark: Correcting a Myth in Astronomy Teaching," *Journal of the British Astronomical Association*, 99 (1989), no. 1, p. 11.

[8] *Ibid.*

[9] *Ibid.*, p. 12.

[10] Donald Sheff, "Izzy, Did You Ask a Good Question Today? [Letter to the Editor]," *The New York Times*, 19 January 1988, available at www.nytimes.com/1988/01/19/opinion/l-izzy-did-you-ask-a-good-question-today-712388.html?pagewanted=1.

Chapter 3 – Get Involved

[1] A.B. Cobban, *The Medieval Universities: Their Development and Organization*, London: Methuen & Co. Ltd, 1975, p. 21.

[2] Charles Homer Haskins, *The Rise of Universities*, Ithaca: Great Seal Books / Cornell University Press, 1957, pp. 76-7.

[3] *Ibid.*, pp. 77-8.

[4] *Ibid.*, pp. 79-80.

[5] Ernest Rutherford, quoted in Fred Dainton, "Fools and Pedants," *Nature*, 300, 18 November 1982, p. 295.

[6] William Bowen and Sarah A. Levin, *Reclaiming The Game: College Sports and Educational Values*, Princeton: Princeton University Press, 2003.

[7] For example, see Nigel Spivey, *The Ancient Olympics: A History*, New York: Oxford University Press, 2004, and Judith Swaddling, *The Ancient Olympic Games*, 2nd edn, Austin: University of Texas Press, 1999.

[8] Charles Darwin, *The Autobiography of Charles Darwin* (1887), New York: Barnes & Noble Books, 2005, p. 58.

[9] Dumbledore, quoted in J.K. Rowling, *Harry Potter and the Sorcerer's Stone*, Toronto: Scholastic Canada, Ltd, 1999.

[10] Ludwig van Beethoven, quoted in Gary Stith, *The Conductor's Companion*, Delray Beach, FL: Meredith Music Publications, 2017.

[11] F.M. Cornford, *Microcosmographia Academica: Being a Guide for the Young Academic Politician*, Cambridge: Bowes & Bowes Publishers Ltd, 5th edn, 1953, p. 1.

[12] *Ibid.*, p. 2.

[13] *Ibid.*, p. v.

[14] *Ibid.*, p. 14.

[15] *Ibid.*, p. 15.

[16] *Ibid.*, p. 16.

[17] *Ibid.*

[18] Charles de Gaulle, in Francis Williams, *A Prime Minister Remembers: The War and Post-war Memoirs of the Rt. Hon. Earl Attlee*, London, Melbourne, Toronto: Heinemann, 1961, p. 56.

[19] Aristotle, *Politics*, 1291b35-37, in Aristotle, *The Complete Works of Aristotle*, vol. 2, edited by Jonathan Barnes, Princeton: Princeton University Press, 1984, p. 2050.

Chapter 4 – Be an Active Reader

[1] John Sutherland, *How to Read a Novel*, New York: St Martin's Press, 2006, p. 12.

[2] David Stove, "Did Babeuf Deserve the Guillotine?" in *On Enlightenment*, edited by Andrew David Irvine, New Brunswick (NJ), London: Transaction Publishers, 2003, pp. 3-4.

[3] *Ibid.*, p. 4.

[4] William Cobbett, *A Year's Residence in America* (1795), quoted in Marshall McLuhan, *The Gutenberg Galaxy*, Toronto: University of Toronto Press, 1962, p. 171.

[5] Northrop Frye, *The Stubborn Structure*, London: Metheun & Co. Ltd, 1970, p. 95.

[6] William Shakespeare, *Romeo and Juliet*, act 2, scene 2, in *The Annotated Shakespeare*, edited by A.L. Rowse, 3 vols, New York: Clarkson N. Potter, Inc., 1978, vol. 3, p. 91.

[7] William Shakespeare, *Hamlet*, act 2, scene 2, in *The Annotated Shakespeare*, edited by A.L. Rowse, 3 vols, New York: Clarkson N. Potter, Inc., 1978, vol. 3, p. 219.

[8] "For dust you *are*, And to dust you shall return." *Genesis*, 3:19, in *Holy Bible: The New King James Version*, Nashville, Camden, New York: Thomas Nelson Publishers, 1982, p. 3.

[9] "The spirit indeed is willing, but the flesh is weak." *Matthew*, 26:41, in *Holy Bible: The New King James Version*, Nashville, Camden, New York: Thomas Nelson Publishers, 1982, p. 963.

[10] Ezra Pound, *How to Read*, London: Desmond Harmsworth, 1931, p. 21.

[11] Translations of the quotations listed in the box in this chapter entitled "Reading with Comprehension" are as follows:

Braille: "All human beings are born free and equal in dignity and rights." Article 1(f) of *The Universal Declaration of Human Rights,* adopted by the United Nations General Assembly on December 10, 1948 at the Palais de Chaillot in Paris. (See Johannes Morsink, *The Universal Declaration of Human Rights: Origins, Drafting and Intent*, Philadelphia: University of Pennsylvania Press, 1999, p. 331.)

C: "Print the line: hello, world." An example of the original print command in the popular computer language C. (Brian Kernighan and Dennis Ritchie, *The C Programming Language*, Englewood Cliffs (NJ): Prentice Hall, 1988, p. 7.)

Chess: "White opens by moving his King's Pawn to square e4 and Black responds by moving his King's Pawn to square e5. White moves his Queen to square h5 and Black moves his Queen's Knight to square c6. White then moves his King's Bishop to square c4 and Black responds by moving his Queen's Pawn to square d6. White then moves his Queen to square f7, capturing a Black Pawn and placing Black in checkmate." One of chess's shortest games, variously known as the schoolboy's mate, the scholar's mate, the barber's mate, the shoemaker's mate, etc. (David Hooper and Kenneth Whyld, *The Oxford Companion to Chess*, 2nd edn, Oxford, New York: Oxford University Press, 1992, p. 359.)

Chinese: "A journey of a thousand miles starts from beneath one's feet" or, as it is sometimes also translated, "A journey of a thousand miles starts with one step." One of the most famous aphorisms attributed to Lao Tzu, the founder of Taoism. (Lao

Tzu, *Tao Te Ching,* 64, 153, in Lao Tzu, *Tao Te Ching,* translated by D.C. Lau, Harmondsworth (UK): Penguin Books, 1985, p. 125.)

Chemistry: "Carbon dioxide together with water [together with light energy] yields a carbohydrate [such as glucose] together with oxygen." The chemical formula for photosynthesis, the process by which most plants (and some other types of organism) use sunlight to synthesize foods from carbon dioxide and water. (See D.O. Hall and K.K. Rao, *Photosynthesis,* 6th edn, New York: Cambridge University Press, 1999, pp. 2 ff.)

English: The opening phrase of Charles Dickens' famous novel about the years leading up to the French Revolution in 1789 and the love Sydney Carton, a British lawyer, has for the wife of another man. (Charles Dickens, *A Tale of Two Cities* (1859), New York: Bantam Classics, 2003, p. 3.)

French: "I think, therefore I am." The slogan encapsulating René Descartes' reply to the sceptic who doubts that certain knowledge can ever be attained. (René Descartes, *Discourse on Method* (1637), part 4, in René Descartes, *Discours de la méthode / Discourse on the Method: A Bilingual Edition and Interpretation of René Descartes' Philosophy of Method,* translated by George Heffernan, Notre Dame, London: University of Notre Dame Press, 1994, p. 51; later translated into Latin as *"ergo cogito, ergo sum"* or as *"cogito ergo sum"* in René Descartes, *Principles of Philosophy* (1644), part 1, art. 7, in René Descartes, *Principles of Philosophy,* translated by Valentine Rodger Miller and Reese P. Miller, Dordrecht: D. Reidel Publishing Company, 1984, p. 5, and in René Descartes, *The Philosophical Writings of Descartes,* translated by John Cottingham, Robert Stoothoff, and Dugald Murdoch, vol. 1, Cambridge: Cambridge University Press, 1985, p. 195.)

German: "Ah, still delay – thou art so fair!" or, as it is also translated, "Stay a while, you are so beautiful!" One of the most famous lines in German literature, in which Faust, an astronomer hungry for knowledge, meets the Devil (Mephistopheles) and is enthralled. Yearning for "more than earthy meat and drink," Faust soon agrees to sell his soul to Mephistopheles in return for knowledge and power. (Faust, in Johann von Goethe, *Faust: A Tragedy* (1808), part 1, scene 4, translated by Bayard Taylor, New York: The Modern Library, 1967, p. 58.)

Greek: "The unexamined life is not worth living." Perhaps the most famous line of Socrates' defence speech, delivered in 399 BCE in front of an Athenian jury while Socrates was being tried for corrupting the young and failing to honor the traditional gods of his city. (Plato, *Apology*, 38a, in Plato, *Euthyphro, Apology, Crito, Phaedo, Phaedrus*, Loeb Classical Library, *Plato I*, translated by Harold North Fowler, London: William Heinemann Ltd, and Cambridge, MA: Harvard University Press, 1943, pp. 132, 133.)

Japanese: "The train came out of the long tunnel into the snow country." The first line of Yasunari Kawabata's *Snow Country*, which tells the story of a love affair between a provincial geisha, Komako, and a wealthy Tokyo dilettante. Kawabata was the first Japanese author to receive the Nobel Prize for Literature. (Yasunari Kawabata, *Snow Country* (1935-7), translated by Edward G. Seidensticker, in *Snow Country and Thousand Cranes*, New York: Alfred A. Knopf, 1973, p. 3.)

Latin: "Knowledge and human power meet in one." Francis Bacon's most famous aphorism, often paraphrased simply as "Knowledge is power." An early advocate of what is now called the inductive method in science, Bacon also served as both Attorney General and Lord Chancellor of England. (Francis Bacon, *Novum Organum* [*New Organon*] (1620), bk 1, aphorism 3, in Francis Bacon, *The Works of Francis Bacon*, vol. 14, edited by Basil Montagu, London: William Pickering, 1831, p. 31.)

Mathematics: "Euler's number [the base of the natural logarithm] raised to the power of the imaginary unit times *pi*, plus one, equals zero." Euler's identity, often called the most beautiful theorem in mathematics because of its stark simplicity. Although the equation is a special case of Euler's formula in complex analysis (which states that $e^{ix} = \cos x + i \sin x$), it is not known whether Euler himself ever proved the simpler identity. (See Paul J. Nahin, *Dr Euler's Fabulous Formula: Cures Many Mathematical Ills*, Princeton, Oxford: Princeton University Press, 2006, pp. 1-3 ff., cf. p. ii.)

Morse Code: "SOS". The universally recognized symbol of someone in distress. (See Peter Carron, *Morse Code: The Essential Language*, 2nd edn, Newington, CT: American Radio Relay League, 1993, p. 3-2.)

Music: "This music is to be played in the treble clef in the key of C minor in two/four time. The first bar begins with an eighth-rest, which is followed by three g eighth-notes. The second bar contains a single e-flat half-note, held slightly long. The third bar begins with an eighth-rest, which is followed by three f eighth-notes. The fourth bar contains a single d half-note that is tied to the single d half-note in the fifth bar. The d half-note in the fifth bar is held slightly long." The opening five bars of Ludwig van Beethoven's *Symphony No. 5 in C minor*. (See Ludwig van Beethoven, *Symphony No. 5 in C minor*, Op. 67 (1808), New York: Sony Classical, 1992 [compact disc].)

Physics: "Energy [in joules] equals mass [in kilograms] times the speed of light [in metres per second] squared." The mass-energy equivalence introduced by Albert Einstein in 1905 stating that the mass of a body is simply a measure of its total energy content. (Albert Einstein, "$E=MC^2$," in *Ideas and Opinions*, New York: Bonanza Books, 1954, pp. 337-41.)

Russian: "But the line dividing good and evil cuts through every human heart" or, as it may also be translated, "The line dividing good and evil cuts through the heart of every human being." One of the many memorable lines of Alexander Solzhenitsyn's account of the forced labor camps used to imprison political dissidents in the former Soviet Union. (Alexander I. Solzhenitsyn, *The Gulag Archipelago* (1973), New York: Harper and Row, 1974, p. 168.)

Spanish: "Art is a lie that makes us realize truth." An explanation of why realism in art isn't always desirable, given by Pablo Picasso, founder of the cubist movement and the most-recognized artist of the 20th century. (Pablo Picasso, quoted in Robert Cumming, *Art Explained*, New York: DK Publishing, 2007, p. 98.)

[12] Alfred North Whitehead, quoted in Fred Dainton, "Fools and Pedants," *Nature*, 300, 18 November 1982, p. 296.

[13] Alfred North Whitehead, *The Aims of Education and Other Essays*, New York: The Macmillan Company, 1959, pp. 138-9.

[14] *Ibid.*, p. 139.

Chapter 5 – Be a Demanding Writer

[1] Ernest Campbell Mossner, *The Life of David Hume*, 2nd edn, Oxford: Clarendon Press, 1980, p. 354. Cf. D. Berman, *A History of Atheism in Britain: From Hobbes to Russell,* London: Routledge, 1990.

[2] For example, see his *Treatise of Human Nature: Being an Attempt to Introduce the Experimental Method of Reasoning into Moral Subjects* (1739–40).

[3] David Hume, "Of Miracles" (1748), part 2, 41, in *An Enquiry Concerning Human Understanding: A Critical Edition*, sec. 10, edited by Tom L. Beauchamp, Oxford: Clarendon Press, 2000, p. 99.

[4] Ernest Campbell Mossner, *The Life of David Hume*, 2nd edn, Oxford: Clarendon Press, 1980, ch. 25. esp. p. 350.

[5] David Hume, "Introduction," in *A Treatise of Human Nature* (1739), edited by L.A. Selby-Bigge, Oxford: Clarendon Press, 1888, p. xiv.

[6] *Ibid.*, p. xvi.

[7] David Hume, "Of Miracles" (1748), part 1, 4, in *An Enquiry concerning Human Understanding: A Critical Edition*, sec. 10, edited by Tom L. Beauchamp, Oxford: Clarendon Press, 2000, p. 84.

[8] Aristotle, *Nicomachean Ethics*, 1094b26-27, in Aristotle, *The Complete Works of Aristotle*, vol. 2, edited by Jonathan Barnes, Princeton: Princeton University Press, 1984, p. 1730.

[9] Mark Twain, quoted in Jeffrey and Carole Bloom, *Bloom's Bouquet of Imaginary Words*, New York: Black Dog & Leventhal Publishers, 2004, p. 10.

[10] Charles Dickens, *A Tale of Two Cities*, London: Chapman & Hall, 1859.

[11] J.D. Salinger's *The Catcher in the Rye*, New York: Little, Brown and Company, 1951.

[12] Gabrielle Roy, *The Tin Flute*, translated by Hannah Josephson, New York: Reynal & Hitchcock, 1947.

[13] George Orwell, *Nineteen Eighty-Four,* London: Secker and Warburg, 1949.

[14] Northrop Frye, "A Literate Person Is First and Foremost an Articulate Person," in *Interviews with Northrop Frye* (Collected Works of Northrop Frye, vol. 24), Toronto, Buffalo, London: University of Toronto Press, 2008, p. 341. As one of my students has commented, the phrase *A literate person is an articulate person* is "tattoo worthy." I *think* this was meant as a compliment to Professor Frye. And rightly so.

[15] Northrop Frye, "A Literate Person Is First and Foremost an Articulate Person," in *Interviews with Northrop Frye* (Collected Works of Northrop Frye, vol. 24), Toronto, Buffalo, London: University of Toronto Press, 2008, p. 331.

[16] Northrop Frye, *The Stubborn Structure*, London: Metheun & Co. Ltd, 1970, p. 95.

[17] For a report about one such controversy see Lawrence Solomon, "Wikipedia's Climate Doctor," *Financial Post*, 19 December 2009, available at www.nationalpost.com/opinion/c olumnists/story.html?id=62e1c98e-01ed-4c55-bf3d-5078af9cb409.

[18] "The Declaration of Independence as Adopted by Congress" (July 4, 1776), in *The Papers of Thomas Jefferson, Volume 1: 1760-1776*, edited by Julian P. Boyd. Princeton: Princeton University Press, 1950, p. 429.

[19] Thomas Jefferson, "Jefferson's 'original Rough draught' of the Declaration of Independence" (1776), in *The Papers of Thomas Jefferson, Volume 1: 1760-1776*, edited by Julian P. Boyd. Princeton: Princeton University Press, 1950, p. 423.

Chapter 6 – Calculate Mechanically, Think Creatively

[1] Owen Gingerich (ed.), *The Nature of Scientific Discovery: A Symposium Commemorating the 500th Anniversary of the Birth of Nicolaus Copernicus*, Washington, DC: Smithsonian Institution Press, 1975, p. 496.

[2] E.T. Bell, "The Prince of Mathematicians: Gauss," in *Men of Mathematics*, New York: Simon and Schuster, 1937, pp. 221–2. Like all good stories, this one might be apocryphal. For example, see Joseph J. Rotman, *A First Course in Abstract Algebra: With Applications*, Upper Saddle River (NJ): Pearson / Prentice Hall, 2006, p. 7.

[3] *Ibid.*

4 Euclid, *Elements*, bk 9, prop. 20, in Euclid, *The Thirteen Books of Euclid's Elements*, edited by Thomas L. Heath, vol. 2, 2nd edn, New York: Dover Publications, Inc., 1956, pp. 412-13; published originally, Cambridge: Cambridge University Press, 1925.

5 Aristotle, *Metaphysics,* 1084a1-4, in Aristotle, *The Complete Works of Aristotle*, vol. 2, edited by Jonathan Barnes, Princeton: Princeton University Press, 1984, p. 1713.

6 See Georg Cantor, "Über eine Eigenschaft des Inbegriffes aller reellen algebraischen Zahlen [On a Characteristic Property of All Real Algebraic Numbers]," *J. Reine Angew. Math.,* 77 (1874), pp. 258–62; and Georg Cantor, "Uber ein elementare Frage der Mannigfaltigkeitslehre [On an Elementary Question of Set Theory]" *Deutsche Mathematiker-Vereinigung,* 1 (1890-1), pp. 75-78. A more modern treatment appears in George S. Boolos, John P. Burgess, and Richard C. Jeffrey, *Computability and Logic*, 5th edn, Cambridge: Cambridge University Press, 2007, ch. 2.

Chapter 7 – Discover the Best That Has Been Thought and Said

1 Alan Sokal, *Beyond the Hoax: Science, Philosophy and Culture*, Oxford: Oxford University Press, 2008, p. 153.

2 Lingua Franca, *The Sokal Hoax: The Sham that Shook the Academy*, Lincoln, London: University of Nebraska Press, 2000, pp. 1-2.

3 Alan Sokal, *Beyond the Hoax: Science, Philosophy and Culture*, Oxford: Oxford University Press, 2008, p. 152-3.

4 C.P. Snow, *The Two Cultures and A Second Look: An Expanded Version of The Two Cultures and the Scientific Revolution*, Cambridge: Cambridge University Press, 1969, p. 3.

5 *Ibid.*, p. 4.

[6] For example, see Jerome Kagan, *The Three Cultures: Natural Sciences, Social Sciences, and the Humanities in the 21st Century*, New York: Cambridge University Press, 2009.

[7] Hilda Neatby, *So Little for the Mind*, 2nd edn, Toronto: Clarke Irwin, 1953, p. vii.

[8] *Ibid.*, p. 15.

[9] C.P. Snow, *The Two Cultures and A Second Look: An Expanded Version of The Two Cultures and the Scientific Revolution*, Cambridge: Cambridge University Press, 1969, p. 5.

[10] See Clark Kerr, *The Uses of the University*, 5th edn, Cambridge (MA), London: Harvard University Press, 2001. See also Grace Hechinger, "Clark Kerr, Leading Public Educator and Former Head of California's Universities, Dies at 92," *The New York Times*, 02 December, 2003, available at www.nytimes.com/2003/12/02/us/clark-kerr-leading-public-educator-former-head-california-s-universities-dies-92.html.

[11] Clark Kerr, *The Uses of the University*, 5th edn, Cambridge (MA), London: Harvard University Press, 2001, p. 1.

[12] *Ibid.*

[13] *Ibid.*, p. 14.

[14] *Ibid.*, p. 102.

[15] *Ibid.*

[16] *Ibid.*, p. 1.

[17] *Ibid.*, p. 14.

[18] *Ibid.*

[19] *Ibid.*

[20] *Ibid.*, p. 103.

[21] *Ibid.*, p. 7.

[22] T.H. Huxley, "A Liberal Education and Where to Find It" (1886), in *Science and Education* (Collected Essays, vol. 3), London: Macmillan and Co., 1893, p. 83.

[23] Willis Rudy, *The Universities of Europe, 1100-1914: A History*, London, Toronto: Associated University Presses, 1984, p. 29.

[24] *Ibid.*

[25] *Ibid.*, p. 32.

[26] *Ibid.*, p. 33.

[27] For more information about the founding of the earliest European universities, see Olaf Pedersen, *The First Universities: Studium Generale and the Origins of University Education in Europe*, Cambridge: Cambridge University Press, 1998.

[28] For some of the earliest discussion about the connection between *theoria* (our observation and contemplation of the world) and *eudaimonia* (human flourishing or happiness), see Aristotle, *Nicomachean Ethics*, 1174b21, 1177a11 ff., in Aristotle, *The Complete Works of Aristotle*, vol. 2, edited by Jonathan Barnes, Princeton: Princeton University Press, 1984, pp. 1857, 1860 ff.

[29] For example, see Joseph S. Weiner, *The Piltdown Forgery: The Classic Account of the Most Famous and Successful Hoax in Science*, Oxford: Oxford University Press, 2003.

[30] For example, see the Berkeley Lab Research News press releases dated 07 June 1999, available at www.lbl.gov/Science-Articles/Archive/elements-116-118.html and 27 July 2001, available at www.lbl.gov/Science-Articles/Archive/118-retraction.html.

[31] See Eugenie Samuel Reich, *Plastic Fantastic: How the Biggest Fraud in Physics Shook the Scientific World*, New York: Palgrave Macmillan, 2009.

[32] G.E.R. Lloyd, *Early Greek Science: Thales to Aristotle*, New York, London: W.W. Norton & Company, 1970, pp. 14-15.

[33] *Ibid.*, p. 54.

[34] Plato, *Theaetetus*, 152a, in Plato, *Complete Works,* edited by John M. Cooper and D.S. Hutchinson, Indianapolis: Hackett Publishing Co., 1997, p. 169.

[35] Plato, *Theaetetus*, 171b, *Ibid.*7, p. 190.

[36] *Ibid.*

[37] Mark Mercer, Department of Philosophy, St Mary's University (Halifax), in correspondence.

[38] Matthew Arnold, quoted in Roger Kimball, *Tenured Radicals: How Politics has Corrupted Our Higher Education*, New York: Harper Collins Publishers, 1990, p. 4.

[39] Put another way, the understanding that beliefs can be justified, not on the basis of some private, privileged authority but on observation, reason and open, public debate, requires that a distinction be made between the view that observation, reason and open, public debate are *sources* of knowledge and the view that observation, reason and open, public debate are *infallible sources* of knowledge.

[40] Thucydides, *History of the Peloponnesian War*, bk 6, New York: Penguin Books, 1975, pp. 409 ff.

[41] Doreen Kimura, *Sex and Cognition*, Cambridge (MA), London: MIT Press, 1999, pp. 1-2.

[42] Doreen Kimura, *Sex and Cognition*, Cambridge (MA), London: MIT Press, 1999, p. 3.

[43] For those who may be interested, it may also be worth noting that since the time of Saint Anselm of Canterbury in the 11th century, this view has even been the dominant guiding force for most work in Western theology. For example, see the opening pages of Saint Anselm's *Monologion*, in Anselm,

Saint Anselm: Basic Writings, translated by S.N. Deane, 2nd edn, La Salle, Illinois: Open Court, 1974, pp. 35ff. In this context, the term *natural theology* is used to refer to theology based on reason and experience, rather than revelation. Natural theology is thus contrasted with *revealed theology*.

[44] As mentioned earlier, this doesn't mean there is no room for subjective work in a university. What it does mean is that when it comes time to examine such work, or when it comes time to select one piece of work (a novel or theatrical performance, say) to serve as an object of study, we do so in the hope of learning something objective.

[45] For example, see his comment to the effect that "Both are composed of sets of statements; the statements are 'moves' made by the players within the framework of generally applicable rules; these rules are specific to each particular kind of knowledge, and the 'moves' judged to be 'good' in one cannot be of the same type as those judged 'good' in another, unless it happens that way by chance." (Jean-François Lyotard, *The Postmodern Condition: A Report on Knowledge*, translated by Geoff Bennington and Brian Massumi, Minneapolis: University of Minnesota Press, 1984, p. 26.)

[46] Jean-François Lyotard, *The Postmodern Condition: A Report on Knowledge*, translated by Geoff Bennington and Brian Massumi, Minneapolis: University of Minnesota Press, 1984, p. 8.

[47] *Ibid.*, pp. 8-9.

[48] *Ibid.*, p. 26.

[49] William A. Henry, *In Defense of Elitism*, New York, London, Toronto, Sydney, Auckland: Anchor Books / Doubleday, 1994, p. 14.

[50] For an interesting and thoughtful critique of the idea that increased knowledge necessarily leads to improved quality of life, see David Stove's provocative essay, "D'Holbach's

Dream: The Central Claim of the Enlightenment," *Quadrant*, 33 (12) (December 1989), pp. 28-31; reprinted in David C. Stove, *Against the Idols of the Age*, edited by Roger Kimball, New Brunswick (NJ) and London: Transaction Publishers, 1999, pp. 81-91.

[51] Christopher Marlowe, "Prologue," *The Jew of Malta* (c.1589), in *The Complete Works of Christopher Marlowe*, vol. 1, edited by Fredson Bowers, 2nd edn, Cambridge: Cambridge University Press, 1981, p. 263.

[52] For example, see Plato, *Theaetetus*, 176b, in Plato, *Complete Works,* edited by John M. Cooper and D.S. Hutchinson, Indianapolis: Hackett Publishing Co., 1997, p. 195.

[53] For example, see Socrates, quoted in Plato, *Protagoras*, 35e-357c, in Plato, *Complete Works,* edited by John M. Cooper and D.S. Hutchinson, Indianapolis: Hackett Publishing Co., 1997, pp. 785-6.

[54] *Genesis,* 3:1-6, in *Holy Bible: The New King James Version*, Nashville, Camden, New York: Thomas Nelson Publishers, 1982, p. 3.

[55] A more recent example can be found in Bernard Williams' *Ethics and the Limits of Philosophy* (Harvard University Press, 1986), where Williams argues that to preserve certain (good) ways of life, it is necessary that people living those ways cannot come to discover that values are (only) tastes, for that knowledge would destroy their commitments to various goods.

Chapter 8 – Beware the Fribling, Fumbling Keepers of the Age

[1] For example, see Bettany Hughes, *The Hemock Cup: Socrates, Athens and the Search for the Good Life*, London: Jonathan Cape Ltd, 2010, Robin Waterfield, *Why Socrates Died*, Toronto: McClelland & Stewart, 2009, and Armand D'Angour,

Socrates in Love: The Making of a Philosopher, London: Bloomsbury Publishing, 2019.

[2] For example, see James Reston, *Galileo: A Life*, New York: Harper Collins, 1994.

[3] Howard Mumford Jones, "The American Concept of Academic Freedom," Appendix D in Louis Joughin, *Academic Freedom and Tenure: A Handbook of the American Association of University Professors*, Madison, Milwaukee, London: The University of Wisconsin Press, 1967, p. 234.

[4] For example, see Andrew David Irvine, "Bertrand Russell and Academic Freedom," *Russell*, n.s. vol. 16 (1996), pp. 5-36.

[5] Ray Bradbury, "Coda," *Fahrenheit 451* (1953), New York: Ballantine Books / A Del Rey Book, 1979, p. 177.

[6] *Ibid.*, p. 178.

[7] For example, see Jill Kathryn Conway, *The Politics of Women's Education: Perspectives from Asia, Africa, and Latin America*, Ann Arbor: University of Michigan Press, 1995.

[8] For example, see Brendan O'Malley, "More Academics and Students Suffer Attacks," *University World News*, 111 (14 February 2010), available at www.universityworldnews.com/article.php?story=20100212123612777.

[9] For example, see Charles Lewis, "Support Abortion or Stay Off Campus, Club Told," National Post, 17 November 2010, available at www.nationalpost.com/news/Support+abortion+stay+campus+club+told/3839898/story.html.

[10] For example, see Zhores Medvedev, *The Rise and Fall of T.D. Lysenko*, New York: Columbia University Press, 1969.

[11] For example, see David Gardner, *The California Oath Controversy: The Story of the Loyalty Oath Controversy which for Three Years Convulsed the Nation's Largest Institution of*

Higher Learning, Berkeley: University of California Press, 1967.

[12] Albert Einstein, *Ideas and Opinions*, New York: Bonanza, 1954, p. 30.

[13] Greg Finn, "An Open Letter to the Brock Community," *The Brock News*, 31 October 2020, brocku.ca/brock-news/2020/06/an-open-letter-to-the-brock-community/.

[14] David Robinson, CAUP/ACPPU Letter to Brock University, safs.ca/issuescases/brock-chemistry/6) CAUT letter to President Fearon.pdf.

[15] "Controversial Essay at German Chemistry Journal Leads to Suspensions, Mass Resignations," *Retraction Watch*, retractionwatch.com/2020/06/08/controversial-essay-at-german-chemistry-journal-leads-to-suspensions/.

[16] Charles Darwin, in a letter to Alfred Russel Wallace (1857), quoted in George Seldes, *The Great Thoughts*, New York: Ballantine Books, 1985, p. 101.

[17] In contrast, one study done by University of California-Irvine professor Ellen Greenberger found that approximately two-thirds of undergraduates believed that if students are "trying hard," a professor should give them some consideration with respect to their course grades. (Shannon Proudfoot, "Pass Me, I Tried Hard, Students Say," *The Vancouver Sun*, 11 November 2008, p. B6.)

[18] Conrad Russell, *Academic Freedom*, London, New York: Routledge, 1993, p. 18.

[19] *Ibid.*, pp. 4, 19.

[20] *Ibid.*, p. 11.

[21] It may be important to note that just as one can condemn a specific political movement – Stalinism, for example – without condemning all forms of politics, one can also recognize the anti-intellectualism of some forms of religion – religious fun-

damentalism, for example – without condemning all forms of religion.

[22] Eratosthenes' figure of approximately 25,000 miles also proved to be remarkably accurate; the figure generally accepted today is 24,901.5 miles. See Robert P. Crease, *The Prism and The Pendulum: The Ten Most Beautiful Experiments in Science*, New York: Random House, 2003. See also, J.B. Russell, *Inventing the Flat Earth: Columbus and Modern Historians*, New York: Praeger, 1991.

[23] For example, see Kitcher, Philip, *Abusing Science: The Case against Creationism*, Cambridge (MA), London: The MIT Press, 1982.

[24] For example, see Rita S. Botwinick, *A History of the Holocaust: From Ideology to Annihilation*, Upper Saddle River (NJ): Prentice Hall, 2001, and Ronald Headland, *So Others will Remember: Holocaust History and Survivor Testimony*, Montreal: Vehicule Press, 1999.

[25] For example, see Niki Kitsantonis, "Debate Rages in Greece about Right of Police to Enter University Campuses," *The New York Times*, 09 December 2009, available at www.nytimes.co m/2009/12/10/world/europe/10iht-greece.html?_r=2&emc=tnt&tntemail1=y.

[26] In North America, such organizations include the Foundation for Individual Rights in Education (www.thefire.org), the National Association of Scholars (www.nas.org), and the Society for Academic Freedom and Scholarship (www.safs.ca).

[27] Graeme Hunter, "Coulter Exposes Ottawa's Shame-On U," *National Post Full Comment*, 26 March, 2010, available at network.nationalpost.com/NP/blogs/fullcomment/archive/2010 /03/26/graeme-hunter-coulter-exposes-ottawa-s-shame-on-u.aspx.

[28] *Ibid.*

[29] For example, see University of Cambridge, "University and Colleges: A Brief History – Early Records," available at www.cam.ac.uk/univ/history/records.html.

[30] Willis Rudy, *The Universities of Europe, 1100-1914: A History*, London, Toronto: Associated University Presses, 1984, p. 49.

[31] *Ibid.*, pp. 49-50.

[32] *Ibid.*, pp. 78-9.

[33] Nathaniel Lee, *Lucius Junius Brutus* (1681), Lincoln: University of Nebraska Press, 1967, pp. 95-6.

[34] Sidney Hook, *Academic Freedom and Academic Anarchy*, New York: Cowles Book Company, Inc., 1970, p. 77.

[35] *Ibid.*, p. 100. See, too, John Castellucci, "The Night They Burned Ranum's Papers," *The Chronicle of Higher Education*, 14 February 2010, available at chronicle.com/article/The-Night-They-Burned-Ranums/64115.

[36] Andrew Peyton Thomas, *The People v. Harvard Law: How America's Oldest Law School Turned Its Back on Free Speech*, New York: Encounter Books, 2005.

[37] University of British Columbia, *Trek 2010*, available at www.trek2000.ubc.ca.

[38] *University Act*, RSBC 1996, 468, sec. 66(1), available at www.bclaws.ca.

[39] John Carpay, "Free Speech Dies a Slow Death on Canadian Campuses," *The National Post*, 09 February 2009, available at network.nationalpost.com/np/blogs/fullcomment/archive/2009/02/09/john-carpay-free-speech-dies-a-slow-death-on-canadian-campuses.aspx.

[40] Jytte Klausen, *The Cartoons that Shook the World*, New Haven: Yale University Press, 2009.

[41] CBC News Online, "Muhammad Cartoons: A Timeline," 26 October 2006, available at www.cbc.ca/news/background/isla m/muhammad_cartoons_timeline.html.

[42] David Brooks, "Drafting Hitler," *The New York Times*, 09 February, 2006, available at select.nytimes.com/2006/02/09/op inion/09brooks.html?ref=davidbrooks.

[43] Patricia Cohen, "Yale Press Bans Images of Muhammad in New Book," *The New York Times*, 12 August 2009, available at www.nytimes.com/2009/08/13/books/13book.html.

[44] Roger Kimball, "Yale & the Danish Cartoons: On the Shameful Censorship at Yale University Press," *The New Criterion*, 28, September 2009, p. 1.

[45] Benno Schmidt, quoted in Nat Hentoff, *Free Speech for Me – But Not for Thee*, New York: Harper Collins, 1992, p. 152. Cf. Michiel Horn, *Academic Freedom in Canada: A History*, Toronto, Buffalo, London: University of Toronto Press, 1999, pp. 332-3.

Chapter 9 – *Inoculate Yourself Against Ergophobia*

[1] Although often recounted among mathematicians, I have not been able to discover a reliable source for this quotation.

[2] Dennis Moralee, "The Old Cavendish – 'The First Ten Years'," in *A Hundred Years and More of Cambridge Physics*, Cambridge: Cambridge University Physics Society, 3rd edn, 1995, p. 8, available at www.phy.cam.ac.uk/history/years.

[3] *Ibid.*

[4] James Mark Baldwin, quoted in Martin L. Friedland, *The University of Toronto: A History*, Toronto, Buffalo, London: University of Toronto Press, 2002, p. 124.

[5] For example, see Andrew David Irvine, "Let Truth and Falsehood Grapple," *University of Toronto Quarterly*, 67 (1998), pp. 549-66.

Chapter 10 – Be Honest

[1] For an alternative view, see Peter Gray, *Free to Learn*, New York: Basic Books, 2015.

[2] D.C. Baird, *Experimentation: An Introduction to Measurement Theory and Experiment Design*, Englewood Cliffs (NJ): Prentice-Hall, Inc., 1962, p. 7.

[3] For further information, see The Stanford University Office of Judicial Affairs, at honorcode.stanford.edu.

[4] Kate Zernike, "With Student Cheating on the Rise, More Colleges are Turning to Honor Codes," *The New York Times*, 02 November 2002, available at www.nytimes.com/2002/11/0 2/us/with-student-cheating-on-the-rise-more-colleges-are-turning-to-honor-codes.html.

[5] I am grateful to Neil MacKay for telling me of this case.

[6] Devika Desai, "What's Behind Rise in Academic Cheating During Pandemic?" *National Post*, 28 May 2021, available at epaper.nationalpost.com/national-post-latestedition/20210528/281556588741079.

[7] Anonymous, "Plagiarism Investigation Ends at Virginia," *The New York Times*, 26 November 2002, available at www.nytimes.com/2002/11/26/us/plagiarism-investigation-ends-at-virginia.html.

[8] Anonymous, "44 Students Suspended after Project Plagiarized," *SFU News Online*, 31 October 2002, 25 (5), available at www.sfu.ca/sfunews/_pvw9C438741/sfu_news/sfunews103 10203.shtml.

[9] Paula Wasley, "Indiana U. Punishes 46 Cheaters," *The Chronicle of Higher Education*, 18 May 2007, available at chronicle.com/article/Indiana-U-Punishes-46/21117.

[10] Marcel Berlins, "Cheating has Always been Around in Schools and Universities – but the Internet is Making it Far Worse," *The Guardian*, 20 May 2009, available at www.guard

ian.co.uk/commentisfree/2009/may/20/comment-marcel-berlins-plagiarism-students-internet.

[11] Rebecca Attwood, "143 Students Expelled for Plagiarism," *Times Higher Education*, 12 June 2008, available at www.timeshighereducation.co.uk/story.asp?storycode=402351

[12] Sara, Rimer, "A Campus Fad That's Being Copied: Internet Plagiarism Seems on the Rise," *The New York Times*, 03 September 2003, available at www.nytimes.com/2003/09/03/n yregion/a-campus-fad-that-s-being-copied-internet-plagiarism-seems-on-the-rise.html.

[13] As Michael Shermer puts it in his review of David Goodstein's book *On Fact and Fraud: Cautionary Tales from the Front Lines of Science* (Princeton: Princeton University Press, 2010), "The general environment [within universities] of openness and honesty, though mythic in its idealized form, nonetheless exists and in the long run weeds out the cheats and exposes frauds and hoaxes, as history has demonstrated." (Michael Shermer, "When Scientists Sin," *Scientific American*, July 2010, p. 34, available at www.scientificameric an.com/article.cfm?id=when-scientists-sin.)

[14] In my case, I report the academic work I have done as part of my day job under the name Andrew David Irvine – although I'd be grateful if readers could keep this secret to themselves!

[15] Natasha Singer, "Medical Papers by Ghostwriters Pushed Therapy," *The New York Times*, 04 August 2009, available at www.nytimes.com/2009/08/05/health/research/05ghost.html?_r=1.

[16] Luke Harding, "History of Modern Man Unravels as German Scholar is Exposed as Fraud: Flamboyant Anthropologist Falsified Dating of Key Discoveries," *The Guardian*, 19 February 2005, available at www.guardian.co.uk /science/2005/feb/19/science.sciencenews.

[17] Thomas Bartlett and Scott Smallwood, "Just Deserts?," *The Chronicle of Higher Education*, 01 April 2005, available at chronicle.com/article/Just-Deserts-/4787; Jacques Steinberg, "New Book Includes Passages from Others," *The New York Times*, 31 May 2003, available at www.nytimes.com/2003/05/31/books/new-book-includes-passages-from-others.html; and Scott Smallwood, "The Fallout," *The Chronicle of Higher Education*, 17 December 2004, available at chronicle.com/article/The-Fallout/36364.

[18] Robert F. Worth, "Historian's Prizewinning Book on Guns is Embroiled in a Scandal," *The New York Times*, 08 December 2001, available at www.nytimes.com/2001/12/08/books/08GUNS.html; and J. Lindgren, "Fall from Grace: Arming America and the Bellesiles Scandal," *Yale Law Journal*, 111 (2002), pp. 2195 ff.

[19] Phil Baty, "Whistleblowers: Plagiarism Scandal Returns to Haunt V-C," *The Times Higher Education Supplement*, 21 June 2002, available at www.timeshighereducation.co.uk/story.asp?storyCode=169922&sectioncode=26; and also Editorial, "Monash and its VC: The End of the Affair," *The Age* (Melbourne), 13 July 2002, available at www.theage.com.au/articles/2002/07/12/1026185107089.html.

[20] Anonymous, "U.S. Agency Reprimanded Virginia U.," *The New York Times*, 16 April 1995, available at www.nytimes.com/1995/04/16/us/us-agency-reprimanded-virginia-u.html.

[21] Anonymous, "Ex-President of Morris Brown College Pleads Guilty," *The Chronicle of Higher Education*, 01 May 2006, available at chronicle.com/article/Ex-President-of-Morris-Brown/36951.

[22] Scott Jaschik, "Temple Fined $700,000 in Rankings Scandal," *Inside Higher Ed*, 7 December 2020, www.insidehighered.com/admissions/article/2020/12/07/education-department-fines-temple-700000-rankings-scandal.

[23] Helpful discussion can be found in all of the following: Roger Kimball, *Tenured Radicals: How Politics has Corrupted Our Higher Education*, New York: Harper Collins Publishers, 1990; John Fekete, *Moral Panic: Biopolitics Rising*, Montreal, Toronto: Robert Davies Publishing, 1994; Alan Charles Kors and Harvery A. Silvergate, *The Shadow University: The Betrayal of Liberty on America's Campuses*, New York: Harper Collins, 1998; and Martin Loney, *The Pursuit of Division: Race, Gender, and Preferential Hiring in Canada*, Montreal, Kingston, London, Buffalo: McGill-Queen's University Press, 1998.

[24] John Fekete, *Moral Panic: Biopolitics Rising*, Montreal, Toronto: Robert Davies Publishing, 1994, pp. 244-5.

[25] Michiel Horn, *Academic Freedom in Canada: A History*, Toronto, Buffalo, London: University of Toronto Press, 1999, p. 332.

[26] Much the same is true of university administrators. In 2006, the president of Harvard University was hounded from office in part as a result of his public speculation that innate differences between men and women might be one reason fewer women select careers in science and mathematics. See Marcella Bombardieri, "Summers' Remarks on Women Draw Fire," *The Boston Globe*, 17 January 2005, available at www.boston.com/news/local/articles/2005/01/17/summers_remarks_on_women_draw_fire; and Alan Finder, Patrick D. Healy and Kate Zernike, "President of Harvard Resigns, Ending Stormy 5-Year Tenure," *The New York Times*, 22 February 2006, available at www.nytimes.com/2006/02/22/education/22harvard.html.

[27] Michiel Horn, *Academic Freedom in Canada: A History*, Toronto, Buffalo, London: University of Toronto Press, 1999, p. 5.

[28] Thomas Sowell, *Intellectuals and Society*, New York: Basic Books, 2009, p. 9. See too, Neven Sesardic, *When Reason*

Goes on Holiday: Philosophers in Politics, New York: Encounter, 2016, but also Fareed Zakaria, *In Defense of a Liberal Education*, New York: W.W. Norton & Company, 2015.

[29] For example, York University in Toronto has been accused of favouring one side of the anti-Israel/pro-Israel debate. See David Frum, "Something's Seriously Wrong at York University," *The National Post,* 27 February 2010, A16, available at www.nationalpost.com/opinion/story.html?id=2620345.

[30] Cicero, *De Amicitia*, sec. 5, sec. 8 and sec. 9, in *De Senectute, De Amicitia, De Divinatione* (Loeb Classical Library, Cicero, vol. 20), translated by William Armistead Falconer, Cambridge (MA), London: Harvard University Press, 2001.

[31] *Ibid.*, sec. 10.

[32] *Ibid.*, sec. 12.

[33] *Ibid.*, sec. 23.

[34] *Ibid.*

Chapter 11 – Have Fun

[1] Or more faithfully, "Knowledge and human power meet in one." See Francis Bacon, *Novum Organum* [*New Organon*] (1620), in vol. 14 of Francis Bacon, *The Works of Francis Bacon*, edited by Basil Montagu, London: William Pickering, 1831, p. 31 (bk 1, aphorism 3). See also bk 2, sec. 4, p. 92, and Francis Bacon, *Meditationes Sacrae* [*Sacred Meditations*] (1597), in vol. 1, 1825, p. 219.

[2] Benjamin Franklin, *Advice to a Young Tradesman* (1748), in Anon., *The Life of Benjamin Franklin*, Philadelphia: Desilver, Thomas & Co., 1836, p. 142.

[3] Plato, *Charmides*, 164d-165a, in Plato, *Complete Works,* edited by John M. Cooper and D.S. Hutchinson, Indianapolis: Hackett Publishing Co., 1997, p. 651. This is just one of the three famous phrases that were inscribed in stone at the temple

at Delphi in ancient Greece. The other two were "Know thyself" and "Pledges lead to perdition" (or perhaps "Pledges lead to misfortune").

[4] Aristotle, *Nicomachean Ethics*, 1104a10-26, 1106a25-1109a29, 1133b32, in Aristotle, *The Complete Works of Aristotle*, vol. 2, edited by Jonathan Barnes, Princeton: Princeton University Press, 1984, pp. 1744 ff.

[5] Robert J. Sales, "MIT's Great Dome becomes a Droid as Students Pull Off Star Wars Hack," *MIT News*, 17 May 1999, available at web.mit.edu/newsoffice/1999/r2d2.html.

[6] Anonymous, "Conundrum at Cornell: Pumpkin's Lofty Perch," *The New York Times*, 27 October 1997, available at www.nytimes.com/1997/10/27/nyregion/conundrum-at-cornell-pumpkin-s-lofty-perch.html.

[7] Claudia Joseph, "Pranksters Graduate in Fine Art of Spoofing," *The Independent*, 05 May 2000, available at www.independent.co.uk/news/education/educationnews/pranksters-graduate-in-fine-art-of-spoofing-hoax-698189.html.

[8] Anonymous, "Huskies Won in Rose Bowl but Lost to Ingenuity of Cal Tech Students," *The Washington Post*, 27 January 1961, A21.

[9] Erin Millar and Ben Coli, "I Prank, Therefore I am," *Maclean's*, 08 November 2007, available at www.macleans.ca/education/postsecondary/article.jsp?content=20071107_1414 06_2096&page=1.

[10] James Bieri, *Percy Bysshe Shelley: A Biography*, Baltimore: The Johns Hopkins University Press, 2008, chs 7-10.

[11] Neil Steinberg, *If at All Possible, Involve a Cow: The Book of College Pranks*, New York: St Martin's Press, 1992, pp. 114-17.

[12] Homer, *The Odyssey*, bk 1, 183 and *passim*, in Homer, *Odyssey, I* and *Odyssey, II* (Loeb Classical Library, Homer, vols 3 and 4), translated by A.T. Murray and George E.

Dimock, Cambridge (MA), London: Harvard University Press, 1995, p. 27 and *passim*.

[13] Euripides, *Bacchae*, 272 ff., in Euripides, *Bacchae, Iphigenia at Aulis, Rhesus* (Loeb Classical Library, Euripides, vol. 6), translated by David Kovacs, Cambridge (MA), London: Harvard University Press, 2002, pp. 35 ff.

[14] Aristophanes, *Lysistrata*, 190-239, in Aristophanes, *Birds, Lysistrata, Women at the Thesmophoria* (Loeb Classical Library, Aristophanes, vol. 3), translated by Jeffrey Henderson, Cambridge (MA), London: Harvard University Press, 2000, pp. 293-303.

[15] Plato, *Symposium*, 176a ff., in Plato, *Complete Works*, edited by John M. Cooper and D.S. Hutchinson, Indianapolis: Hackett Publishing Co., 1997, pp. 461 ff.

[16] Alexander Nazaryan, "The Tipsy Hero," *The New York Times* blog, 30 January 2009, available at proof.blogs.nytimes.com/2009/01/30/the-tipsy-hero.

[17] For example, see David Stove, "The Diabolical Place: A Secret of the Enlightenment," *Encounter*, 74 (4) (May 1990), pp. 9-15; reprinted in *On Enlightenment*, edited by Andrew David Irvine, New Brunswick (NJ), London: Transaction Publishers, 2003, pp. 93-110.

[18] Alan Wood, "Marriage and Morals," in *Bertrand Russell: The Passionate Sceptic*, London: George Allen and Unwin, 1957, p. 174; reprinted in Andrew David Irvine, *Bertrand Russell: Critical Assessments, Volume IV: History of Philosophy, Ethics, Education, Religion and Politics*, London, New York: Routledge, 1999, p. 96.

[19] *Ibid.*

[20] C. Shawn Green and Daphne Bavelier, "Action Video Game Modifies Visual Selective Attention," *Nature*, 423, 29 May 2003, pp. 534-7.

[21] P.W. Singer, "War of the Machines," *Scientific American*, July 2010, pp. 56 to 63, available at www.scientificamerican.com/article.cfm?id=war-of-the-machines.

[22] Aristotle, *Politics 1.2, 1253a,* in Aristotle, *The Complete Works of Aristotle*, vol. 2, edited by Jonathan Barnes, Princeton: Princeton University Press, 1984, p. 1987.

[23] Aristotle, *Nicomachean Ethics 1.7, 1097b,* in Aristotle, *The Complete Works of Aristotle*, vol. 2, edited by Jonathan Barnes, Princeton: Princeton University Press, 1984, p. 1735.

[24] Aristotle, *Politics 1.2, 1253a,* in Aristotle, *The Complete Works of Aristotle*, vol. 2, edited by Jonathan Barnes, Princeton: Princeton University Press, 1984, p. 1988.

Chapter 12 – Remember the Past, Look to the Future

[1] If you *do* want to show off, have a look at Eugene H. Ehrlich, *Amo, Amas, Amat, and More: How to Use Latin to Your Own Advantage and to the Astonishment of Others*, New York: Harper & Row, 1985 as well as Eleanor Dickey, *Learning Latin the Ancient Way: Latin Textbooks from the Ancient World*, Cambridge: Cambridge University Press, 2016.

[2] Another good source for information is Hugh Smith, *Academic Dress and Insignia of the World*, 3 vols, Cape Town: A.A. Balkema, 1970.

[3] For further information, see www.bologna.msmt.cz/?lng=EN.

[4] This is also why, when speaking carefully, most universities distinguish between an applicant's *acceptance* to university as a student and a graduand's *admission* to the university as a graduate.

[5] At some universities it is said in Latin: "*Admitto te ad gradum.*"